Politics and Film

Politics and Film

The Political Culture of Film in the United States

DANIEL P. FRANKLIN

ROWMAN AND LITTLEFIELD PUBLISHERS, INC.
Lanham • Boulder • New York • Toronto • Oxford

ROWMAN & LITTLEFIELD PUBLISHERS, INC.

Published in the United States of America
by Rowman & Littlefield Publishers, Inc.
A wholly owned subsidary of The Rowman & Littlefield Publishing Group, Inc.
4501 Forbes Boulevard, Suite 200, Lanham, Maryland 20706
www.rowmanlittlefield.com

P.O. Box 317, Oxford OX2 9RU, UK

British Library Cataloguing in Publication Information Available

Library of Congress Cataloging-in-Publication Data

Franklin, Daniel P.
    Politics and film : the political culture of film in the United States / Daniel P. Franklin.
        p.   cm.
    Includes bibliographical references and index.
    ISBN-13: 978-0-7425-3808-5 (cloth : alk. paper)
    ISBN-10: 0-7425-3808-7 (cloth : alk. paper)
    ISBN-13: 978-0-7425-3809-2 (pbk. : alk. paper)
    ISBN-10: 0-7425-3809-5 (pbk. : alk. paper)
    1. Motion pictures—Political aspects—United States.   I. Title.
PN1995.9.P6F73 2006
791.43'658—dc22
                                                                    2005019455
Printed in the United States of America

⊗™ The paper used in this publication meets the minimum requirements of American
National Standard for Information Sciences—Permanence of Paper for Printed Library
Materials, ANSI/NISO Z39.48-1992.

Contents

Introduction

In 2003 documentary filmmaker Michael Moore began looking for financing for his next project, a documentary that was to allege a close relationship between President Bush's family and Osama bin Laden. Moore—who had been the director of other controversial and left-leaning documentaries, including *Bowling for Columbine* (2002) and *Roger and Me* (1989)—at first was reported in the trade papers to have found financing with ICON productions. But when Mel Gibson, one of the partners in ICON, learned about the proposed deal, the company broke off negotiations. Gibson, who was in Italy shooting his next film, *The Passion of the Christ*, reportedly "didn't want any part of it. He figured he had enough controversy on his hands [with the filming of *The Passion*]."[1]

Moore then managed to secure financing with Miramax Films, a division of Disney Studios. Moore is atypical of documentary filmmakers—his films make money. *Roger and Me* grossed over $6 million on a budget of $160,000,[2] and *Bowling for Columbine* did about $30 million in business on a $4 million budget.[3] This is relatively "small potatoes" for major Hollywood studios. But why should they pass up a chance to make a reasonable profit with a proven winner if the downside is only a few million dollars spent and the upside is a quite substantial return on investment?

Conservatives, however, didn't agree. When they caught wind that Miramax was going to produce *Fahrenheit 9/11*, they began to threaten a boycott against Disney. Conservatives have had for a long time a rocky relationship with Disney over the movies that Miramax has produced, including *Pulp Fiction* (1994), and the gay-friendly policies of the Disneyworld theme park. Nevertheless, production of the film went forward.

However, by May 2004, Michael Eisner, chairman and CEO of Disney, had decided not to distribute the film. Moore claimed that Eisner had told him that Disney was concerned about losing the tax breaks it received from the state of Florida for its Disneyworld theme park. After all, Jeb Bush, the president's brother, was governor of Florida. Eisner disputed Moore's claims of political intimidation but still decided to block Miramax's release of the film.

1

The dispute over the film erupted into a full-blown donnybrook at Disney Studios. Miramax cochairmen Harvey Weinstein and Bob Weinstein threatened to leave Disney over Eisner's decision. Finally, they offered to buy the rights to the film from Disney out of their own pockets and to find another distributor. Eisner agreed to sell the rights to the Weinsteins but only after he exacted a promise from them to donate 60 percent of the net proceeds from the film to charity.

In the meantime, the film was scheduled to be screened at the Cannes Film Festival, where it had been nominated for the prestigious Palme d'Or. The political climate in Europe at the time was highly charged. In March 2003, the United States, against the advice of most of its Western European allies, invaded Iraq and toppled Iraqi dictator Saddam Hussein. The Bush administration had criticized the governments of France and Germany for opposing the war and, as a result, was none too popular on the continent. So when *Fahrenheit 9/11*, a film sharply critical of the Bush administration, actually won the Palme d'Or *and* received an unprecedented fifteen-minute standing ovation, there was a bit more than a suggestion that politics had been involved in honoring the film.[4]

Controversy over the film had generated tremendous publicity. Lion's Gate Films, a small Canadian company, had already expressed an interest in distributing the film in the United States, as had a number of distributors in Europe and Australia, so the Weinstein brothers took their new property out of Disney and distributed it on their own. Despite the fact that the film was given an R rating and despite the fact that conservative groups—by threatening to boycott theaters that screened the film—managed to keep the film below its planned release of one thousand screens and despite the fact that documentaries are rarely commercial successes, *Fahrenheit 9/11* opened to record box office revenues. When the film was released at the end of June 2004, it instantly became the number one box office grossing hit ($23.9 million in its first weekend), this despite the fact that opened in only 848 theaters nationwide. "By contrast, the No. 2 film ($19.6 million), *White Chicks*, played at 2,726 theaters, while the No. 3 film ($18.5 million), *Dodgeball*, played at 3,020."[5]

The story of *Fahrenheit 9/11* is the story, in microcosm, of politics in modern American film. The heads of major corporations that just happen to own movie studios often eschew the controversial. The production of a film can exacerbate internal and external squabbles within the industry. Independent film producers scramble for financing. Then, if funding is secured and the film is actually made, the next step is finding a distributor, then a theater, and, finally, an audience. *Fahrenheit 9/11* surmounted all these hurdles, which just goes to show that the offbeat, unconventional, and controversial film can get made in Hollywood. What this story doesn't highlight is the conventional wisdom concerning the politics of Hollywood.

It is now in vogue for politicians, film critics, and academics to decry the degeneracy of American film. In general, the argument goes something like this: Hollywood movie moguls, out of touch with the mainstream of American society, are producing films that appeal to our basest instincts. Moreover, because the Hollywood movie community is generally leftist in its political orientation, American feature films have become a medium for promoting all sorts of radical left-wing political and social agendas. The more society sees of this degeneracy on-screen, the more likely that the members of the viewing public will become inured to the fictional violence and sexual promiscuity on-screen and vote Democratic. Eventually, the argument goes on, public tolerance of violence and sexual promiscuity has very real consequences. The epidemic of teenage pregnancy, violent crime, and the spread of sexually transmitted diseases are all the results of profligate attitudes and behavior promoted by the images that the public sees on television and movie screens. As conservative commentator Thomas Sowell has written,

> What we are seeing in the media today is a degeneracy that is by no means confined to the media, and is indeed actively promoted in many of our schools that are busy breaking down moral standards instead of educating children.[6]

Assuming that these behaviors are in some ways influenced by the media, we as viewers are then left to ponder the remedies necessary to reverse these trends. Do we have the tools and will in society necessary to address the challenge of the media message?

The willingness of candidates from both political parties to adopt some form of this argument is an indication of their reading of the public's belief that the media are at least partially responsible for a moral "decline" in America. Disgust with media content, including what is in the movies, spans the political spectrum, from the radical Right, who worry about liberal influence in Hollywood, to feminists and socialists on the Left, who decry the use of the media to promote capitalist exploitation of women, minorities, and Third World peoples. But it is not just radicals who believe that the American entertainment medium causes trouble. In a 1997 survey by the Roper Organization, 71 percent of those responding said that the quality of television and entertainment was in "strong to moderate decline."[7] Politicians who are attuned to this sort of thing have taken up the cause. The question is, are they right? Is the "decline" in the entertainment media leading to the moral degradation of America?

This book is a discussion of film and politics in American political culture. The influence of the entertainment media is only a very small part of the overall picture, and feature films are a smaller part even still. In this book I want to make it clear that I am not evaluating the media as a whole. The "media" can more accurately be divided into the entertainment and journalistic media.[8] This book is not about journalism, and what I may say about entertainment media will not necessarily attain to journalists. For example, I argue that the marketization of the entertainment industry is generally to the good. The marketization of journalism, however, may not have the same beneficial results. But that is a topic for another book. This book is about entertainment and a limited portion of the entertainment medium at that. *Feature motion pictures* are those films made for commercial exhibition by commercial enterprises. I am not studying television here except to the extent that movies are screened on VHS/DVD/digital format, television, cable, and pay-per-view. Television entertainment is a different medium. I am not studying not-for-profit films produced by organizations funded by public or private foundations. I think those productions *are* fraught with the kind of ideological baggage about which the Right and the Left are so concerned. Rather, I am interested in film as a commercial product. I am interested in the subtle connections between film and American politics. To what extent do films guide or reflect American political culture?

Political culture, or the societal context in which distributive decisions are made, is influenced by a myriad of historical, geographical, and cultural factors. While there is quite a bit of disagreement over the definition of the term and even its relation to politics and culture,[9] the classic formulation of the concept is contained in the groundbreaking work of political scientists Gabriel Almond and Sidney Verba. In their 1963 cross-cultural opinion survey of five countries, *The Civic Culture*, Almond and Verba seek to identify differences in the political cultures of states and thereby explain, among other things, differences between nations in regard to their public policy and planning. They define political culture as "the specifically political orientations—attitudes towards the political system and its various parts, and attitudes towards self in the system."[10] As such, Almond and Verba identify political culture as the "connecting link" between micropolitics (the attitudes of the individual) and macropolitics (the structure of the political system).[11] What makes political culture political is that attitudes, particularly in a democracy, are translated into public policy through political participation. To the extent that the media form and reinforce this political culture, they become part of the process that guides the formation of public policy. For example, if the public perceives that the level of crime has increased, a perception that can be created by the media (as we shall see), there is likely to be pressure on the government to adopt more extensive public policy measures against crime.

American political culture is shaped by a unique national heritage.[12] As an isolated land—separated for most of its early history from the rest of the world by thousands of miles of ocean, with a relatively wide-open frontier—the United States has developed a culture that is unlike any other. Furthermore, because the United States was populated de novo by political and economic refugees of one kind or another, the political context of this country is heavily influenced by this shared experience of flight from governmental oppression and economic upheaval in foreign lands.[13] Finally, because most of the original settlers (at least those who had any say in matters of politics) were from Western Europe, American politics reflects the overwhelming influence of European politics of the eighteenth century, when our constitution was written. The result is a culture that is on the one hand the ethic of the Wild West, where anything goes, and the culture of the Puritans, Pilgrims, and Plymouth Rock. These two strains of thought, Protestant asceticism and liberal freedom, come to clash in matters of freedom of thought and expression.

There are any number of reasons that make the politics of film a difficult topic to discuss in any systematic way. The main problem with evaluating the psychological and political effects of film is that, at a superficial level, films are so easy to understand. Who am I to say what a film means or doesn't mean? Films are so intentionally accessible that even the most uneducated viewer can have a legitimate opinion about whether or not *Citizen Kane* (1941; considered one of the greatest films of all time) is a good film. But the popularity and praise of *Citizen Kane* may have subtle meaning beyond the film's artistic merit. To explore the subtle meaning of an art form so purposely designed for popular consumption is a very difficult task requiring the observer to go beyond the superficial level and put the film in societal context.

This is not a book about the techniques of film production. That topic is handled with much skill elsewhere.[14] Rather, this is a book that explores the meaning of film within a societal context. In examining the political role of films, we become real-time cultural anthropologists, sifting through the artifacts of modern society to determine what our culture really is all about.

In the main the problems of discussing film and society are associated with making connections. What is the influence of film, if any, on the individual and thus on society? What is the direction of causality, and, even if there were an established link between movie viewing and behavior, is that behavior necessarily a problem at all? The evidence is not altogether clear that, for most of us, there is any relationship between what we view on the screen and how we behave. Furthermore, even if it is true that viewing a motion picture influences behavior, it is not clear whether the "good" balances or even compensates for the "bad" in motion pictures. Finally, what if it is the case that films "influence" the behavior of particularly susceptible individuals? Even if that is true, what then do we do? We can forbid children from viewing objectionable material, but can we selectively ban certain individuals from the theater or restrict what the rest of society sees because a film negatively affects just a few?

CAUSALITY AND THE INFLUENCE OF FILM

It is difficult to even establish a direction of causality. Is film an influence on or a mirror of society? The answer is that it is probably both. Filmmakers decide what we are going to see on-screen. However, we decide what we are going to pay to see. Thus, filmmakers are constrained by financing at both the front end and the back end of production. Backers will not come up with the money to produce a script without at least some assurance that the film will make a profit. However, that sort of judgment is by no means a science. Audiences are notoriously fickle. What looks profitable on paper may not be so in the suburban multiplex cinema. Thus, if anything, we would expect filmmakers to be rather conservative in making decisions about what type of films to produce, at least for the consumer market. This is not to say that filmmaking is politically conservative but that the choices made in producing a film are driven by market demands that emphasize reliance on proven formulas.

Common sense tells us that, from a business perspective, filmmakers—if they want to make a profit—have to be responsive to the market. This doesn't just mean that they have to produce a product that delights the eyes, nor does it mean that special effects alone are enough. Anyone who doubts this should see the film version of an already mediocre television series, *Lost in Space* (1998). Films also must be made to please the mind, not just in terms of satisfying our desire to be entertained (although that alone is sometimes enough) but also in those of satisfying our curiosity about people, ideas, and problems that we may confront in everyday life. In that respect, even commercial films are political. They reflect the values with which we are comfortable or interested, or else we wouldn't go to see these films at all. This is not to say that there isn't lots of brain-dead filmmaking. But when it comes to successful films, in those expansive box office receipts is a message about American political culture. In the tradition of those who have said, "You are what you eat," I would further assert, "You are what you pay to see." Consequently, I argue in this book that to a certain extent American film reflects the culture of American society.

Thus, there are three central questions in discussing the relationship of film and politics in the United States. At the individual level, is film a behavioral influence, and, if so, in what direction does the influence flow? At the societal level, is commercial film "art" or simply another product with all the attendant legal and constitutional implications thereof? Finally, at the systemic level, which beliefs, values, and notions of justice special to the American political context and culture are promoted by and reflected in American film? The answers are, respectively, yes (but in both directions), product, and American liberalism. Allow me to elaborate.

In the chapters to follow I answer each of these questions in turn. At the individual level I examine the question of causality. There is extensive evidence to suggest that at least some individuals are influenced by what they see in the movie theater. But this doesn't necessarily mean that films "cause" certain types of behaviors. To make that connection requires establishing a set of links in a chain that connect behavior on a screen with an actual act. Establishing this connection requires some sort of actual evidence, and just because a theory seems to make sense, doesn't make it true. In the chapters to follow I examine the strength of the evidence in this regard. For instance, is it in fact true that film violence causes likewise behavior? And, if so, how widespread is the effect, and does the effect of influence extend to other areas of thought and behavior?

There seems to be quite a bit of evidence to suggest that the media influence our behavior. This behavior is affected by what I call *first-, second-,* and *third-order effects.* First-order effects are the direct connections between what we see on the screen and what we do. Violence in films, racism in film, or simple incivility can influence our behavior by increasing our tolerance for such behavior and, at times and for some people, suggest a mode of seemingly acceptable behavior. Thus, children who see people punch one another in cartoons may tend to do the same with their peers. That is an example of a first-order behavioral effect. At another level, the media and film create a worldview that influences our behavior. If young black men are seen in handcuffs at the beginning of every evening television newscast, then the perception is created that, in general, young black men are dangerous. People will respond to this perception, and the second-order behavioral effect will become manifest. Finally, when someone watches a film, they cannot be doing something else; thus, this form of entertainment has a "crowding out" effect. What is lost to society when someone is in a theater or at home watching a video is a third-order effect. For example, it has been suggested that the effect of television is to atomize a society in which people are increasingly less likely to interact in social settings.[15]

To the extent that it can be established that the viewing of film violence causes actual violence, we are obligated to act. Already as a society we have adopted a number of strategies to mitigate what we perceive as the negative effects of film content on behavior. These strategies range from outright government censorship, to an industry-imposed ratings system, to reliance on the controls of the market better known as laissez-faire. But the suppression of undesirable film content does not come without a cost. At risk are other societal values just as important, such as the freedom of speech and artistic expression. A clear and sober analysis of exactly what negative effects films have on societal behavior is the first step in deciding in what ways and how far we should go in controlling film content. I would add that it's not just film violence that should be of concern. There are those who find equally as dangerous in films explicit sexual relations and just plain, old-fashioned immorality. If film content causes those behaviors, just what trade-offs should we make to control film content in that regard? More to the point, what is a "bad" movie and what should we do about it?

CONTROLLING THE CONTENT OF FILM

The whole question of whether we can or should "do" something about the content of film is strongly related to whether film is product or art. Our laws and customs make it easier, in both the legal and the philosophical sense, to regulate a dangerous product, through product-liability laws, for example, over an objectionable work of art that is presumably protected under the First Amendment. Part of the controversy concerning the content of film can be traced at its source to disagreements over whether films should be considered product or art. A commercially produced film is not strictly a work of art. In the consumer market, art may not sell, which is the case more often than not. Therefore, commercial motion pictures can best be described as a product, shaped by a craftsman's or craftswoman's touch and with perhaps an artistic influence. Primarily, however, motion pictures are commercial goods.[16] As noted, this question of art versus industry is not as esoteric as it seems. Depending on what we judge feature motion pictures to be, art or commercial good, may determine their legal status, including the banning of commercial film.

This brings us to the legal-constitutional component of the politics of film—the problem of regulating the motion picture industry. If motion pictures are simply another industrial product, there is no reason that the government cannot intervene to protect the public interest. However, motion pictures exist on the cusp of expression and industry. Filmmakers are fond of asserting their right of protection pursuant to the First Amendment admonition against restrictions of free expression. Is this a phony claim? Does the commerce clause of the constitution or the right of the federal government to regulate interstate commerce trump the First Amendment in this case? All of this exists in the gray area of the law because of the hybrid status of motion pictures. Furthermore, do local communities have the right to restrict the screening of films that they find objectionable? Not only is this a First Amendment issue, but it is an issue of states' rights as well. With the "new federalism" that is now so much in vogue, can we expect local governments to be more active in the censorship of film, and will the federal government let them get away with it?

THE SUBLIMINAL MESSAGES OF FILM

What are the subtle and not-so-subtle messages sent to the public through the medium of film? What do we learn and what do we allow? I assume that there are messages so repulsive to the public that they would not be acceptable when translated into films. Those films would at least fail in the box office (if not effectively end the careers of those people associated with the films' production). Public beliefs probably form a sort of philosophical and moral range within which film content is acceptable. A film that attacks an American icon—the recent miniseries produced by CBS on the presidency of Ronald Reagan, for example—violates the sensibilities of a large portion of the American public and is therefore rejected whether it is true or not.

What are the dimensions of that range is certainly one of the most important questions to ask. The answer gets at the bedrock foundations of American beliefs. Why is it more acceptable to an American audience to watch two men kill each other, something we see all the time on-screen, than it is to see them make love to each other, an act that even today would incite considerable comment? On the other hand, is the high level of societal permissiveness in regard to homosexuality (and violence and liberal/conservative politics) a function of the subliminal messages of film? Presumably, filmmakers have room to maneuver within that range. But, within that range also lies considerable leeway to suggest, connote, and imply certain types of behaviors. Indeed, under the restraints of the now defunct Motion Picture Production Code, filmmakers became masters at implying the forbidden.

What is the nature of the interaction between audience beliefs and the apparent increasing violence and explicit sexuality in American films? Are we more tolerant of that sort of thing because of the influence of the rest of the media film or because of some other factor? The answer to this question is probably so complex and nuanced as to not be completely knowable. Nevertheless, it is almost certainly the case that some of what we learn about how to dress, how to act, and how to think comes from the movies.

WHO GOES TO THE MOVIES?

This brings to mind yet another consideration. Who goes to the movies? I assume that the filmgoing audience is not necessarily representative of a cross section of American society—that is, films are geared toward a special, moviegoing public and not the American public at large. Thus, the objections so commonly heard about the nature of film content may be largely the complaints of a group of people who don't go to movies in general or to a film not made with them in mind. If I go to an X-rated movie (now NC-17), I will certainly see a lot of nudity and explicit sexuality. I really can't complain about that. No one forced me into the theater. If there is a market for those types of films, then my public complaints about nudity and sex in X-rated films are a thinly veiled attempt to control the viewing habits of others— presumably a violation of rights of individuals in a free society. I might assume, then, that those who complain about film content and seek government controls have a hidden antidemocratic agenda. I can only assume that to be the case because, if those films (with excessive sexuality or violence) were really objectionable to the moviegoing public, nobody would go to see them. The films would wither on the economic vine (and, indeed, many do). Thus, the ongoing controversy about film content and our degenerate moral culture is almost certainly part of a much larger political debate.

Ultimately, I argue that commercial film is a reflection of a large part of American political culture, warts and all. While sexism, racism, and social Darwinism are generally not, and increasingly less so, a strain of American political ideology, they are a part of our history. As such, and being that films reflect and guide our culture, American motion pictures are often racist, sexist, and violent even still. By the same token, film can also reflect the good in society, the power and scope of democratization, or the positive effects of capitalism. Thus, the effect and reflections of American film can be a mixed bag. At their best, films inspire and motivate us in the best of American tradition. At their worst, film taps the darker side of our nature and of our society. In that way, films are a twentieth-century historical record of American popular culture—modern hieroglyphics if you will. For instance, films of the 1950s reflect a concern for the Soviet communist menace; films of the 1930s reflect the burden of the Great Depression; and so on. I also argue that whatever the decade or the studio or the stars or the screenplay, American films reflect enduring notions of justice in American political culture.

OUTLINE OF THE BOOK

In the first chapter of this book, I examine American political culture and how that culture influences the stories that are told in the movies about American life. Thus, commercial films become a marker of the evolution of American ideologies but only a partial marker. Commercial films have been produced since only the beginning of the twentieth century. I want to distinguish between political culture, which is an enduring iconography of American society, and popular culture, which is reflective of a more transient form of expression.[17] Furthermore, as we shall see, film content tends to interact with the political economy of the modern film industry.

Chapter 2 puts the development of American film into context. This chapter is a short history of the political economy of American film—a transformation from the monopoly of the "golden era" to the relatively unfettered market for and production of American films today. What are the consequences for the content of American film of such a transformation?

Chapter 3 is an examination of who makes the movies and who watches them. What are the connections between the producers/consumers of the product and the product itself? Included in this chapter are the results of a Georgia State/*Atlanta Journal Constitution* survey that shows that frequent moviegoers are more socially liberal and less religious than those people who don't go to the movies. Thus, in service to its most lucrative market, Hollywood makes films that may be objectionable to the religious Right—who don't go to the movies anyhow. Why are they so concerned about what the rest of us watch in the theater?

Chapter 4 gets to the heart of the matter of causality. What evidence is there to suggest that feature films stimulate or discourage some types of behavior? Ultimately, I argue in this section that because the financing of feature films is so expensive, investments made in movie projects generally follow rather than lead the market. Financiers take enough of a risk when they sponsor an expensive film venture without having to anticipate the market. Thus, feature films are more a reflection of perceived demand than they are a stimulant to any particular interest or behavior. Nevertheless, there may be an interactive influence at work in the sense that films reinforce existing perceptions and behaviors.

In chapter 5, I discuss the evaluation of films. In order to criticize the content of films, we must attempt to develop some standards. More simply put, we must answer, what is a "bad" movie? It is my contention that because moviegoing is a very personal experience, a bad movie is one that offends the person but not the society. Films that offend the broad expanse of the viewing public will not get made and, if they do, will not get seen (or, in other words, will not make a profit). This argument, however, comes with a qualifier. Given the marketization of the industry, it is now possible to make and profit from niche films that may offend many to appeal to the few. Thus, there is more of a chance than ever that someone may wander into a film that is made for another audience and may be offended.

In chapter 6, I address the issue of why films "aren't what they used to be." The fact of the matter is that times and taste change. What was acceptable in the past may be unthinkable today and the other way around. I have some fun with this idea by rewriting the story line of classic films so that they conform to modern sensibilities. I hope to illustrate in this exercise the transient nature of American tastes and beliefs. Nevertheless, there are, as I argue in chapter 1, certain ideas and standards that endure.

In chapter 7, I turn to the constitutional debate. Can movies be censored, and can communities act to forbid the screening of a film? At first this seems to be a simple, open-and-shut case, governed by the dictates of the First Amendment. However, feature films are not "speech" in the strictest sense. They are also commercial products manufactured for the market. As such, they may also be subject to the commerce clause of the constitution. In this chapter, I examine the constitutional case for both restricting and not restricting the exhibition of feature films. Does the First Amendment trump the commerce clause? Probably not, but the issue is far from settled.

At the end of each chapter, I write about a feature film. This feature film is examined from the perspective presented in the chapter. Each of these minireviews illustrates how the issues presented here can be translated into a perspective from which a film can be viewed. Readers are then invited to review a film of their own choosing from that particular historical, philosophical, economic, or legal perspective.

In the end, I argue that feature films are the hieroglyphics of our time. Future generations may be able to tell more about our culture from viewing our films than from any other single source. That is why this subject is so important. While the answers to the questions of cause and effect and of societal limits may be difficult to answer, there lies at the end of that pursuit perhaps one of the most insightful and fruitful examinations of American society going into the twenty-first century.

On a final note, this book is about film and politics in the United States. This limitation should not be taken to mean that other nations do not have a tradition of filmmaking worthy of mention. In fact, I believe that choosing to examine the films of France, Italy, Germany, or Japan can tell us much about the politics and sensibilities of those countries, giving us the types of insights that would take years to obtain in any other way. I hope that with this book I can establish a model that other scholars can follow in examining and explaining the countries with which they have more familiarity. Furthermore, I hope that in publishing this book, I further legitimize the study of culture as way to gain insight into the politics of ours and other states.

Feature Film: *Master and Commander: On the Far Side of the World* (2003)

This is a review of a current, successful, big-budget production, Hollywood film. Basically, any film of this type can be chosen at random and analyzed as to its meaning in the sense of the transient popular culture and more enduring political culture (defined earlier) of the United States. This film is "political" in the sense that it reflects, reinforces, and may in fact drive the political attitudes of those who go to see it.

In this very successful feature film, bankable Australian star Russell Crowe plays a British ship captain in pursuit of a French privateer during the Napoleonic Wars. Through pluck and individual (meaning unauthorized) determination, Captain Jack Aubrey, played by Crowe, succeeds in his mission but not so completely as to preclude a sequel (just in case the film is a resounding success).

From the political perspective, it is interesting to note that in the book upon which this movie is based, the British captain is pursuing an American warship

Master and Commander: On the Far Side of the World. *Photo by Stephen Vaughan. Courtesy of M.P. & T.V. Photo Archive.*

during the War of 1812. It is not hard to see why the theme of a British frigate pursuing and ultimately destroying an American warship wouldn't work well given the tenor of the times and the market for American films.

The French make such a more convenient enemy in the aftermath, from the American perspective, of their reprehensible behavior leading up to the war with Iraq. Indeed, the French are portrayed in the film as being devious and ultimately dishonorable. But since there is a large market for American films in Britain and in most of the rest of Europe, and because the French have placed restraints on the screening of American films anyhow (to protect French "culture" and the French film industry), there is no reason that the British can't be the good guys as long as the French are the bad. After all, the British have been fairly reliable allies since that unpleasantness leading up to the burning of the White House in 1814 (including their stalwart support and participation in the recent invasion and occupation of Iraq).

The film is a ripping yarn with marvelous special effects. It is a wonderfully crafted product. It should be noted that the violence in the film, while fast paced and skillfully choreographed, is not particularly graphic, with much of the dismemberment taking place offscreen. After all, this is a PG-rated film.

The narrative itself is pretty standard, relying on one of the most common and well-tested story lines in American commercial film, that of the "buddy" film. The British captain and his ship's doctor have a wholesome manly relationship based on a loose but not too demonstrative affection that could not be mistaken for a homosexual attraction, even though there are virtually no women in the film. And when a woman does appear, the captain gazes lustfully upon her just to accentuate the point that he is a man's man.

Okay, so you don't agree. What do you think?

EXERCISE

Select the film that is currently leading in box office receipts. Write a review of the film from the perspective of a social scientist. What does the popularity of the film tell us about the politics of the audience that watches it and the filmmakers who produce it?

NOTES

1. Studio News, "Gibson Passes on Moore's Documentary; Miramax Picks It Up," www.imdb.com/news/sb/2003-05-13#film3 (accessed February 1, 2005).

2. Internet Movie Database, "Business Data for *Roger & Me*," www.imdb.com/title/tt0098213/business (accessed February 1, 2005).

3. Internet Movie Database, "Business Data for *Bowling for Columbine*," www.imdb.com/title/tt0310793/business (accessed February 1, 2005).

4. Parenthetically, Quentin Tarantino, director of *Pulp Fiction*, was the chair of the Cannes Festival Awards Committee.

5. Internet Movie Database, "News for *Fahrenheit 9/11*," www.imdb.com/title/tt0361596/news (accessed February 1, 2005).

6. Thomas Sowell, "The Hyena Press," *Human Events Online*, www.humaneventsonline.com/article.php?id=4015 (accessed November 22, 2004).

7. Roper Center, "Our Country's Main Challenges Are in the Moral Dimension, Not in Economics or Power," *Public Perspective* 8, no. 2 (February/March 1997): 10.

8. The media can be defined as "organizations of communication that take different forms, such as broadcasting and print, and create and transmit a vast array of content." David L. Paletz, *The Media in American Politics: Contents and Consequences* (New York: Longman, 1998), 4.

9. For a strong critique of the entire notion of political culture as it is commonly used, see Margaret R. Somers, "What's Political or Cultural about Political Culture and the Public Sphere? Toward an Historical Sociology of Concept Formation," *Sociological Theory* 13, no. 2 (July 1995): 113–44.

10. Gabriel Almond and Sidney Verba, *The Civic Culture: Political Attitudes and Democracy in Five Nations* (Boston: Little, Brown, 1965), 12.

11. Almond and Verba, *Civic Culture*, 30.

12. For a good recent discussion of American exceptionalism, see Byron Shafer, ed., *Is America Different? A New Look at American Exceptionalism* (New York: Oxford University Press, 1991).

13. I should note that most African Americans and Native Americans did not share in this immigrant experience. Thus, the black and Native American political culture is somewhat different. However, inasmuch as these peoples are in the minority, when I talk about mainstream American culture, I refer to the largely shared experience of flight from economic and political oppression. This is not to ignore the role that African Americans and Native Americans have played in the formation of American political culture. They have both influenced and been influenced by the mainstream. Thus, American political culture is even more complex than the generalities outlined here.

14. For an outstanding discussion of the techniques of film production, see James Monaco, *How to Read a Film*, 3rd ed. (New York: Oxford University Press, 2000).

15. See Robert Putnam, "Tuning In, Tuning Out: The Strange Disappearance of Social Capital in America," *PS: Political Science & Politics* 27, no. 4 (December 1995): 664–83.

16. There is the rare exception of the documentary or the "art" film that is produced not so much for the market but for the purpose of individual expression. However, the price of making a film is so dear as to exclude all but the most intrepid artist. For example, Francis Ford Coppola sank much of his personal fortune (earned from the making of the *Godfather*, 1972) into making a series of artful and ultimately commercially unsuccessful films, including *Apocalypse Now* (1979) and *One from the Heart* (1982). Few filmmakers have that kind of personal courage and conviction.

17. For a discussion of the transient nature and effects of popular culture, see James B. Gilbert, "Popular Culture," in "Contemporary America," special issue, *American Quarterly* 35, nos. 1–2 (Spring–Summer 1983): 141–54.

SUGGESTED READING

Deming, Barbara. *Running Away from Myself: Dream Portrait of America Drawn from the Films of the Forties.* New York: Viking, 1969.

Jowett, Garth. *Film: The Democratic Art.* Boston: Little, Brown, 1976.

Monaco, James. *How to Read a Film: Movies, Media, Multimedia.* 3rd ed. New York: Oxford University Press, 2000.

Paletz, David L. *The Media in American Politics: Contents and Consequences.* New York: Longman, 1998.

Scott, Ian. *American Politics in Hollywood Film.* Chicago: Fitzroy Dearborn, 2000.

Sklar, Robert. *Movie-Made America: A Cultural History of American Movies.* New York: Vintage Books, 1994.

Wood, Michael. *America in the Movies.* New York: Basic, 1975.

1

Film, the Media, and American Tales

In his classic examination of political systems, David Easton suggests that the media play an important role in what he calls the "feedback loop" of politics.[1] Feedback in political systems is the information transmitted to the public, mainly by the media that inform the public as to the actions of government and guide the public to their responses, which in turn gives direction to the government for further action. In most political systems, even authoritarian ones but particularly in democracies, the government is constantly adjusting policy to conform to public opinion. The media play a crucial role in this feedback process. Particularly for those not directly affected by a particular policy, the media play a crucial role in providing information and interpreting the effects of public policy. Thus, the conversation of politics is carried on through this feedback loop. While we generally think about media primarily as a journalistic enterprise (the journalistic media can include anything from television and radio journalism to the newspapers), as a subset of the media there is also the entertainment industry, of which feature films are a part. While the role of the entertainment media in this feedback loop is much more subtle, what we view as entertainment informs, forms, and transmits our concerns. How the entertainment industry addresses social problems should be of interest to decision makers. After all, in viewing and thus financing films, the public "votes" with its dollars in expressing its interests, concerns, and beliefs.

Decision makers do seem to monitor our moviegoing. The language of movies often slips into the political debate. "Read my lips" ("no new taxes") and "make my day" (in reference to a presidential veto threat) are just two recent examples of how movie lines have become political jargon.[2] Politicians assume, and rightly so, that most people will know what complex ideas a phrase like "make my day" connotes. That phrase captures exactly the point that political candidates are trying to make, and, in being test-marketed at the theater, the language of the movies becomes a surefire appeal to a specific audience. In fact, after sports analogies (the sports industry is another component of the entertainment media), references from the movies are some of the most commonly used metaphors in the language of American politics.

Feedback through the media is not purely in one direction or the other, through the bottom up or from the top down. Not only does the public register its concerns and interests in its consumption of entertainment and news, but there is also clearly an influence going in the other direction. News editors are constantly making decisions about what stories to cover, what points in a news story to emphasize, and how to place a news story into a broader context. So it is too with the movies. Movies (and literature in general) place a spin on the events of the world. The choices that film producers make in editing, marketing, financing, casting, and scripting all represent editorial decisions of a kind. Who decides what we see in the theater and how that product is presented is an editorial decision. Whether those decisions are a function of the personal bias of the people who make those decisions is a matter for debate. One thing seems to be certain, however—the journalistic and entertainment media are not clear, unfiltered reflections of public interests and concerns.[3]

Thus, we need to think of films as being influenced by and influencing public opinion. A most obvious example of this sort of phenomenon is that of *The China Syndrome* (1979), a film that evoked the concern shared by many about the dangers of nuclear power. That film is an obvious example of popular culture reflecting current problems. Cable and network television produce shows that are almost contemporaneous with current events and our modern lives. Given the longer lead time for their production and the broader market for their product, filmmakers are somewhat less current but are nevertheless cognizant of current events and political trends. *The Contender* (2000), a story about a politician accused of sexual indiscretions, along with *Primary Colors* (1998), are clearly comments on the politics of the Clinton era. But the contemporary political and social commentary of film can be even subtler than that. In the era of the Great Depression, *Mr. Smith Goes to Washington* (1939), *Gabriel over the White House* (1933), and *Meet John Doe* (1941) all evinced a growing concern about the viability of democracy in the face of fascism, political corruption, and economic decline. In the 1940s, during the Second World War, films taught us about how to act as patriots and why we should fight our enemies. And after the war came the doubts about American life in peacetime, evoked in an entire genre of films collectively known as *film noir* (one of the best examples of which is *The Big Sleep*, 1946). In the 1950s both directly and in metaphor, the red menace was on display and so on throughout the twentieth century.

To what extent and in what ways the entertainment media reflect and drive the concerns of the public who consume its product is hard to say. It is not necessarily true that the financial success of *Silence of the Lambs* (1991) or *The Godfather* (1972) expresses an overwhelming public fascination with mass murderers and the Mafia, but it is not too difficult to suggest that the focus on crime in film in general both reflects and transmits some degree of societal enthrallment with the Mafia and a concern with violence and crime. Certainly, the increasing acceptance of graphic violence on-screen indicates, if nothing else, a higher degree of tolerance for that sort of depiction.

Whether this tolerance then translates into greater tolerance for real-life violence in the form of, say, the death penalty or war is an open question. Establishing that sort of connection would require exploring one more link on the causal chain. Does film violence beget actual violence?

But even if that were true, film violence could work in the opposite way. Depictions of violence can lead to a certain type of revulsion and outrage. Steven Spielberg, it is said, made the battle scenes in *Saving Private Ryan* (1998) as graphic as they were in order to accurately depict the horrors of war. Anyone watching those scenes would probably think twice about favoring war as a policy option. News footage of civil rights demonstrators being clubbed by local police in Selma, Alabama, in 1964 had the effect of nudging a large segment of the American public to support civil rights legislation. By the same token, it makes sense that films extolling the glory of war or the repulsiveness of crime would drive public sensibilities in another direction.

As part of the feedback loop, the entertainment media play a subtle but important role in American politics. To the extent that public opinion in a democracy influences politics and to the extent that politics determines "who gets what, when and how,"[4] the media and even the entertainment media become an important influence on how we prosper and how we lead our lives. In the chapters to follow, I discuss in detail some of the issues introduced here. I am particularly interested in the issue of films as cause and effect—at both the market and the individual level. How much influence does the market have on the content of film as opposed to the beliefs and prejudices of filmmakers themselves? Furthermore, at the individual level, how do film messages translate into actual behavior? In other words, where does film exist on the feedback loop?

There are three general ways that the information transmitted through the feedback loop can be altered. At one level the message of the media can be affected by the biases of the industry itself. This encompasses the debate concerning the liberal or conservative bias of the media. I examine those biases in chapter 3. At another level the media can be influenced by their structures. The fact that in the former Soviet Union *Pravda* was published in a totalitarian state and that the *New York Times* is published in a capitalistic democratic state certainly affects the journalistic tone and content of those newspapers. I examine this political economy of the film industry in chapter 2. Finally, media can be influenced in their relationships to a state's political culture. In this chapter, I examine the effects on the media feedback loop of American political culture.

FILM AS PART OF POLITICAL CULTURE

Easton also writes of the environmental context in which a political system operates. By environmental context, I mean the deep-seated beliefs of our society that affect public policy. More specifically, political culture has been described as "a 'mind set' that has the effect of limiting attention to less than the full range of alternate behaviors."[5]

For example, the selection or tolerance by the public of an overtly authoritarian government may be possible in Algeria or Russia or even Italy but would be unlikely in largely libertarian political systems such as the United States. After all, libertarians believe, as do most Americans, that the government that governs best governs least.[6] While there is some intramural disagreement over the size and scope of government, the communitarian perspective—or the belief in the importance of a collective identity and response[7]—never gained much traction in the United States. By the same token, the heroic sacrifice of the individual to the needs of the all-encompassing state, a perspective central to fascist ideology, never gained much leverage in the United States either. Americans are just too independent for that sort of political involvement. Thus, the spectrum of American political debate and the range of the acceptable political message are delimited by a rejection of the communal approach to politics. Even rather limited proposals that require Americans to act as a community, such as affirmative action (or national health care or social security for that matter), are highly controversial because they regard certain persons as part of a protected class rather than as persons deserving reward on the basis of individual merit.[8]

These parameters of political debate influence the media. As noted film critic Andrew Sarris has written,

> Simply by looking at movies again and again I began to see them in terms of recurring myths and fables deep within our psyches rather than as transient impressions of the surface of our society. Also, I began to realize that the cinema did not faithfully record all the realities of politics. . . . The enormous expense of production, and the publicity attendant on exhibition make it mandatory for films to be in tune either with their society or with at least a sympathetic subculture within that society.[9]

Thus, a serious (not mocking) rendition or depiction of socialism is rarely seen on American television or at the movies. With the exception of the film *Reds* (1981), a reasonably successful film about the life of socialist writer Jack Reed, most American films ignore the socialist revolution in Russia (*Enemy at the Gates*, 2001), mock its results (*Dr. Zhivago*, 1965), or remember nostalgically the rule of the czar (*Nicholas and Alexandria*, 1971). Without getting into a discussion of which of these depictions are most accurate, it would be safe to say that the most popular message, the one most likely to succeed commercially, will not paint capitalism as a threat to world peace and prosperity. There are plenty of other examples of this tendency to rewrite or at least selectively remember history in American films. Slavery is whitewashed or ignored, even in recent films (*Cold Mountain*, 2003). The slaughter of Native Americans was for many years viewed as a triumph, only lately being depicted in a more nuanced manner.[10]

The most prominent determinants of a society's political culture are geographic, historical, temporal (point in time), and, for lack of a better term, cultural.[11] Geographic determinants such as location, resources, climate, and so on, are vital determinants of a nation's development. In the case of the United States, its relatively large size, self-sufficiency, and isolation have contributed greatly to the American character. The history of the settlement of the West is a significant totem in the American psyche that reflects our geographical heritage. Also, our relative isolation, bounded on both sides by vast oceans, has allowed our culture to develop in a unique manner, largely unsullied by recent changes in the Far East and Europe. For example, while the world drifted into the totalitarianism of the 1930s, the United States remained relatively aloof.

The largely shared historical experiences of American citizens—most prominently, the immigrant experience, our relative isolation, our relative resource self-sufficiency, our struggle with slavery and its aftereffects, and our attempt to build a multicultural society—are all fundamental determinants of dominant attitudes in the United States. The status of the United States as a mature democracy with an advanced capitalist economy reflects the fact that there are widely shared notions of equality (and the meaning of equality) and justice. Finally, while the ethnic diversity of the United States is quite remarkable, the dominant cultural influence at this time is the English language and the European subcontinent. In terms of religion, Americans are only somewhat devout but fairly unanimous in their support for the Judeo-Christian ethic. All of these factors add up to an exceptional and, given the diversity of our population, surprisingly homogeneous political culture.[12]

All of these environmental influences combine to delimit the range of policy options available to politicians in the American political system. And if feature films are reflective of the political culture, the political environment, too, delimits these films. As noted, it is hard to imagine that a film explicitly extolling the virtues of a centralized, state-controlled economy would have much commercial potential in the United States. By the same token, foreign films in the United States generally receive a quite limited release, which says something not only about the perceived marketability of those films but also about cultural sensibilities in the United States. Foreign themes and sensibilities as depicted in films don't play well in the mall cineplex. On the other hand, it is interesting to note that American films are widely accepted abroad as one of our country's most profitable and important exports.

HOLLYWOOD AND ITS EFFECT ON/BY AMERICAN POLITICAL CULTURE

By answering three general questions, we can analyze American films to trace the contours of American political culture. First, what are the special characteristics of American political culture represented in American films? As discussed, there is much about American culture that is exceptional. That exceptionalism is reflected in the films that are produced in the United States. For example, the plots of American films present us with explanations of who is responsible for what. In successful films, these are explanations that resonate and ring true. In looking for the politics of American films, we can look for the explanatory conventions. For example, is the criminal a "bad person" or the product of a deprived upbringing? Are people poor because they are lazy or because they are beset by disadvantages not of their own making? Are people successful because of their own individual efforts or because of the advantages they inherit or the opportunities provided to them by living within a nurturing community? In answering these questions and accepting those explanations as logical and just, we are told much about our American view of the world. And through repetition on television, in the theater, and on the news, these explanations become reinforced.

Second, does American culture dictate the content of American film, or is it the other way around? This is an important question. If film content is simply the plotting of an ideologically distant and isolated community ("Hollywood"), then films tell us nothing about the beliefs of the majority of Americans. However, if films are truly made to meet the demands of the consumer, then the logic of the influence of film is simple. Filmmakers are businessmen and businesswomen. They want to make money. They make money by giving the public what it wants. Films then come to largely reflect the sensibilities of their audience. Even if that is true, the influence could work, in some limited sense, in the other direction as well.

Third, can films influence the behavior and perceptions of Americans as well? Most of this influence, I suggest, is simply reinforcement of beliefs already held. Since films are made in the service of the market, then the biases they reflect also become the biases they promote. For example, the recent film *Road Trip* (2000) portrays a picture of college life that is hardly the norm, but it sure looks like a lot of fun. And, to be honest, I found the film funny and entertaining even though that's not college life as I experienced it or as I see it taking place around me on campus. As a professor, I do see at least the surface veneer of campus life. Nevertheless, the film is so attractive and pleasing that it can't help but influence behavior as, say, *Animal House* (1978) did in an earlier generation.

What is just as interesting about this notion of the direction of causality is not only what it does to a domestic audience but also what it does to a foreign audience. After all, movie sales abroad constitute about 60 percent of American feature-film revenues, and what goes on in *Road Trip* probably has very little to do with what happens at a university in Istanbul or Mexico City. And maybe such an influence is not so bad. One can only guess at how the perceptions (and perhaps the behaviors) of foreigners are influenced by this important American export.

AMERICAN IDEOLOGY—WHAT THEMES TO LOOK FOR IN AMERICAN FILMS

There are several core concepts of American political ideology that permeate feature motion pictures. Far and away the most dominant features of American political culture are the principles of its founding, classical liberalism. This is not the liberalism of Ted Kennedy, although that is part of it. Nor is it exclusively the philosophy of the Libertarian Party, although it is part of that too. Rather, liberalism, what I call *classical liberalism*, is the philosophy of the commercial middle class, those people who earn their living in the marketplace. Liberalism relies on the market to coordinate economic activity and leans toward the protection of private property. Liberalism, as an ideology, justifies a capitalist economic system and the American variant of democracy.[13]

According to these "classical" liberals, society is like the marketplace, where the value of ideas, people, and products are determined by the preferences of consumers. Those goods that are in demand will be valued, and those that are not, will not. Thus, the market for one's product determines one's worth—and the market delivers perfect justice. All of this should sound pretty familiar to the American reader since in one way or another, most of us are classical liberals.

Classical liberals will tolerate interference in the marketplace (and, thus, people's lives) only insofar as those limitations are imposed by a government, controlled through a democratic process that is respectful of basic human rights, often called "natural" rights. Thus, according to the classical liberal, it is appropriate for a government to provide police protection, enforce contracts, and provide for national defense. Strict adherence to classical liberalism will result in a limited government guided by democratic participation. There are some exceptions to the rule concerning government interference, such as in the areas of civil rights, social welfare, and so-called moral values. But even in these instances Americans are deeply conflicted about the need for government to intervene.[14]

Democratic rule is important to classical liberals because democracy is as close to the absence of government as is possible without the actual absence of government. Through the democratic process we rule ourselves. Therefore, the laws imposed by a democratic government, in essence, are restrictions that we have placed upon ourselves. As long as the government respects the rights of individuals, citizens are obliged to obey the law (as if they were being true to themselves). However, when a government violates the rights of its citizens, citizens have a right and even an obligation to rebel. Thus, classical liberalism was an attractive justification for a Declaration of Independence and, ultimately, the design of our government.

Besides the essential role of democracy and capitalism in a liberal state is the notion of natural rights. John Locke, one the founders of the liberal tradition, argues in his *Second Treatise on Government* that all persons by virtue of their humanity are deserving of certain "natural rights." The centerpiece of this Lockean notion of rights is the concept of property. Individuals, according to Locke, have the right to possess property free from the violation of those rights by individuals or the government. Locke defines property rights rather broadly. Property can be defined as a possession or as the "property" rights one has in one's own person. In other words, an individual in a just society should be free from assaults to his or her own person or possessions.[15] The founders of the United States adopted this concept of natural rights more or less intact as reflected in the words of the preamble of the Declaration of Independence.[16] According to Locke, all individuals have the right to life, liberty, and property (later converted to "the pursuit of happiness" by Thomas Jefferson in the Declaration of Independence).

As prominent as Lockean liberalism is in constitutional design, it has persisted as an ideological strain throughout American history and is being reinforced still. Two important historical processes have served to lock the American body politic into an eighteenth-century philosophy in a twenty-first-century world. The fact that the United States has been predominantly settled by Protestant Christians has generally reinforced Lockean liberalism in the United States. Protestantism was born of a revolt against the Catholic church. Among other things, Protestants believe that Christians can have a direct relationship with God, without the necessary intercession of a priest or the hierarchy of an official church. Along with the liberal rejection of strong hierarchical government, these beliefs mesh quite well with the individualism of Lockean liberalism, where the fate of the individual in the market is determined by his or her own actions.[17]

Besides religion and the tradition of Lockean liberalism, American individualism is reinforced by yet another widely shared American backdrop, the immigrant experience. For almost every American, with the exception of the Native American, there is a shared experience of flight. In almost every family tree in the United States is an ancestor who dropped a plow, waded out of a rice paddy, or swam the Rio Grande in search of a better life in the United States. That shared history of flight reinforces the individualism of American political culture in a couple of important ways. First, the United States is, and continues to be, populated by the world's dispossessed. For those whose lives are comfortable and connected in the Old World, there is no need to flee. But for those who are persecuted or simply put at a disadvantage by the social hierarchy of the Old World, the United States offers a legitimate and desirable alternative. Thus, most immigrants who come the United States are distrustful of governments and the established order. They desire that people be judged not by their origins but by their individual merits. More than anything else, they hope that the government will leave them alone. This is as true today for Vietnamese, Nigerian, or Cuban immigrants as it was one hundred years ago for immigrants from Poland, Ireland, or Italy.[18]

It is important to note that I intentionally include African Americans in this category (of immigrants) because so many fled the South to find work in the North and, in doing so, had the experience of flight. In addition, a large percentage of African Americans arrived well after the end of slavery, from Africa or the Caribbean, and have been exposed to more or less the standard immigrant experience. Nevertheless, it would be impossible to argue that the black community has had a typical American historical experience. Thus, the current of Lockean liberalism does not run as strong in the black community—which is precisely the reason that in many ways the black community is more a distinct community than many others in the United States.

The immigrant experience is a recurring theme in many American films. *America, America* (1963), *Hester Street* (1975), *Coming to America* (1988), *Moscow on the Hudson* (1984), and *The Godfather* (1972) series are just a few examples of what is a standard film plot genre in American political culture. These films resonate not only in the story they tell, a story to which most Americans can relate, but also in the metaphors they elicit. The immigrant is a risk taker, entrepreneurial and courageous. These are the positive traits of the immigrant that we admire and hope to emulate in this country.

However, there are traits in the immigrant that are also not so attractive, which are also part of the immigrant tradition (if not the myth) and thus American political culture. Immigrants are not a little hedonistic; they are loners, often abandoning their families and the other "problems" of their society. They are isolationist, insensitive to the plight of others, aggressive toward those who impinge on their freedom, and generally antisocial. It is this hedonism that was on display in the genocide committed against Native Americans, in the failure of the United States to join the League of Nations, and in the smallest per capita humanitarian assistance budget for any developed nation.[19]

Thus, the immigrant experience produces a relatively consistent and somewhat unique notion of "freedom." Freedom for Americans is the absence of constraint. This is in contrast to the freedom "to" as opposed to the freedom "from."[20] In many other societies, freedom is evaluated in the functional sense: it is not enough for someone to have the right to do something, but they must also have the functional ability to do something as well. This is not generally true in the United States. For example, in theory anyone can influence political decision making in the United States. In practice, however, there is a certain class bias in our American political system. More simply put, all things being equal, the rich have more influence than do the poor. Nevertheless, in the United States we are loathe to define that as an insult to the freedom to participate. Thus, the freedom to participate as equals in politics exists in theory but not in practice. This concept of rights is important because it defines a wide range of story lines so popular in American films. For example, in many variants of the "rags to riches" story, characters overcome their disadvantaged circumstances to make good or have themselves heard. Whether that is an accurate depiction of the American story is neither here nor there. The fact that the allegory of rags to riches persists and is constantly reinforced in our popular culture creates a reality of consciousness, if not a reality of fact.

Individualism, as opposed to communalism, is a powerful strain of American political ideology. Consequently, socialism and fascism, ideologies that have on occasion been central to European politics, have never gained much of a toehold in the United States. The subjugation of personal preferences to the needs of the state in socialism and fascism are just too much a violation of the American notion of freedom to resonate in the United States. Thus, story lines in praise of the rugged individual (Horatio Alger) and in support of the individual against the state (Ayn Rand) are a prominent and popular part of the American literary tradition and, thus, film tradition as well.

Of course, there are limits to even theoretical freedom. The actions of one person in society affect others. Thus, there is a constant conversation in American politics about the limits of freedom. For example, we witness the spirited debate in the United States over laws related to the possession of guns. Where these limits are is the source of endless and intense debate. These debates, which are intensely fought in Congress and the courts, are also a recurring theme in the literature of American political culture. But in many other political cultures, these issues would be beside the point.

What is not generally discussed in the American context is functional freedom. In theory, anyone can become president. However, is that functionally true? Judging by the past, the only people who can qualify for the presidency are relatively wealthy Protestant white males—with the exception of John Kennedy, who fits the bill in all other ways save for his religion. Of course, there is an equal opportunity for education or advancement in the United States. But in reality, do we live in a meritocracy or in an aristocracy based not on title but on wealth? This is an issue that is less explicitly debated. After all, such a discussion would tend to undermine the legitimacy of many of our politicians and business elite whose status is as much inherited as it is earned. Furthermore, an explicit discussion of the real opportunities available in American society would discomfit the moviegoing public, which, we shall see, is also from the high economic strata. Nevertheless, when in *Mr. Smith Goes to Washington* (1939), or more recently in *Dave* (1993), regular guys find themselves in high office, they do so through a series of accidents and not through the more traditional route of winning an election. It is almost inconceivable that a common person could otherwise attain political office.

AMERICAN TALES

American political culture has generated a set of stories that serve as metaphors for American history. These American tales (designated as such in deference to an animated feature of the same name) provide a sort of oral tradition of American nationhood. In every community there is such an oral tradition. These stories exist to explain history, to condone some behaviors and condemn others, and to pass on the culture of the community from one generation to the next. In a complex, technologically advanced society such as ours, these tales are told and retold through the media. It is not up to the media to challenge these myths. In fact, to challenge these myths would be dangerous for media that in our country are so dependent on market success. The fact that much of what these stories say is true reinforces their credibility. But not everything in the American tales is true, or it is at least subject to question. And, yet, these tales are repeated over and over, in one form or another, and go pretty much unquestioned in American film. Thus, American movies serve an important role in perpetuating and promoting our culture. There are several important American tales. Here is just a sample.

The Conquest of the West

One of the most enduring themes of American film is the conquest of the West. In this story rugged individualists, overcoming all sorts of adversity, settle the virgin wilderness frontier and thereby spread American civilization from the Atlantic to the

Pacific. There are so many films of this genre that it is near impossible to list even a representative sample. However, some of the classic favorites include *The Gold Rush* (1925), *High Noon* (1952), *My Darling Clementine* (1946), *The Searchers* (1956), *The Wild Bunch* (1969), *Little Big Man* (1970), *McCabe and Mrs. Miller* (1971), *Paint Your Wagon* (1969), *Unforgiven* (1992), and many others. There are, of course, some inaccuracies in this story as depicted in the movies. Much of the West was conquered by the American military in the Mexican-American and Indian Wars. The West was hardly uninhabited anyhow. The U.S. government actively subsidized the railroads (built by slave and immigrant labor) that played such a significant role in the settlement of the West and so on. Nevertheless, the conquest story is true enough to resonate whenever it is depicted in films. Besides, the conquest story reinforces the liberal notion of minimal government; individualism; and justice in hard work, enterprise, and true grit.

Kudos go to Clint Eastwood and the makers of *Unforgiven* (1992). In that excellent and Academy Award–winning film, we see a counter to the traditional Western. All of the elements of the formula are there: the gunfighter, the sheriff, the sidekick, the whore with the heart of gold, and the apprentice; but what is missing is that none of them seem to play their assigned roles. The gunfighter is sensitive, disgusted with what he has been asked to do. The sheriff is brutal and lawless. The African American sidekick is every bit an equal to the protagonist and so on. But more to the point, as if doing penance for his previous work, Clint Eastwood depicts violence as shocking, with permanent and heartrending consequences. Is this film a more accurate depiction of the West? My guess is that the film is not much more historically accurate than *Shane* (1953). But what is different is that in this film the conversation about the West and its myths has changed. Thus, *Unforgiven* is a modern film about the West that tells us as much about America in the 1990s as in the 1890s.

The Cult of the Individual

The main focus for justice in a liberal society is the individual. To the greatest extent possible, individual rights are to be honored in the United States even at the expense of the community. That is a core value of a liberal society. The cult of the individual as played out in movie plots goes something like this: a resilient resourceful individual with personal courage and ingenuity overcomes the odds and succeeds without help against the grain of an oppressive environment often depicted as the government.

As noted, because the rights of the individual are so well respected in our country (even over the rights of the community), European and Asian communitarian traditions have never taken hold. Furthermore, the individualism of American society is constantly reinforced by the inflow of immigrants who generally share the core American values of self-reliance, thrift, and enterprise (the protestations of the nativist anti-immigration crowd notwithstanding). This focus on the individual is mainly all to the good. It promotes a dynamic, vibrant, and creative society. Thus, the benefits of individualism are constantly celebrated in the story lines of film. One of my favorite films in this regard is *Lonely Are the Brave* (1962), but there are many others, including much of the rags-to-riches genre—see *The Truman Show* (1998), *Conan the Barbarian* (1982), *The Fountainhead* (1949), *Mr. Smith Goes to Washington* (1939), and *Mr. Deeds Goes to Town* (1936).

The problem with this point of view, however, is that the rights of the individual must sometimes be put into context. Unless you live in an uninhabited wilderness, what you do has consequences for other people. Since the Wild West no longer exists, the rights of the individual in this country are to a certain extent limited for no other reason than for the shortage of space. Nevertheless, there may exist a disconnect between the ability of our society to protect individual rights (as we define them) and our sometimes ineffective attempts to address the problems of urban sprawl, environmental degradation, and other pressing problems. Collective action in response to these problems is hampered by our tendency toward deference to individual rights over community action, deference that is constantly reinforced by the repetition of this American tale. Thus, the movies affect public policy by reinforcing certain beliefs in our political culture.

Rags to Riches

There is a tremendous amount of controversy in the scholarly community in regard to the true nature of American opportunity. To what extent are the opportunities provided to us in this society functional as opposed to illusory? In other words, to what extent can individuals get ahead in our political and economic system? The nuanced answer to this question is that, by and large, income disparity is increasing in the United States, but that is not the same as saying that the opportunity for the individual (to get ahead) isn't there.[21] Thus, it is not entirely inaccurate to suggest that, as the American literary tradition presented in the movies tends to reassure us, all holdings are earned and thus deserved and that we live in a meritocracy in the sense that hard work and perseverance are richly rewarded. One of the most time-honored and richly rewarded genres in American fiction is the tale of rags to riches.[22] In this story, those who are born poor have a real opportunity to overcome their disadvantage, and those who are wealthy have earned and thus deserve their prosperity. Some would argue, however, that in general, people who are born poor tend to stay that way and that in order to reinforce that belief, Americans are fed a steady diet of films and literature that extol the virtues of our economy that are actually the exceptions to the rule.[23] Nevertheless, some of the best films in this rags-to-riches genre are *Citizen Kane* (1941), *The Godfather* series, *The Getaway* (1972), *Mildred Pierce* (1945), *Stripes* (1981), and *An Unmarried Woman* (1978). In each of these movies, the protagonist is beset by a set of circumstances that make it near impossible to get ahead. In seeing these obstacles overcome, we come to believe that we too have a chance.

For example, in the enormously popular film *Pretty Woman* (1990), the best-looking, healthiest, most intelligent, nonaddicted streetwalker on the planet manages through pluck and charm to win the heart of a billionaire client. There are some real ironies in this story. The protagonist, rather than going to school or working hard at her job, manages to sleep her way to the top. While probably unintentional, this film can be seen as being basically anticapitalistic. Since the story is so preposterous, and because the "work" that the protagonist does involves performing sex for money, a viewer might well conclude that the film is a paean to Marxist Leninism—the suggestion here being that the only way a woman in her station can get ahead in our free market economy is to sleep with and marry money. But I don't think that is why the film was so popular. This weird story line (admittedly very nicely acted and produced) appeals to the underdog, rags-to-riches hopes of the moviegoer. But it doesn't tell us much about how getting wealthy can actually happen.

I am not going to argue that all holdings are inherited and thus in some sense undeserved (at least from the perspective of a meritocrat). Much too much evidence suggests that real opportunity exists in the United States—with Ross Perot, Ronald Reagan, Bill Clinton, and Bill Gates being prime examples of those who have succeeded from humble beginnings. Nevertheless, much of the wealth and privilege held in the United States is inherited, and much of the law in the United States is intended to keep it that way (making the lives of Clinton, Gates, Reagan, and Perot all the more remarkable). It is this disconnect between the myth of a meritocracy and the actuality of an oligarchy of inherited wealth that makes this genre in American literature and popular entertainment somewhat distorted.

If, according to the rags-to-riches myth, all wealth is earned and thus deserved, then poverty is earned and deserved as well. This myth too is highlighted in American popular culture. Throughout American history, not just in the history of American motion pictures, the poor and oppressed are often depicted as deserving their fate. Blacks, particularly in the past, were disparagingly depicted as slow and lazy. Native Americans were traditionally depicted as primitive and brutal. Hispanics, Asians, and other groups in society have been subject to depiction through cultural and gender stereotypes that have been used at one time or another to explain and justify the existing hierarchy in society.

Some of these cultural values and beliefs are rather consistent across time. The American commitment to democracy and the free market is pretty much bedrock solid. However, other values wax and wane. Thus, the timing of films is also important. The sensibilities of a film made in the 1950s were different from the content of a film made in the 1990s. In some cases, the myths have changed and so have the stories. In American political culture, a new set of stories is being told.

TIMING

It would be inaccurate to say that the movie industry is consistently insensitive to the plight of those who are less fortunate in society. As public attitudes change, so do audiences' tastes for entertainment. Times do change, and the movies change along with them. For example, many films have chronicled Custer's last stand. But there is a profound difference in the representation of General George Armstrong Custer's character in the 1942 film *They Died with Their Boots On* and the 1970 film *Little Big Man*. Certainly, historical fact did not change, but the attitudes of those who make and watch motion pictures reflected different sensibilities thirty years apart. The substantive equivalent of *Little Big Man* could no more have been produced and screened in the 1940s than *They Died with Their Boots On* could have been screened in the modern era. One of the most significant films of all time, *The Birth of a Nation*, is deeply troubling when viewed in the modern context, but it is also a window into the past.

Overall, the movie industry has been in existence for only a relatively short time. Even so, it has been in existence through some of the most tumultuous and significant changes in American history. What we see when we review the brief history of American motion pictures is a study of change in American political culture in the twentieth century.

Some of the major events faithfully recorded in American film that profoundly influenced the United States in the twentieth century were the Depression, World War II, the Cold War, the Vietnam War, and the civil rights and environmental movements. The Depression, for example, as depicted in *The Grapes of Wrath* (1940), is presented as a deeply troubling and somewhat ambiguous failure of capitalism. The narrative of the film never really answers the central question of the film: Why are the Joads (the family at the center of the film) in the fix that they are in? Is the plight of the dispossessed family farmer a function of individual failure, systemic changes within a basically sound capitalist market, or a total and inevitable collapse of the capitalist system? The answer to that question is important because through the interpretation of history we determine solutions. If the Joads are simply shortsighted and inefficient, then all we can recommend is charity. If the Joads are in trouble through no fault of their own, maybe we should ease their transition into another line of work. But if the Joads fail because the system fails, then we may need to change the system.

Not only is political culture reflected in historical film, but movies also often reflect modern sensibilities through metaphor. *Braveheart* (1995), the story of a medieval Scottish revolutionary, was seen by members of the House Republican freshman class as being analogous to the Gingrich "revolution" of 1994 right down to the Democrats as the effete (and sometimes gay) English occupiers to the Republican moderate accommodationists as the Scottish nobles.[24] In fact, the more fantastic the setting of the film, the more freedom the narrative has to reflect contemporary concerns. In the 1950s, *The Thing* (1951) and *The Invasion of the Body Snatchers* (1956) came to underscore the communist menace. *The Invasion of the Body Snatchers* was remade in 1978, and it reflects some of the same, and some of the different, concerns mainly related to people's fear of loss of individuality. *The Planet of the Apes* series reflects the fear of nuclear war; the *China Syndrome* reflects concerns raised by nuclear power; and so on. These are not just films with a message; they are films of a message. These are films that resonate with viewers not just as an escape but also as a release. In viewing our nightmares on-screen, we confront our fears and put them into context. Sometimes these fantasies, such as the multifilm *Star Wars* saga, not only help us confront our fears of the evil empire (the Soviet Union) but also provide us with a cathartic release—the military and spiritual defeat of our adversaries.

CONCLUSION

This chapter is a brief examination of feature film as part of the feedback loop of politics. The entertainment media in a subtle way serves our political culture by repeating our stories, reinforcing our beliefs, and providing an emotional release for our fears. While some of the assumptions underlying the story lines in American film could at least be questioned, it is generally the case that American movies pretty much repeat the same themes in one context or another, over and over. Thus, I would argue that American films are nowhere near the corrosive influence that they are purported to be by the cultural Right.

In the next chapter, I discuss the political economy of the American film industry. American film doesn't deviate from American core values because it is a business like any other. It cannot market products that will not sell. Thus, American films reflect rather than guide American culture, particularly in the modern context. More than ever before, films come to reflect rather than drive the sensibilities of the viewing public. There need, however, to be several provisos added to this argument. Not everyone goes to the movies. Not all films accurately reflect the market. And a lot of filmmaking is just plain bad. I make each of those arguments in turn—but first to the political economy of American film.

Feature Film: *The Coneheads* (1993)

Science fiction often serves as metaphor for concerns and events of political culture. In this comedy, a family of illegal aliens (literally) encounters and overcomes most of the obstacles common to others cast upon these shores. Thus, this film serves to reinforce and even promote certain popular beliefs concerning immigration, tolerance, and upward mobility in the American economy. As such, this film becomes part of the language of American politics by implying that immigration is generally for the good, that opportunities for upward mobility exist in the United States, and that government bureaucracies tend to get in the way.

Beldar and Primat Conehead have been sent from the planet Remulak to conquer Earth. Through a series of misfortunes, their spacecraft crashes in suburban New Jersey. Like many an immigrant cast upon our shores, they are penniless and innocent to the ways, in this case literally, of the New World.

Setting himself to the task at hand, Beldar finds a job and place for them to live. As he is an illegal "alien," he is forced to work off the books as an appliance repairman and later as a taxicab driver. The vast immigrant community of which they are a part accepts the Coneheads and their strange customs as they

The Coneheads. *Photo by Murray Close. Courtesy of M.P. & T.V. Photo Archive.*

would any other foreigners. There is no class or race distinction here where everyone comes from somewhere else.

Because the Coneheads are illegal aliens, Beldar is forced to buy forged immigration documents. As a result, he comes to the attention of the Immigration and Naturalization Service. The INS bureaucrats are petty and vindictive. They go to ridiculous lengths to pursue the now peaceful and prosperous Coneheads.

Because he works hard and is industrious, Beldar is eventually able to buy for himself and Primat (and their new baby) a house in the suburbs. Beldar joins the golf club and Primat the PTA. One of the running jokes throughout the film is the fact that no one seems to be particularly put off by the Coneheads' large and pointy heads. The explanation, of course, is that they are from France. And, in some sense, the French are as foreign to the New Jersey suburbs as aliens from another world would be. No one questions the French connection because no one in New Jersey knows, needs to know, nor wants to know about France. The old country for most immigrants exists in the past. Americans look to the future.

Eventually, the Coneheads are rescued (along with, by accident, two of the INS agents) and returned to Remulak. On Remulak they find a robotic, oppressive, totalitarian state that is as foreign to them now as Earth had been some years before. Ironically, at least one of the sycophant bureaucrats fits in just fine. Through a series of fortunate accidents, the Coneheads are again returned to Earth to conquer the planet. Instead, they stage a disaster and disappear, presumably to return to their suburban lives.

The point is that it is better to live in suburban New Jersey than to rule the planet Earth as a vassal of Remulak. Isn't this the classic immigrant story? Don't agree? What do you think?

EXERCISE

Trace the history of race relations in the United States as depicted in film. Start with the film *Birth of a Nation* and contrast that to the film that is currently leading in box office receipts.

NOTES

1. See David Easton, *The Political System: An Inquiry into the State of Political Science* (New York: Knopf, 1971).

2. It should be noted that President George H. W. Bush uttered these words in an attempt to transmit not just an idea but also an image. President Bush labored under the general perception that he was somewhat removed on the basis of his privileged background from the problems and concerns of regular citizens. Using lines from a popular film, in this case a film that also happened to embody a rather conservative perspective (*Dirty Harry*), Bush implied that he was a "regular" guy to a specific target audience.

3. See Vivian C. Sobchack, "Beyond Visual Aids: American Film as American Culture," *American Quarterly* 32, no. 3 (1980): 280–300.

4. For a good discussion of the definition and nature of politics, see Harold Lasswell, *Politics: Who Gets What, When, How* (New York: Henry Holt, 1938).

5. Quoted from David J. Elkins and Richard E. B. Simeon, "A Cause in Search of Its Effect, or What Does Political Culture Explain?" *Comparative Politics* 11, no. 2 (January 1979): 127–45. Alexis de Tocqueville writes, "In order that society should exist and, *a fortiori*, that a society should prosper, it is necessary that the mind of all citizens should be rallied and held together by certain predominant ideas." Tocqueville, *Democracy in America*, vol. 2 (New York: Knopf, 1945), 8, quoted in John Street, "Review Article: Political Culture—from Civic Culture to Mass Culture," *British Journal of Political Science* 24, no. 1 (January 1994): 95–113. See also, Young C. Kim, "The Concept of Political Culture in Comparative Politics," *Journal of Politics* 26, no. 2 (May 1964): 313–36.

6. This statement is often attributed to Thomas Jefferson but is found in none of his recorded writings. See Paul F. Boller and John George, *They Never Said It* (Oxford: Oxford University Press, 1989), 56.

7. "Communitarians are skeptical about efforts to base a conception of justice on abstract individual rights and on the priority of the right over the good." John Arthur and William H. Shaw, *Justice and Economic Distribution*, 2nd ed. (Englewood Cliffs, N.J.: Prentice Hall, 1991), 242.

8. On this topic, see Theodore Lowi, "The Public Philosophy: Interest-Group Liberalism," *American Political Science Review* 61, no. 1 (March 1967): 5–24; Neil Mitchell, Rhoda E. Howard, and Jack Donnelly, "Liberalism, Human Rights, and Human Dignity (in Controversies)," *American Political Science Review* 81, no. 3 (September 1987): 921–27; or Robert Y. Shapiro and John T. Young, "Public Opinion and the Welfare State: The United States in Comparative Perspective," *Political Science Quarterly* 104, no. 1 (Spring 1989): 59–89.

9. Andrew Sarris, *Politics and Cinema* (New York: Columbia University Press, 1978), 4–5.

10. John A. Price, "The Stereotyping of North American Indians in Motion Pictures," *Ethnohistory* 20, no. 2 (Spring 1973): 153–71.

11. For a discussion of the formation of political culture, see Samuel C. Patterson, "The Political Cultures of the American States," *Journal of Politics* 30, no. 1 (February 1968): 187–209.

12. For more on American exceptionalism, see Byron Shafer, ed., *Is America Different? A New Look at American Exceptionalism* (Oxford: Clarendon Press, 1991). See also, Michael Kammen, "The Problem of American Exceptionalism: A Reconsideration," *American Quarterly* 45, no. 1 (March 1993): 1–43.

13. The classic text on this subject is Louis Hartz's *The Liberal Tradition in America* (New York: Harcourt Brace Jovanovich, 1955).

14. Stanley Feldman and John Zaller, "The Political Culture of Ambivalence: Ideological Responses to the Welfare State," *American Journal of Political Science* 36, no. 1 (February 1992): 268–307.

15. See John Locke, "Of Property," in *Second Treatise of Government*, ed. C. B. Macpherson (Indianapolis, Ind.: Hackett, 1980), chap. 5.

16. "We hold these truths to be self-evident, that all Men are created equal, that they are endowed by their Creator with certain inalienable Rights, that among these are Life, Liberty, and the Pursuit of Happiness."

17. On this topic see, Michael S. Rabieh, "The Reasonableness of Locke, or the Questionableness of Christianity," *Journal of Politics* 53, no. 4 (November 1991): 933–57.

18. For a powerful rendition of the immigrant story, see Oscar Handlin, *The Uprooted: The Epic Story of the Great Migrations That Made the American People* (Philadelphia: University of Pennsylvania Press, 2001); and for a nuanced refutation, see Rogers M. Smith, "Beyond Tocqueville, Myrdal, and Hartz: The Multiple Traditions in America," *American Political Science Review* 87, no. 3 (September 1993): 549–66.

19. A solid repudiation of the notion that American liberalism is unsullied by retrograde nativism is authored by Rogers M. Smith, "The 'American Creed' and American Identity: The Limits of Liberal Citizenship in the United States," *Western Political Quarterly* 41, no. 2 (June 1988): 225–51.

20. The classic discussion of this distinction can be found in Thomas Hill Green's "Lectures on the Principles of Political Obligation," in *T. H. Green: Lectures on the Principles of Political*

Obligation and Other Writings, ed. P. Harris and J. Morrow (Cambridge: Cambridge University Press, 1986).

21. See Carole Shammas, "A New Look at Long-Term Trends in Wealth Inequality in the United States," *American Historical Review* 98, no. 2 (April 1993): 412–31; and Daniel H. Weinberg, Charles T. Nelson, Marc I. Roemer, Edward J. Welniak Jr., "Economic Well-Being in the United States: How Much Improvement? Fifty Years of U.S. Income Data from the Current Population Survey: Alternatives, Trends, and Quality," in "Papers and Proceedings of the 111th Annual Meeting of the American Economic Association," *American Economic Review* 89, no. 2 (May 1999): 18–22.

22. Named in reference to the writings of Horatio Alger, a nineteenth-century author who supposedly extolled the virtues of and opportunities available in our capitalist economy. As it turns out, Alger's writings may have been misinterpreted, as noted in Michael Zuckerman's convincing "The Nursery Tales of Horatio Alger," *American Quarterly* 24, no. 2 (May 1972): 191–209. Nevertheless, the general perception is that Alger is the herald of justice of American capitalism, and the story is so oft repeated that the perception has become reality.

23. For example, see Clarke A. Chambers, "The Belief in Progress in Twentieth-Century America," *Journal of the History of Ideas* 19, no. 2 (April 1958): 197–224, for a disquisition on the illusory nature of American opportunism. Also see Larry J. Griffin and Arne L. Kalleberg, "Stratification and Meritocracy in the United States: Class and Occupational Recruitment Patterns," *British Journal of Sociology* 32, no. 1 (March 1981): 1–38.

24. See Jeffrey Goldberg, "Adventures of a Republican Revolutionary," *New York Times*, November 3, 1996, sec. 6, 42.

SUGGESTED READING

Ball, Terrence, and Richard Dagger. *Political Ideologies and the Democratic Ideal.* 5th ed. New York: Pearson Longman, 2003.

Cripps, Thomas. *Slow Fade to Black: The Negro in American Film, 1900–1942.* New York: Oxford University Press, 1977.

Geertz, Clifford. *Myth, Symbol, and Culture.* New York: Norton, 1974.

Handlin, Oscar. *The Uprooted: The Epic Story of the Great Migrations That Made the American People.* Philadelphia: University of Pennsylvania Press, 2001.

Haskell, Molly. *From Reverence to Rape.* New York: Penguin, 1977.

Locke, John. *Second Treatise of Government.* Edited by C. B. Macpherson. Indianapolis, Ind.: Hackett, 1990.

Rollins, Peter C., and John E. O'Connor. *Hollywood's White House: The American Presidency in Film and History.* Lexington: University of Kentucky Press, 2003.

2

Industry and Bias: The Political Economy of Film

In the previous chapter I suggest that film content, indeed media content, can be influenced from both the top down and the bottom up. From the bottom up, the market influences the content of film through box office receipts. The film industry is a business, and as a business it must turn a profit. Therefore, in some sense, the market for films tells us about our interpretation of history because there are literally some stories we buy and others we don't.

From the top down, film content is biased by the nature of the industry and the people who make the product. As the film industry has evolved, there have been both internal and external pressures that have influenced film content. Politics and economics are not the same thing. Economics is the study of the distribution of goods; politics is also the study of the distribution of goods but with an important difference. Political scientists consider the influence of public policy on the distribution of goods—or who gets what according to the rules of the game. Government regulation is the most obvious case in point of public policy's influencing the distribution of goods. Everything, from government regulation that can restrict certain economic activities to government subsidies that can encourage others, involves a political dimension. But besides the direct intervention of government, economic activities influence politics in other ways.

The unfettered market—the free exchange of goods and services—is basically apolitical, but it can have political results. Consider the market for health care. In the free market, relatively scarce health care services will go to the highest bidder. But illness is egalitarian: it comes to us all. In a free market for health care, some people who are sick will not get treated because they don't have the money to pay. It is up to us as a society to decide whether this is a morally defensible state of affairs. If we believe on balance that it is more important to protect the rights of doctors, pharmaceutical companies, and the insurance industry to ply their trades without restriction than it is to guarantee health services, then some sick people will go untreated. If, on the other hand, we believe that health care is a right and not a privilege, then access to the free market by the aforementioned sectors can be restricted. This is not an either-or proposition. There are varying degrees of regulation. In the case of health care, doctors are licensed; pharmaceutical and insurance companies are regulated; and patients are at least partially subsidized.

Superficially, it may seem that the politics of media control are not on a par with the importance of health care services. But upon further consideration, the media can have a profound influence on the way we think and behave. Advertisers certainly believe (and can prove) this to be true, as they spend billions on media outlets to sell their products. Politicians spend millions, too, to influence how we think. So it stands to reason that the entertainment media influence how we view the world, a view that is crucial to the way that we behave in a democratic society.

In this chapter, I discuss the political economy of the film industry and how the economics of filmmaking produce the particular slant of the final product. The study of political economy can be defined as

> a branch of the social sciences that takes as its principal subject of study the interrela-
> tionships between political and economic institutions and processes. That is, political
> economists are interested in analyzing and explaining the ways in which various sorts
> of government affect the allocation of scarce resources in society through their laws and
> policies as well as the ways in which the nature of the economic system and the behavior
> of people acting on their economic interests affects the form of government and the kinds
> of laws and policies that get made.[1]

The central focus of this chapter is not only how the free market affects the content of film but how the industry's structure, unique historical development, and interaction with government have shaped the content of films. It is fairly reasonable to assume that in an unfettered market, most films tend to appeal to the lowest common denominator. But that is clearly not the case. Many fine (and terrible), financially successful films have and are being made. This is true for three reasons. First, marketing isn't just the science of supplying consumers with what they want. Marketing is also the science of creating a demand for something consumers didn't know they needed—soft drinks, tissues, dryer sheets, Humvees, and so on. Therefore, the industry can shape the market—that is, quality films can be sold. Second, there are forces internal and external to the industry that expand the possibilities for making films, regardless of the market. Furthermore, there are increasing technological opportunities (and limitations) in the making of commercial films. As we shall see, technological limitations on the making of films, patents on technology, and availability of the raw materials for making film have influenced the industry. Times have changed and so has filmmaking.

THE THREE MONOPOLIES OF HOLLYWOOD FILM

Some critics argue that films are becoming ever more explicitly sexual and violent. It is hard to deny that the body count in the movies has been increasing. The question is, why? While self-censorship has been the rule rather than the exception in the movie industry since almost the beginning, the effectiveness of that self-restraint in terms of limiting the pandering to prurient interests has been in decline since the 1960s. What changed between 1910 and 2004 is the film industry's loss of monopoly. Throughout much of its history, the film industry in the United States was structured as some form of monopoly—and the influence of monopoly on movie content was profound.[2]

Economists tell us that monopolies create distortions in the market in a couple of ways. First, monopolies create distorted pricing. Consumers pay more than the market-clearing price for monopoly goods. Second, in a related sense, monopoly industries are less sensitive to consumer demand. By definition a monopoly for a product excludes alternatives. Because the movie industry was in one way or another a monopoly until about 1960, I argue that the movie industry was capable of controlling the content of its films, including their body count, up to that time. However, when the movie monopoly was challenged and more or less broken, the industry was forced to be more competitive. In this case, being more competitive meant being more graphic (by appealing to the lowest common denominator). Thus, the movie industry changed its product not because the culture of Hollywood changed but because the environment of the entertainment market changed.

The First Monopoly: The Edison Trust

Still photography has been in general use since before the American Civil War. By the late nineteenth century there were already some forward thinkers who had envisioned photographic moving pictures. In fact, the novelty use of drawings flipped past the eye in the pages of a book or on some kind of roller had been in use for quite some time. The problem for making moving pictures from photography, however, was that photographs were shot on individual plates with very slow exposure times. In order for action to appear seamless to the human eye, frames must be "flipped" at a minimum of about fifteen frames a second. As a practical matter, until the late nineteenth century, it was impossible to shoot action fast enough with the still photography of the day to capture actual events in motion.[3]

But then the technology changed. A much faster chemical-exposure process was introduced for film, and exposure plates were placed on continuous, flexible ribbons. But there remained one major technological hurdle to overcome. Just because exposure times for film were faster—fast enough to shoot film at the minimum speed for motion pictures of fifteen frames a second—the camera to shoot the film had yet to be invented. The problem was that in photography, even that shot at fifteen or the now standard twenty-four frames a second, photographs have to be shot as stills. In other words, a camera mechanism had to be invented that advanced the film, stopped the film, shot a picture, and advanced the film at a smooth, continuous rate, and it had to perform this process quickly. Such a "pull-down" device (now known as a rotary shutter) was invented in Europe and the United States in about 1895. The motion picture was then technologically possible.[4]

The final stage in the technological process was to devise a means for displaying this film. One of the earliest inventors of the film-display process was Thomas Edison.

Edison envisioned motion picture display to be a logical extension of his phonograph technology. Therefore, when he designed a device for showing films, known as a kinetoscope, it was in some ways similar to the phonograph. The picture on a kinetoscope was meant to be seen by no more than a few persons, and it was designed as that for private viewing. Indeed, the kinetoscope had a successful introduction as a novelty in carnivals, sideshows, and pinball parlors. The films shown by kinetoscope lasted for only a couple of minutes, and the subjects were, sometimes, of what was considered in those days to be of a prurient nature. Thus, because of their subject matter and because of their marketing to some of the seamier segments of society, the film industry almost immediately garnered a reputation for being somewhat seedy and immoral.

On the other side of the Atlantic, however, the development of film projection went in a different direction. Projectors were designed using technology similar to the camera to project films to a mass audience. Projection technology moved quickly back across the Atlantic, where the first film was shown in a theater in New York City in 1896.

After a series of patent disputes, Edison managed to make peace with his competitors by forming an alliance, a trust (monopoly) based on control of motion picture technology. The Motion Picture Patents Company that formed in 1908 was Edison's attempt to monopolize motion picture production and distribution. Since the Edison trust held the patents to most forms of motion picture technology of the day—and in agreement with the Kodak Corporation, the only supplier of film stock—the trust also held the key to film style and content. This technology cartel was doomed from the beginning and lasted only a few years. However, the creation of the Edison trust had the ironic effect of bringing outsiders, many of whom were immigrants, into the movie production business and, at the same time, encouraging technological development beyond the rather crude capabilities available at the time. Despite the fact that Edison and his cohort fought a vigorous rearguard action in the courts to protect their industry against alleged patent infringements, a new movie industry was born.[5]

The strongest challenge to the Edison trust came from film exhibitors. Most of the films that were made by the cartel were short "one reelers," each with a running time of no more than a few minutes. In order to put together a half-hour screening, exhibitors were forced to prepare a program of as many as three one-reel films. That fact alone created a tremendous demand for the cartel's products. However, at the same time, the market for these films was limited. With a running time of only a few minutes, one-reel films had no capacity for the type of story line development that would attract a clientele better educated and classier (as well as better connected). On the midway of a carnival or in the amusement parlor, one-reel films were intended to pique the interest of the viewer in a few moments. Thus, films of this era tended to feature violence, chases, and/or nudity with little or no plotline. The unsavory content of early sideshow films attracted the attention of religious groups and thus local governments. Censorship boards were set up in a number of cities to screen and edit the content of films shown to the public.

At least one major exhibitor—Carl Laemmle, who owned a chain of nickelodeons and theaters in the Midwest—began to chafe at the supply-and-content restrictions imposed by the cartel. Furthermore, he feared the consequences of attempts by some communities to censor films and close down theaters. He began to explore other sources of films by dealing with independent film producers, who were not controlled by the cartel. At first, independent filmmakers were at a technological disadvantage. Film stock was generally unavailable, and to avoid discovery by the cartel and its lawyers (as well as its goons), independent films were shot covertly in what then was the film capital of the world, New Jersey. But with the introduction of new equipment, a new kind of filmmaking, and government antitrust prosecutions, the Edison trust began to crumble. In turn, this escape from monopoly led to a number of innovations in the film industry, not the least of which was the production of feature-length motion pictures.

Feature-length motion pictures had the effect of attracting a different and wider audience to the movie theater. Heretofore, in the United States motion pictures had been more or less carnival sideshow attractions that were fashioned to appeal to a rougher crowd. Because the decision makers in the Edison trust still had a limited vision of the future of motion pictures, the cartel refused to produce a more substantial product. But in Europe, filmmakers had already produced several feature-length films. The advantage was that the market for these films was much broader and much more respectable. After all, feature-length films didn't necessarily have to rely on titillation to attract an audience. Stories could be developed that would be compelling enough in their own right. Furthermore, feature-length films could be produced for a profit, a huge profit. When *Birth of a Nation* (1915) was made for what was then the outlandish sum of $110,000 and returned by some estimates $100 million, the independents knew they had a business. From the societal perspective, the exhibition of feature-length films expanded the audience for movies from a limited segment to almost the entire population. Movies became a mass medium and entertainment for the masses.

Thus, the movie industry was built from the bottom up. Exhibitors began to produce films on their own when, collectively, Carl Laemmle founded Universal Studios; William Fox founded Fox Film, which was later purchased in a bankruptcy sale by Twentieth Century Pictures; Louis B. Mayer founded Metro Pictures, which later became Metro-Goldwyn-Mayer (MGM); the Warner brothers (Albert, Sam, Jack, and Harry) founded Warner Bros. Pictures; and Adolph Zukor founded Paramount Pictures. The retailers took over production, and they were not just any retailers. It just so happened that many of the movie moguls who built Hollywood were Eastern European Jews. In founding a new, completely unique business, they were able to make a fortune for themselves and their families, unhindered by the Protestant political and social establishment that dominated almost every other major industry. This pattern has been repeated constantly over the course of the twentieth century, as each new wave of immigrants becomes ensconced in some tiny corner of American industry. In many cities, even today, parking businesses, motels, taxicabs, laundries, and corner grocery stores come to be associated with one ethnic group or another. In

Los Angeles, Jews were associated with the nascent movie industry. That fact alone, as we shall see, has conditioned the content and public perception of the film industry even to this day.

The Second Monopoly: The Golden Age of Hollywood Cinema

As exhibitors began to get into the filmmaking business, the monopoly character of the film industry began to change. From a film monopoly based on technology, the film industry moved to a monopoly based on distribution. Unlike the technology trust that was fragile from the beginning (because there is no way to restrain innovation in technology), the distribution monopoly was extremely resilient and was helped along by some lucky historical accidents.[6] The vertical integration of the film industry almost guaranteed that small, independent film producers would have trouble screening their products without the support of the major studios. While this is somewhat the case today, it was even more so in the past.

During the so-called golden age of American cinema, in the 1930s and early 1940s, eight major studios had a virtual lock on the moviemaking industry. The majors owned or controlled not just the production of film but practically every movie theater in America. Theaters owned by the big eight were permitted to screen only their own products. Not only that, even theaters that were not owned by the majors were forced to display the works of the majors and the majors only. If they attempted to screen an independently owned film or if they refused to purchase only part of a package of films, a practice known in the parlance as "block booking," they would simply be cut off from the source.[7] And with no alternative, the majors (and a couple of secondary studios) were the only game in town.

This worked to restrict the options of all who worked in the industry, as long as the studios agreed to collude and as long as there was no foreign competition. The Hollywood moguls caught a break when the film industry that had been thriving in Europe was halted by World War I and then, after a brief respite, by the rise of fascism, the Second World War, and the reconstruction of Europe. But the fact is that European filmmakers would have had trouble selling their wares in the United States in any event by the distribution cartel.

The entire industry was therefore controlled from the top down by a few studio moguls—from the star system in Hollywood (in which stars were in essence "owned" by the studio to which they signed) to the collusive relationship between the studios and the film production labor unions to the distribution and screening of the final product. While this monopoly was stronger than the Edison technology trust, it too came under attack as an antitrust violation by the Justice Department of the Roosevelt administration.

In May 1948, the Supreme Court decided in *United States v. Paramount Pictures, Inc.* that the Big Eight studios were in violation of the Sherman Antitrust Act. The issue at hand was the practice of block booking. The big eight had virtually guaranteed a market for their products, no matter what the quality, by requiring theater owners to book the good films along with the bad. The Court tried to end block booking by requiring the studios to sell off their theater holdings. Independent theater owners would then, theoretically, be able to book only those films that they wanted to screen. In practice, however, this solution did not work. Because the major studios still had a monopoly on the production of films, they could require the now independent theater owners to buy the good films with the bad by threatening to withhold blockbuster hits from operators who failed to cooperate. In some sense, collusion in the distribution of films exists to this day: the top studios still control the lion's share of the market.[8] However, in an environment where entertainment comes from so many sources, the studios have nowhere near the power they did when there was no television and when foreign film industries were supine.

Thus, the golden era of Hollywood film was in part a result of trade restraint. During these halcyon years, the studios cranked out thousands of quality films. But because these films were produced in a truncated market, they tended to have a kind of industrial feel. The lack of competition that results from any monopoly stifles creativity. While the films of the golden era tended to be bright and sunny, they were also noncontroversial and bland. In the golden era, movies were produced as if they were any other industrial product. While there were subtle differences between the films produced by different studios—MGM was the class of the industry; Universal specialized in Westerns and horror films; Paramount was known for its sophisticated comedies and so on—there was a distinct (often quite fine) uniformity to their output.

Furthermore, as discussed, the major studios (with the exception of Walt Disney Productions and Twentieth Century Fox) were mostly run by a group of first-generation immigrant Jews.[9] To understand why that is important is to understand what it was like for Jews in Europe during the late nineteenth and early twentieth centuries. Anti-Semitism was open and rampant. Jews were treated as the outsiders, even to a large extent in their adoptive United States. Therefore, the films of the moguls reflected not only their ethnic sensitivities but also their ethnic insecurities. Just as many immigrants had rejected the Old World to become almost caricatures of the new, most of the moguls tried hard to assimilate, and their effort was reflected in the conventions of their films. Add to that the U.S. immigrants' natural affinity to the ideology of classical liberalism, and the films of the golden era become as American as apple pie, if at the same time their producers become as American as apple strudel.

Thus, when the movie business was mainly a sideshow attraction at a carnival or in a storefront and literally a nickel-and-dime business (hence the term *nickelodeon*), the ownership of the business was really irrelevant to the rest of society. However, by luck, accident, and hard work, the movie business became a major industry, almost overnight. At that point, the ownership of the business became an issue. Unlike other major industries, the moviemaking industry was clearly dominated by a population of ethnically uniform and religiously unrepresentative new money—that is, heavily Jewish and Catholic. American culture has always harbored an unattractive characteristic of distrust toward immigrants, especially immigrants from non-Protestant denominations. Thus, it was natural that the American political establishment came to have, and continues to have, a love-hate relationship with the film industry. The public loves the product, but they are vaguely distrustful of the crowd that produces it.

The film industry in the second monopoly certainly contributed to this love-hate relationship. The purpose of the film business is entertainment. One way to entertain is to titillate. It was sometimes the case that filmmakers in the early years of the second monopoly would violate the sensibilities of the general public—gangster films in the 1920s were particularly alarming. Furthermore, the film industry has a way of creating instant millionaires who just happen to be very much in the public eye. The lives of Hollywood actors, producers, and directors, many of whom were accumulating money for the first time in their lives, were glaringly exposed. The perception was that Hollywood was an insulated bohemian enclave outside of the American mainstream. Certainly to the extent that its community was wealthy, living on the West Coast, and ethnically diverse, Hollywood was different. But were its members less moral than, say, the average real estate, railroad, steel, or oil tycoon of the time? It is difficult to say. They were certainly more exposed.

The Hollywood community was definitely sensitive to these criticisms. Jews in particular have been constantly conscious of being a minority in an environment that can turn hostile at a moment's notice.[10] Thus, the movie moguls of the golden era of Hollywood film were more than willing to accede to the demands of those who would censor film content. The production code, as it came to be known, was written in 1930 and later strictly enforced by something called the Catholic Legion of Decency (under the threat of a boycott), implemented by Production Code Administration (PCA), and willingly adhered to by the film moguls of the second monopoly, who saw the code as providing a veneer of respectability for their products.

The code required that the PCA approve every new script and changes to scripts in production. Even today, at the beginning of most American films produced before 1960, one can still see the production code "bug" (the cursive letter *a*) signifying approval by the PCA. The production code was quite intrusive. It regulated not just nudity and violence but plotlines as well. While the censorship board was often arbitrary, movie plots were forbidden if they allowed criminals to get away with their crimes or couples to engage in romance without getting married. Note, for example, that during most of the years governed by the code, couples would never be shown in bed together without at least one foot on the floor.[11]

Films that did not conform to the code were simply not exhibited, were subject to a boycott by the Legion of Decency, and were thus never made. This applied not just to films with prurient content but also to films that might be considered subversive—critiques of capitalism, the church, and the like. The studio executives willingly practiced this form of self-censorship not just because they were intimidated but also because they were indeed capitalists themselves who had been richly rewarded by the American system. Their view of America was honestly that of Horatio Alger. The films of the golden era of Hollywood cinema overwhelmingly conformed to the unwritten code that reflected such a perspective.[12]

This was truly a halcyon era of film when content and message of the movies was mainly about all that is good and right about American culture. What eroded this foundation of the production code was the bust of the movie distribution trust and the entry into the market of new competitors for the audiences' attention. Starting with the government's efforts to force the big eight to divest themselves of their distribution monopoly, and ending with the advent and general popularization of television, the film industry began to change—and so did film content. As television began to siphon away the movie audiences and as foreign filmmakers from the recovering economies of Europe and Japan began to export a new and more adventurous class of films, Hollywood began to respond in kind. Picking up on a trend begun in the late 1930s, Hollywood produced in the 1950s a whole new genre of films that skirted the edge of the written and unwritten production code.

This second monopoly, commonly referred to as the golden era of Hollywood film, was relatively short-lived, and its fall—albeit briefly delayed by World War II—was facilitated by the forced divestiture of theater chains controlled by the studios, the advent of television, and competition from outside and inside the industry. Thus, modern-day calls for a return to the halcyon years of Hollywood cinema really are calls for the return to ownership of the studios by executives long since dead and a return to an economic monopoly that could only be reproduced by no less than getting rid of television. It is remarkable that many of the current attacks on the politics and profile of the film industry are so out of date. The problem of subversive film content to the extent that it now exists is a function of the third monopoly of Hollywood film, the monopoly of money.

The Third "Monopoly": The Marketization of Hollywood

Even before the end of World War II, producers and directors began to skirt the edge of the production code. Film classics such as *Citizen Kane* (1941), *Double Indemnity* (1944), and *The Big Sleep* (1946) spawned a whole genre of film that explored a darker aspect of American society. This film genre came to be known as *film noir*. As one author describes it, "What film noir was, what was so revolutionary about it, was its inherent reaction to decades of forced optimism."[13] The themes and indeed the techniques explored in these films were edgy and innovative and viewed by some as not just a little subversive. It is not surprising then that in combination with the latent aversion toward the otherness of the Hollywood moguls at the end of World War II, when the Soviet Union and world communism came to be viewed as America's primary threat, Hollywood was ripe for attack. The McCarthy era blacklist attacked not so much the communist threat in the industry—it is now fairly clear that most of those who were blacklisted were not communists or even particularly political—as it did the departure from the mainstream of American political culture.[14] In that sense, the McCarthy era blacklist reflected and carried on in practice a general, historical distrust of the entertainment industry.

Thus began, in at least the economic sense, the darkest days of Hollywood cinema. Despite the fact that in the 1950s some fine feature films were made, the studios were reluctant to air subversive themes, even as they were slowly losing market share to television. The studios tried to compensate by offering technological innovations such as wide-screen cinemascope and 3-D special effects, by filming elaborate musicals borrowed from Broadway, and by exploring more mainstream and upbeat themes. But despite a steady stream of biblical epics, Broadway musicals, mainstream Westerns, war movies, and frothy bedroom farces, the audience hemorrhage continued. Given their limitations on content, censored by the code, and intimidated by the blacklist, what could the studios offer that the viewer couldn't get with less bother and expense on television at home?

In some ways, this was a repeat of the pattern that brought to an end the first monopoly, except now for their intransigence it was the moguls turn to be outsmarted. Because movie executives refused to embrace the possibilities of television or were prevented from moving into television production by the federal government because of anti-trust concerns, they were overtaken by the new technology and its new potential for profit.[15] For example, not recognizing the value of their extensive film libraries, the studios sold the rights to them for much less than their market value. After all, who would want to watch a rerun of a film such as *Casablanca* on television? Who indeed? Many people did, and the individuals who bought these film libraries made a fortune. What emerged from this second monopoly was a third monopoly of corporate ownership and independent production.

By the late 1960s, all the major studios began to fail and were forced to sell out, most often to large corporate conglomerates. Gulf and Western (commodities) bought Paramount, which was in turn briefly owned by Coca-Cola; Transamerica (insurance and Budget Rent a Car among others) bought United Artists; Kinney National Services (funeral homes and parking lots) bought Warner Bros.; and so on. To the corporations who bought them, the studios were little more than the sum of their component parts. This is generally the case in corporate fire sales. The acquiring companies see value in the bankrupt company's component parts. Kirk Kerkorian bought MGM for its film library and apparently for its brand (Kerkorian built the MGM Grand Hotel in Las Vegas). The former production back lot of Twentieth Century Fox was converted into a glittering office, hotel, and retail complex—Century City. Only the shells of the studios survived. The actual production of films was passed on to independent production companies such as Orion, the Ladd Company, Tri-Star pictures, and New Line Cinema.

The advent of television was a devastating blow to the movie industry. To compete, it had to change. What could the film industry offer that was not available on the television screen, and what new audiences could be tapped to make up for the loss of audiences who stayed home?

The answers to these questions tell us a lot about why film content is the way it is today. First, to make up for a loss in domestic viewership, the film industry began a much more aggressive pursuit of international audiences. As noted, depending on the exchange rate for the dollar and the release of blockbuster films, such as *Titanic* (1997), foreign sales of American films can constitute up to 60 percent of the American film industry's annual film revenues. As a percentage of sales abroad, American films are crowding out foreign domestic producers. Fully 70 percent of all admissions to theaters in the European Union market are to American films. In 2000, Hollywood's share of the world market was twice what it had been in 1990.[16]

Second, the film industry began to look for new ways to distribute its product. Instead of trying to beat television, the film industry decided to join it. By the end of the 1950s, most of the major studios began to get into the television production business. Ultimately, the spread of cable television allowed film producers to market their products on television cable outlets, such as on the so-called superstations, on movie channels, and on pay-per-view television. Finally, the development of home videocassette playback and recording allowed filmmakers to directly market their product for viewing at home. In the year 2000, some $20 billion in consumer spending was generated from home video sales and rentals while movie ticket sales amounted to a little more than a third ($7.5 billion) of that amount.[17] Many films have no theatrical release at all and go straight to the video store and pay-per-view. Indeed, the functional distinction between television and motion picture production has begun to disappear as television networks and cable outlets produce original films and miniseries that can be rented in video stores and are on a par in quality with any feature film.

Third in the evolution of the film industry is the creation of a new star system. In the days of the golden era, studios owned stars the way that sports teams own athletes, the one difference being that they could "loan" their contract players out to other studios. With the collapse of the studio cartel, movie stars became free agents. That is both good news and bad news for the film-acting profession. On the one hand, actors and actresses in demand can command enormous salaries. Russell Crowe received $20 million for *Master and Commander* and Nicole Kidman got $15 million for *Cold Mountain* (2003). The bad news is that with so much of the fate of a film dependent on bankable stars, the work available for other fine actors is limited. In the studio system, careers were nurtured; there was plenty of work available for actors to hone their craft—in the modern market, promising careers are often stillborn. The good news is that actors who succeed have control over their own careers. The bad news is that Mel Gibson has the clout to play *Hamlet* (1990) and produce his own interpretation of the *Passion of the Christ* (2004).[18]

Fourth, as the Hollywood film industry passed on from private to corporate management (ownership by diversified publicly owned corporations), the film business took on attributes more or less common to any industry. The first thing that the corporate managers of the new Hollywood did was cut costs by divesting themselves of many of the ancillary activities of the studios under the second monopoly that had the movie executives involved in everything from contracting and developing talent to providing schooling for child stars. It should come as no surprise to anyone who works in, say, the automobile industry that outsourcing, one of the quickest ways for a business to cut costs, was instituted in the film industry starting in the late 1960s. In that way manufacturers pay piecework wages for labor. And while hiring

Spielberg to direct or Redford to act may be expensive, it is nothing compared to having Spielberg and a lot of less-successful directors (and actors, writers, editors, and other technicians) on the payroll while paying for their development.

To further cut costs, studios have moved a large portion of film production overseas. According to the U.S. Department of Commerce, in 1990, 29 percent of all U.S.-developed film projects were shot overseas; by 1999, 37 percent were. Again, according to the Department of Commerce, the main reason that these productions were moved overseas was not for creative purposes (to shoot on location) but to cut costs.[19] Just like many other American manufacturers, the film business is taking its production overseas to cut costs.

Finally, the nature of corporate ownership of the film industry has changed. There was never a lot of natural synergy between sales of Coke, insurance, parking lots, funeral homes, or rental cars and the movie business. In the latest transformation of the movie industry, giant media conglomerates have been formed to take advantage of the synergies between film and related technologies and entertainment outlets. For example, *Time* magazine bought out Warner Bros. Pictures. Later, CNN was added to the mix. This means that films produced by Warner Bros. can be promoted "in house" both in print and on television without going into the commercial market for advertising. The same can be said for Twentieth Century Fox, which is owned by News Corporation, with its enormous holdings in newspapers and television. In addition, vast studio film libraries can be shown on corporate television outlets for free or rented at corporate retail outlets such as Blockbuster Videos (Viacom).

There may be problems, however, with this sort of media ownership. The entertainment divisions of these corporations may come to be indistinguishable from their journalistic outlets. Consider this one small problem. While the news divisions of these corporate giants are supposed to be hermetically sealed from their entertainment divisions, it is hard to imagine that film reviewers working for newspapers, magazines, or media outlets can be totally objective in reviewing films produced by their own corporations or those of others.

At the same time, the film production business has become more segmented and specialized. The studios are more a financier, coordinator, and distributor of production than a genuine factory for films. The actual creative process is contracted out to powerful talent agencies and independent production companies. This is not to say that the creative process is completely out of the control of the studios. Rather, creative control has passed from the studio executive to the market. And the market is an ever-changing place. With the advent of widespread VCR ownership and cable pay-per-view, the market itself is also highly segmented. Films that once would have never been made, because they would never turn a profit, can now be made and marketed to discrete segments of the viewing audience. The shelf life of a film can be extended as well. In foreign markets or on home video, a film can get a second life after its theatrical release.

What this last transformation of the movie industry has meant is simply that the film industry must now appeal to either a new lowest common denominator or a very specialized segment of viewing public. To justify the costs of big-budget blockbusters, film producers must aim to attract the largest possible domestic and now international audience with films of a lowest common denominator that avoid complex dialogue, plot development, and ethnocentric themes. Complex and ethnocentric themes simply do not translate well in foreign markets.[20] On the other hand, to make a film for a specialized audience, filmmakers must keep their production costs low enough to recoup their expenses on a limited number of screens and through nontheatrical release outlets.

The film industry is no longer even a shadow of the monopoly it once was. Independent film producers have a multitude of outlets for their product. And while it is difficult for independent film producers to get the financing and distribution of their films without the support of the major studios, it is not impossible. In fact, the market for independent filmmakers seems to be expanding as more theaters exhibit such work.[21] Thus, because of the new outlets for independent films, independent producers are more likely to be able to produce profitable films for niche audiences.

Consequently, the balance of power has changed in the film industry—from the executives in Hollywood to the market. Any recent changes in the content of films, therefore, are more a product of market demands than of the degenerate culture of Hollywood.

So what has changed in the content of film? The product has changed because the industry has changed. Clearly, a massive increase in foreign viewership has influenced motion pictures in several ways. One is the general subject matter of film. Complex plots or ethnocentric themes that may lose something in the translation are much riskier enterprises for Hollywood producers. For example, black actors, writers, and directors have leveled charges of racism against the entertainment industry.[22] However, big-budget films that are meant to appeal to an Afrocentric audience are less likely to do well in the foreign market and are thus not as willingly financed by the major studios. This may say something about the racial intolerance of film consumers, but it doesn't necessarily attack the proclivities of the producers themselves.[23]

On American television or as part of a segmented domestic audience, black patrons are such a large share of the audience that networks can devote entire prime-time programming slots to black-oriented television shows.[24] By the same token, while the international markets may demand the lowest common denominator for blockbusters, lower-budget films appealing primarily to black audiences can turn a profit. This homogenization of the blockbuster movie market and this heterogeneity of the domestic entertainment market have led to a two-track film-production environment. Big-budget Hollywood spectaculars must appeal to an international audience in order to attract the attention and financing of the Hollywood majors. At the same time, there exists in the domestic market quite a few niche audiences who will support the small-scale, low-budget production of independent producers. In addition, there are many more outlets besides the mall multiplex cinema for independent productions, including art house screenings, DVD, and pay-per-view television. Besides a large and growing market for Afro-American–oriented cinema, there are viable markets for low-budget art films, foreign films, gay-lifestyle films, Hispanic films, X-rated films, family-oriented films, and so on.

It would be easy for one to draw the conclusion from watching blockbuster releases of the major studios that the film content is becoming more un-American, more violent, less complex in terms of plot development, and more graphically sexual. And this conclusion is probably true. The question is, why the change and what to do about it?

The answer to the first question, why the change in movie content, requires a two-part response. First, the audience for American films has changed. In the 1990s, with 60 percent of revenues coming from foreign markets (the percentage for blockbuster films is probably higher), producers must pay attention to the bottom line. The safest and most easily financed projects are those that take the least risks in terms of content. In other words, filmmakers must respond to a new lowest common denominator. If kung fu action films sell well in Asia, then our version of the kung fu action film—for example, the *Rambo* series—is the safest bet for American producers. In addition, there are certain themes that are almost certainly going to create trouble abroad. Besides specialized topics that have little relevance for foreigners, such as the plight of the African American in the United States, there are also plotlines that are downright subversive in a foreign context. How would the Chinese, Saudi Arabian, or Zairian governments react to *Mr. Smith Goes to Washington*? This film and others like it would almost certainly be banned in authoritarian countries. This is a sad comment on the state of the world, but it is hardly a condemnation of Hollywood.

Second, along with the proliferation of television channels on cable comes increased competition for the entertainment dollar. During the golden age of cinema, the same theater owners and movie producers who busted the Edison trust in the 1910–1920 period controlled the movie production monopoly. The movie industry of the1930s and early 1940s was vertically integrated, meaning that the movie cartel owned or controlled movie distributors as well as film exhibitors. Independent and foreign filmmakers couldn't get their films screened in the United States. But all of that began to change in the 1940s and 1950s as the federal government began its first moves toward imposing antitrust requirements.

Has this improved the quality of American films? The answer is yes and no. Many more films and many different types of films can be made and expected to turn a profit. In that sense, there is a lot more variety, and there is the actuality and potential for some terrific films. Terrific films, however, may be hard to find. Even though there is so much product, theater owners will still be reluctant to take a chance on films without brand-name directors and actors and cookie-cutter plots. Cineplex theaters still tend to enforce a de facto monopoly. From their perspective, theater owners will want to book the film with the highest sales. Even excellent films with a little-known cast and director may not make money. Without a large advertising budget, word-of-mouth films may take a long time to catch on, well beyond the carrying capacity of an average multiplex theater. Thus, independent films produced by unknown directors with unknown actors may only receive theatrical release in the largest cities. With luck those films will receive good reviews and attendance. Eventually, such films will percolate down through the distribution system to smaller and smaller markets. *Sling Blade* (1996) was such a film. Even so, despite its acclaim, the film was hard to find in the suburban multiplexes of my hometown, Atlanta.

Furthermore, because the market is so segmented, the studios are much more reluctant to invest in blockbuster, expensive productions without the participation of high-profile, well-established writers, actors, and directors. This is both a good news, bad news story. Worthy projects proposed by relative unknowns may not receive blockbuster funding. Nevertheless, there is a way that low-budget films can be produced and turn a profit. Thus, the marketization of Hollywood cinema has been mostly for the good. While it may be difficult to find a particular movie or get to the theater before the film closes, there are a variety of interesting films for a variety of tastes available on the market. Of course, blockbuster, high-profile films with large advertising budgets and wide releases may tend to be formulaic and brain-dead, more dependent on technology and the reputations of the producer, director, and cast than on the quality of the product. But it is just as likely that they will be exceptionally well crafted and entertaining for the largest possible audience. *Titanic* was such a film. This production behemoth, which is really a pretty good film, was the seventh-highest grossing film of 1997 in less than two weeks of theatrical release and has to date grossed $1.8 billion worldwide, nine times its production costs of about $200 million.[25]

One also has the possibility of walking into the wrong film. In a more extreme example, conservative film critic Michael Medved has gotten a lot of mileage out of criticizing *The Cook, the Thief, His Wife, and Her Lover* (1990), a film in limited theatrical release that received some positive reviews but not much else in terms of audience.[26] This film is a good example of how some film critics are out of touch with the viewing public. Most viewers would probably be a little put off by some of the scenes in this movie. But Medved is mistaken if he thinks that that film was made with him and his religious audience in mind. By the same token, if nonreligious moviegoers never see another rendition of the *Greatest Story Ever Told* (1965), it will be too soon. But they should understand that Bible stories in film are not made for them. By the same token, gross-out dismemberment films with nudity and violence are not made for Michael Medved.

The third monopoly of American film is therefore not so much a monopoly as it is the final marketization of American cinema. Now that the film industry has begun to outsource and export, compete with foreigners, and justify its operations to millions of stockholders, it is more or less just another industry. More to the point, the audience now for Hollywood films is not just the one sitting in theaters but just as much the one sitting in boardrooms and the stock market. This is where conservative (and some liberal) critics of Hollywood tend to miss their mark. The problem with the film industry today is not that it is immoral but that it is *amoral.* But that is a problem of business in a free market in general. The violence, the nudity, and the muddled messages of many of today's films are produced not so much as a reflection of the subversive visions of a film industry elite out of touch but as a marketing strategy for filmmakers in a market increasingly competitive for entertainment dollars. To the extent that the film industry is a monopoly at all, it is not the artistic talent that is in control but the financiers, distributors, and exhibitors.

Feature Film: *X2* (2003)

As discussed in an earlier review of a feature film, science fiction is a flexible genre for discussing in metaphor matters of contemporary concern. Without making reference to the actual racial tensions that exist in our society, this film is about racism. At another level this film, in its appeal to a particular audience, tells us something about the market for commercial films and why those films are limited to certain story lines and why they feature certain theatrical conventions.

X-Men 2. *Photo by Kerry Hays. Courtesy of M.P. & T.V. Photo Archive.*

I would like to summarize the plot of this film, but I haven't the faintest idea of what it is about. As best as I can tell, it has something to do with "good" mutants, who are being whipsawed between evil mutants (who want to use their special powers to take over the world) and bad humans (who see all mutants as threats). My students tell me that I would understand the film better if I had seen the first film in this series, *X-Men* (2000), which I have, and if I had read the comic book, which I haven't. That second point is worth examining.

It seems to me that if the requirement for enjoying a film is having read the book, that film is destined for failure. After all, how many people have actually read the *X-Men* comics, and would that number sustain the profitability of a feature motion picture? Probably not, except for the fact that this film could be about practically anything, and it would still likely be a financial success. *X2* is not a movie; it is a product.

The formula goes something like this. Take a premise, practically any premise; add a lot of noisy special effects, a couple of cute teenagers with the problems of teenagers, and some very grown-up actresses dressed in revealing but not too revealing outfits. After all, the producers don't want the film to be rated NC-17. This formula is designed to accommodate practically every subliminal and not-so-subliminal fantasy of a typical teenage boy. That's why I yawn now—actually, I fell asleep but found the film too noisy for a really good snooze—but would have been thrilled just a few years ago (well, more than a few years ago).

I can't really say this is a "bad" film. It's a film that wasn't made with me in mind. The production values are terrific; at least somebody gets the story line; and, for the target audience at least, the movie provides actors and actresses who are not hard on the eyes—for example, Hugh Jackman and Famke Janssen. My sources tell me that this sequel is better than the original, which puts it, in at least one way, on a par with *The Godfather: Part II* (1974). So who am I to say that this is a rotten movie?

To be fair, the *X-Men* series is supposed to be a metaphorical examination of the issue of tolerance—tolerance for the other. And I suppose that is a good thing, to teach our kids to tolerate those who are different. But let's be honest. That's the story Hollywood tells your mother to get her to lend you the keys to the car. Any real discussion of tolerance is covered up by the sound of explosions. On the other hand, maybe for all the special effects, skimpy outfits, and teenage trauma, this film does teach its young audience something about courage, loyalty, and moral decision making in a language they can understand.

Don't agree? What do you think?

EXERCISE

Choose a recent commercial film and describe how the production of this film could be justified as part of a corporate business plan.

NOTES

1. From the online edition of "A Glossary of Political Economy Terms," by Paul M. Johnson, Auburn University, www.duc.auburn.edu/~johnspm/gloss/ (accessed November 24, 2004).

2. Literally, a "single seller"—a situation in which a single firm or individual produces and sells the entire output of some good or service available within a given market. If there are no close substitutes for the good or service in question, the monopolist will be able to set both the level of output and the price at such a level as to maximize profits without worrying about being undercut by competitors (at least in the short run). Johnson, "Glossary," www.duc.auburn.edu/~johnspm/gloss/ (accessed November 24, 2004).

3. For an excellent introduction to the invention of motion picture photography, see Martin Quigley Jr., *Magic Shadows: The Story of the Origin of Motion Pictures* (Washington, D.C.: Georgetown University Press, 1948), chap. 11.

4. To read a much more detailed account of the invention of the movie camera, see James Monaco, *How to Read a Film: Movies, Media, Multimedia*, 3rd ed. (New York: Oxford University Press, 2000), chap. 2.

5. For a detailed account of this process, see Lewis Jacobs, *The Rise of the American Film: A Critical History* (New York: Harcourt Brace, 1939), particularly chap. 6.

6. For the story of the development of one of these distribution behemoths, see Douglas Gomery, "The Movies Become Big Business: Public Theatres and the Chain Store Strategy," in "Economic and Technological History," *Cinema Journal* 18, no. 2 (Spring 1979): 26–40.

7. Block booking means that "a studio would sell its films in packages on an all-or-nothing basis—usually requiring theaters to buy several mediocre pictures for every desirable one. Because the studios made mass-produced films, they also sold them in bulk." J. A. Aberdeen, "Block Booking: The Root of All Evil in the Motion Picture Industry," Society of Independent Motion Picture Producers, www.cobbles.com/simpp_archive/blockbook_intro.htm (accessed August 17, 2005).

8. Erwin A. Blackstone and Gary W. Bowman, "Vertical Integration in Motion Pictures," *Journal of Communication* 49, no. 1 (1999): 123–40.

9. For an excellent history of the Jews in Hollywood, see Neil Gabler, *An Empire of Their Own* (New York: Anchor, 1988).

10. See Philip Hanson, "Against Tribalism: The Perils of Ethnic Identity in Mamet's *Homicide*," *CLIO* 31, no. 3 (2002): 257+, www.questia.com/ (accessed November 24, 2004), for an exploration of Jewish paranoia in America in the larger sense but, in particular, in David Mamet's film *Homicide* (1991).

11. For an excellent book-length examination of the production code, see Gregory Black, *Hollywood Censored: Morality Codes, Catholics, and the Movies* (New York: Cambridge University Press, 1994). See also, by the same author, a discussion of the anti-Semitic seeds of the movement to impose the production code, *The Catholic Crusade against the Movies, 1940–1975* (New York: Cambridge University Press, 1998).

12. For a discussion of the content censorship enforced by the production code, see Ruth Vasey, *The World according to Hollywood, 1918–1939* (Madison: University of Wisconsin Press, 1997).

13. Jon Tuska, *Dark Cinema: American Film Noir in Cultural Perspective* (Westport, Conn.: Greenwood, 1984), 152.

14. Dorothy Parker once commented that "the only ism adhered to in Hollywood is plagiarism."

15. For a discussion of Hollywood's venture into television production, see J. A. Aberdeen, *Hollywood Renegades: The Society of Independent Motion Picture Producers* (Los Angeles: Cobblestone Entertainment, 2000), chap. 14.

16. Data cited in Toby Miller et al., *Global Hollywood* (London: British Film Institute, 2001), 4–5.

17. These figures, according to Ernst and Young, were cited by the Public Broadcasting Service, "Frontline: The Monster That Ate Hollywood," www.pbs.org/wgbh/pages/frontline/shows/hollywood/business/windows.html (accessed November 29, 2004).

18. For an excellent history of the star system in Hollywood to date, see Paul McDonald, *The Star System: Hollywood's Production of Popular Identities* (London: Wallflower, 2001).

19. McDonald, *Star System*, 56–60.

20. M. Mehdi Semati and Patty J. Sotirin, "Perspectives: Hollywood's Transnational Appeal," *Journal of Popular Film and Television* 26, no. 4 (1999): 177.

21. Scott Sochay, "Predicting the Performance of Motion Pictures," *Journal of Media Economics* 7, no. 4 (1994): 15.

22. See Vincent F. Rocchio, *Reel Racism: Confronting Hollywood's Construction of Afro-American Culture* (Boulder, Colo.: Westview Press, 2000).

23. Sharon Willis, *High Contrast: Race and Gender in Contemporary Hollywood Film* (Durham, N.C.: Duke University Press, 1997), would disagree but not very convincingly in my opinion.

24. It is also important to remember that syndication is an important source of revenue for television shows that is not available to the film industry. Thus, a popular television show made for a niche audience can make good money in the long run through syndication.

25. Box Office Mojo, "Titanic (1997)," www.boxofficemojo.com/movies/?id=titanic.htm (accessed August 24, 2005).

26. See Michael Medved, *Hollywood vs. America* (New York: Harper Collins, 1993), especially 18–22.

SUGGESTED READING

Black, Gregory D. *Hollywood Censored : Morality Codes, Catholics, and the Movies.* New York: Cambridge University Press, 1994.

Gabler, Neil. *An Empire of Their Own: How the Jews Invented Hollywood.* New York: Anchor, 1988).

Goldman, William. *The Big Picture.* New York: Applause, 2000.

Lewis, Jon. *The New American Cinema.* Durham, N.C.: Duke University Press, 1998.

McDonald, Paul. *The Star System: Hollywood's Production of Popular Identities.* London: Wallflower, 2000.

Medved, Michael. *Hollywood vs. America.* New York: Harper Collins, 1993.

Miller, Toby, Nitin Govil, John McMurria, and Richard Maxwell. *Global Hollywood.* London: British Film Institute, 2001.

Rosenbaum, Jonathan. *Movie Wars: How Hollywood and the Media Conspire to Limit What Films We Can See.* Chicago: Cappella, 2000.

3

Who Makes 'Em and Who Watches 'Em

I often walk out of the movies shaking my head. "Who," I wonder, "thought that one up?" Who felt it necessary to explore the lives of porno filmmakers in the 1970s (*Boogie Nights*, 1997) or a brother and sister who dress up as John and Jackie Kennedy, re-create the president's assassination, and have sex—with each other (*The House of Yes*, 1997)? Some of what we see in the theater is pretty sick and strange. But then again we also see the remarkable and the reflective. The opening sequence of *Contact* (1997) says more in three minutes than does an hour's lecture in astrophysics. The film then goes on to intelligently muse on the relationship between man and God and between faith and science, which brings us to the subject of this chapter. How do producers decide what films to make?

If, as social conservatives argue, films are made without regard to the sensibilities of their audience, then we can argue that films are "art" (and sick art at that). If films are made with the sole purpose of turning a profit, then we can argue that film is just another product, like laundry detergent or furniture, and that the content of film simply reflects the demands of consumers. Are the movies art or product? Does the market drive the content of films or is content driven by a bunch of beatniks/capitalists in California?

Art is a form of human expression that often disregards the marketplace.[1] It represents the personal vision of the artist. It is sometimes revolutionary in the sense that good art stretches our senses. Good or at least compelling art is something that we haven't seen before and, in the best case, gives us a new perspective on color, light, sound, or the human condition. Product, on the other hand, is a function of the market. Product is manufactured to meet some real or perceived need of the public. Something of an intersection exists between art and the market in the sense that artists sell their wares to survive and manufacturers utilize art to manufacture demand. Nevertheless, good art (well regarded in retrospect) generally doesn't follow the market, and good capitalists don't get too far out in front of the consumers. A good many of the greatest artists in history have died broke, and a good many of the greatest capitalists in history have died rich.

Therefore, we generally assume that businesspeople, regardless of their personal beliefs, will endeavor to produce marketable products and that artists, regardless of their financial status, will strive to produce their art. It doesn't make a lot of sense, then, to assume—as do so many of the critics of the American film industry from both the Right and the Left—that studio executives, producers, actors, theater owners, and everyone else involved in the film business are not capitalists, that filmmakers in their desire to promote their personal beliefs disregard market realities. At least one author goes so far as to argue that the movies are neither liberal nor conservative but "contested terrain, and that films can be interpreted as a struggle over representation of how to construct a social world and everyday life."[2] It is simply not enough to demonstrate that one segment of the film industry, the creative (manufacturing) "elite," are overwhelmingly liberal and then assume that films will be the same way. There is a causal connection here that is missing. What difference would it make if, say, the engineers at Ford Motors were frustrated sculptors and their creative energies were held in check by stockholders, management, financiers, and, most important, the market for Ford automobiles. It is therefore somewhat perplexing that film critics who are erstwhile capitalists throw their core economic beliefs out the window when it comes to the entertainment industry.

Why would movie executives, regardless of their beliefs, consciously turn out a product that, because of its unpopular and weird appeal, is likely to fail? Now there is such a thing as a bad businessperson—one who fails to recognize the market. But for the bad capitalist, market retaliation is swift and terrible. One who is bad in business will not be in business for long. Unless critics of the film industry can demonstrate that there exists within it some sort of market distortion, we must assume that the market itself is the driving force. Unless our understanding of capitalist economics is seriously mistaken, it cannot be otherwise.

In the last chapter I suggest that there did exist for a time in Hollywood a market distortion in the form of a monopoly—first in technology (the Edison trust) and later in the vertical integration of the industry (the golden era of Hollywood cinema). The product of that second monopoly was commercial film produced according to a strict production code. But now that the film industry monopoly has been broken, all bets are off. The Motion Picture Association of America (MPAA) rating system is a mere shadow of what the production code once was. If modern films appeal to the lowest common denominator or if they appeal to a particular politics or to prurient interests, the reason is that they are largely driven by the market, which brings us to two recent scholarly examinations of the film industry.

Until now much social film criticism has been based on several articles of faith that have yet to be thoroughly examined. In two recent books on the political economy of the film industry, the authors survey mostly filmmakers from mainly the creative side of the industry. Specifically, in *Risky Business: The Political Economy of Hollywood* and in *Hollywood's America*, the authors conduct a survey of film professionals and come to the conclusion that Hollywood filmmakers as a group are more liberal and more

Jewish than are other businesspeople. Whether that fact is relevant to the content of modern motion pictures, however, is debatable. Commentators from both the Left and the Right assume that the ethnic, political, and class backgrounds of the production side of the movie industry constitute a slam-dunk case for a particular political bias in entertainment content. But it would probably make more sense to assume that because the film industry is a business—that Hollywood movies are largely product, not art. Therefore, film content is no more a reflection of the filmmaker's beliefs than an automobile is the reflection of the automobile engineer's frustrated desire to be a sculptor. Thus, attempts to promote the big conspiracy theory of media are in reality an attempt by two groups in society, either conservative social critics or the radical Left, to assert their control over media content and so restrict our general constitutional rights. Consequently, this discussion of the political economy of the film industry is more than academic—it is a discussion of the politics of control.

WHAT IS THE "FILM INDUSTRY"?

In *Risky Business: The Political Economy of Hollywood*, professor David Prindle interviews thirty-five "studio heads, presidents of artists' unions, trade association leaders, editors and publishers of trade papers, leaders of interest groups, and various industry people who were active in social and political organizations."[3] Not surprisingly, he finds that his sample, from mainly the creative side of the movie industry and the West Side of Los Angeles, is significantly more liberal, less likely to be identified with the Republican Party, and more likely to be Jewish than the general public is. In summarizing his sample, he states,

> Whatever the explanation, artistic liberalism seems to exert a strong influence over the general political outlook of Hollywood. It is not, however, the only force for left-wing politics. Hollywood contains a much higher percentage of Jews than does American society as a whole. Hollywood was virtually founded by Jews (the only important early industry business figure who was not Jewish was Walt Disney), and its important decision making positions have been dominated by them ever since. All of today's studio heads are Jewish.[4]

Nevertheless, he concludes that regardless of their ideological or ethnic profiles, executives in the industry are primarily motivated by economic concerns. But not all observers arrive at the same conclusion. Another author writes,

> In summary, Jews, both on screen and off, span the entire history of Hollywood cinema. As producers, screenwriters, directors, composers, and actors they have been a dominant force in the industry and provide for its creative sustenance.[5]

While it is probably true that on the production side Hollywood filmmakers are more liberal (and Jewish) than the population as a whole is, it is not clear that it is liberals and Jews who "dominate" Hollywood. In fact, liberals and Jews may not have dominated Hollywood for a long time—maybe even from the time of the imposition of the production code.[6] It is essential to reiterate that even during the golden era of Hollywood cinema, the production code was imposed on the Hollywood moguls by outside forces. Consequently, even during the second monopoly, the moguls were not total masters of their own house.

The fact is that even a representative survey of filmmakers in Southern California is not representative of the industry. It would be more accurate to rethink what we mean when we talk about "Hollywood" in the modern era. It is probably more accurate now to think of Hollywood as not so much a place as an abstraction. As an industry, Hollywood is no longer dominated by the moguls but by the market. If those market forces are distorted at all, they are influenced by the large integrated media corporations that make decisions influenced by the requirements posed by their corporate structures.

The seven companies that constitute the MPAA are responsible for the production and release of films that generate about 92 percent of all domestic box office receipts.[7] All of these studios are part of corporations that are publicly held, meaning that their stock is traded on the open market. Twentieth Century Fox is a wholly owned subsidiary of Rupert Murdoch's Australian corporation, the News Corporation. Universal Studios is owned by Vivendi Universal Corporation, the French telecommunications giant (CEO Jean-Bernard Levy). Paramount studios is a wholly owned subsidiary of Viacom, the second-largest media conglomerate in the world (CEO Sumner Redstone). Walt Disney Studios has merged with the American Broadcasting Corporation, or ABC (CEO Michael Eisner). Columbia Pictures is a subsidiary of Sony, a Japanese corporation (CEO Goran Lindahl). Time Warner (CEO Richard Parsons), the largest media corporation in the world, owns Warner Bros. Pictures. Metro-Goldwyn-Mayer (now known as MGM Mirage) is also a member of the MPAA (CEO J. Terrence Lanni Terry). While there are prominent Jews in management and in the employ of many of these corporations, to suggest that they dominate the industry is subject to challenge. Nor are these CEOs particularly liberal. To the contrary, Murdoch is an unabashed conservative; Redstone was a strong supporter of the reelection of President George W. Bush; and, as noted, for one reason or another Michael Eisner blocked the release of *Fahrenheit 9/11*. Furthermore, movie studios are part of publicly held corporations, required by the Securities and Exchange Commission to submit quarterly statements to their shareholders. While they may hold large positions in the stocks of companies they manage, CEOs are managers, not owners. Murdoch and any one of the CEOs listed here would not tolerate, nor would they be in compliance with their fiduciary responsibilities, if they allowed an underperforming subsidiary to lose money because of its penchant to embark on some kind of ideological crusade. For one thing, their stockholders would not allow it. And there is another thing to consider: a substantial portion of the film industry is foreign owned.

It is also worth noting that the persistent focus on the ethnic and political background of movie executives may reflect at least some of the vestigial anti-Semitism that has dogged the industry from its beginnings. In different times, anti-Semitism against Hollywood manifested itself in different ways: first, in the form of nativist distrust of the "foreigners" who founded the industry, then in the imposition of the production code by the Legion of Decency, after that by isolationist elements in the lead-up to America's entry into World War II,[8] after that in the vigorous pursuit of antitrust investigations against the industry, then in the blacklist and communist witch hunt of the McCarthy era, and now in the rabid attacks on "Hollywood" by the conservative Right (including a morbid fascination with the political pronouncements of Barbara Streisand).[9]

But, in reality, there is no more "Hollywood." Decisions about film production are ultimately approved in corporate boardrooms in New York, Tokyo, Paris, and only sometimes in Los Angeles. Consequently, it is fascinating that so much attention is paid to the ethnic backgrounds of members of the media—liberal journalists and all that—as if it makes a difference. And if it does, why aren't the ethnic backgrounds of bankers, politicians, general officers in the military, and other corporate and societal leaders examined with the same vigor? It wouldn't be accurate to say that the personal backgrounds of journalists or filmmakers make no difference at all in the content of films, entertainment, or the news. But it could be more than plausibly argued that the influence of their personal backgrounds is overrated because of the influence of a much more powerful force—capitalism. To suggest otherwise is to suggest that the employees (or contractors) in the film industry are more important to corporate decision making than the owners are. Not only is that suggestion hard to believe, but there is also no incontrovertible evidence to that effect. Again, unless it can be demonstrated that there exists some sort of market distortion, such as a monopoly or government regulation, the argument that a bunch of liberal Jews are corrupting the youth of America is hard to accept. The movie business is now a free-for-all, and for that, capitalism is a much more powerful force—and for that, feature films are more product than art.

In *Hollywood's America: Social and Political Themes in Motion Pictures*, Stephen Powers, David J. Rothman, and Stanley Rothman attempt to be more systematic in their survey of their movie "elite." They draw a random sample from "a list of writers, producers, and directors of the fifty top grossing films made between 1965 and 1982."[10] Their final sample size is 96, with a response rate of 64 percent, out of a pool of 150 candidates. While their sample is somewhat larger and more systematically drawn than that of the Prindle survey, the authors find that, again, the Hollywood elite is different from other elites but not radically so, except to the extent that the former is much less religious than the latter and much more liberal in some respects. According to Powers and colleagues, the liberalism of the Hollywood elite is cultural, meaning that Hollywood filmmakers, on average, are more tolerant of alternate sexual lifestyles, divorce, and a broad range of freedom of expression. In other words, they are more cosmopolitan. But the influence may be not industry specific but geography specific—that is, the same result might be expected if researchers were to interview a group of, say, lawyers, bankers, or real estate brokers all from west Los Angeles.

On economic matters, however, moviemakers are almost as much capitalists as are other economic elites. They are only slightly more liberal on economic matters than are other businesspeople. Nevertheless, even these modest differences in economic liberalism would probably be washed out if the authors controlled for the regionality of their sample. Thus, their study indicates that Hollywood filmmakers are just as interested in making a buck as any other businessperson. Consequently, if this survey is a modestly accurate sample of Hollywood filmmakers, even on the creative side, would they be willing to suppress their personal political preferences when it comes to making a film for popular consumption? Furthermore, were we to include in the sample those who finance the films or show the films in their theaters, would we find that the influence of cultural liberalism overall among those who make and market commercial feature films is minor indeed?

I believe that critics of Hollywood liberalism, in a manner of speaking, have been seduced by Hollywood. In defining the producers of feature films as part of the "cultural elite," too much credit is given to the editorial influence of the creative side of the business. Filmmakers would like to think of themselves as artists and are anxious to convince anyone within earshot of such. It has to do with their self-image—Hollywood filmmakers like to think of themselves as artists. But to take Hollywood filmmakers at their word is to ignore some of the verities of capitalism. In feature films, more often than not, art does not sell. Art certainly doesn't sell well enough to justify a $100 million investment. The makers of the *Batman* series, the *Star Wars* series, the *Jurassic Park* series, and *Twister* are consummate capitalists. They are masters of their craft as well. But the fine craftwork of their films hardly makes them artists. The star of *Twister* (1996), the tornado, is a technological achievement to be sure, but it is no more a work of art than a dishwasher or Cuisinart. Thus, in parsing their sample in such a way as to separate the creative side from the business side of the movie industry, Powers and colleagues create a problem—the liberalism of the cultural elite—by constructing a study that merely compares the political beliefs and lifestyles of liberals and conservatives without considering the movie business as a whole.

While their surveys regarding the attitudes of one segment of the moviemaking industry are no doubt accurate, right-wing critics of Hollywood liberalism err in drawing conclusions from unrepresentative samples. Surveying filmmakers from the creative side of the business biases results in favor of that side of the industry. However, we should also consider the input of corporate CEOs, financiers, distributors, and consumers, who are at least as much a determinant of the content of movies as are moviemakers. To assume that the opinions of writers are on a par with that of producers is to equate the power of those who write screenplays with those who seek financing for production.

According to someone who ought to know, Martin Scorsese,

> In the old days the director dealt with moguls and major studios; today he faces executives and giant corporations instead. But there is one iron rule that has never changed: every decision is shaped by the moneymen's perception of what the audience wants.[11]

To his credit, conservative social critic and commentator Michael Medved, in his critique of Hollywood, *Hollywood vs. America* (1993), confronts the economic argument head on.[12] He does not ignore the economic verities of capitalism but instead argues that Hollywood filmmakers ignore the capitalist impulse to produce broadly popular films because of peer pressure. In seeking the acceptance of their peers, Medved argues, Hollywood filmmakers will ignore the dictates of the market.

Psychologists suggest that peer acceptance is a powerful motive in group decision making. *Groupthink* is a powerful dynamic that can drive decision making in small groups in all sorts of weird directions.[13] That is particularly true for decision making that takes place outside of democratic control or market incentives. Thus, we need to guard against the degenerative effects of groupthink in the decision-making processes of bureaucracies or other nonprofit institutions; but in a for-profit business, the penalty for flawed decision making of the groupthink variety is swift and terrible. Hollywood peers may give awards, but they can't pay for a $100 million film. The desire to have the respect of one's peers or to live north of Sunset Boulevard (the toniest address in Los Angeles) is an important motivation, but it is not a moneymaker. Making films that sell is all that matters, unless there exists some kind of market distortion.

Michael Medved goes on to suggest that there is indeed a market distortion in modern-day Hollywood. He argues that a kind of monopoly exists in Hollywood in the sense that certain films simply will not get made because of the nepotism and insularity of the industry. In other words, family-oriented films are less likely to receive backing because of the degeneracy of the self-perpetuating Hollywood elite. To a certain extent, it is hard to argue with this logic. Almost all businesses resort to some degree of nepotism to promote people into positions of responsibility. Indeed, Jews and other immigrants got into the movie business in the first place because it was a new industry and thus without an existing hierarchy and the informal barriers to entry that go with a nepotistic structure. It is not difficult to understand why Michael Douglas, Tori Spelling, or Jane Fonda (to name only a few) had an edge in getting jobs in the movie business—they had connections.

There can be several responses to this argument. First, the insularity of Hollywood does limit the types of themes that are explored but only to the extent that the industry may be slow to react. While Hollywood filmmakers may be cultural outliers, they are still rabid capitalists. Any market-driven industry will have a lag between market changes and product development. Nevertheless, unless there exists some sort of market distortion, an industry that fails to adapt to changing market conditions will experience falling profits. That has certainly not been the case for what has been a very profitable time for the movie industry.

If there is a market for films more sensitive to conservative social values, it will be developed, even in Hollywood. One of the problems with the points made by most of the authors discussed here is that they adopt a static approach in their analysis—meaning that their surveys are locked into one period of time. One weakness of this approach is trying to project past results into the future. Consequently, as they say in the stock market, "past performance is no indicator of future results." For example, during political campaigns, news organizations and candidates will run a series of tracking polls. Tracking is necessary to trace changes of public opinion—and public opinion can change very quickly, sometimes dramatically over the span of days. The fact is that the movie business is ever changing. Much of this change has historically been, and is currently being, driven by technological developments.

The development of VCRs, DVDs, and cable has transformed the market for motion pictures. This means that there is now a huge market for feature films outside the theater. There is now an audience for feature films that, if production costs are kept down, can be shown to segments of the population who are less likely to go to the theater because of, say, mobility problems, financial constraints, or small children at home. When the market for feature films was primarily the audience that would go to the theater, films were geared toward generally younger audiences without children. Times have changed and so have films. In the much more segmented market that now exists, there *are* more films made that are oriented to a stay-at-home audience. Television in particular has been on the cutting edge of this transition. Television now produces shows that appeal to a wide range of audiences, including religious conservatives. For example, witness the recent success of the CBS series *Touched by an Angel*, which adopts a quasi-religious theme.

This is not to say that slasher, car chase, and sexually explicit films are still not being made and won't, to a certain extent, continue to dominate feature films in theatrical release (for reasons to be discussed later in this chapter). The first-run theater box office continues to yield a more lucrative source of income for moviemakers than that of video rentals. Furthermore, nothing is going to change the fact that religious people and parents with small children in particular are busy on the weekends doing something other than going to the movies.

Finally, if there exists a monopoly in Hollywood based on nepotism, it must be a fragile monopoly indeed. This is not OPEC. For a monopoly to exist, there needs to be some sort of centralized control over the means of production and the marketing of a product. Furthermore, the demand for the product itself has to be nonelastic, meaning that the product is an absolute necessity for which there are no substitutes, such as oil. This hardly describes the film business. Theater ownership is no longer integrated with film production. Film producers are no longer guaranteed screens for their products. In addition, production facilities are readily available for rent, and there are literally tens of thousands of out-of-work actors, directors, and producers who will make a film practically for free. Furthermore, feature films themselves are extremely elastic goods. Going to the movies is not essential for life. Finally, there is a lot of product out there—not just in the theater but also on cable and in the video rental store. Therefore, Medved vastly overemphasizes the monopoly of nepotism in Hollywood because of the overall indefensibility of his argument, which ignores the basic tenets of economics.

MARKET-DRIVEN FILM INDUSTRY: EVIDENCE

In the following, I provide evidence to support my assertions that the film industry is basically market driven. First of all, allow me some disclaimers. What I am talking about here is a general trend. There are individual cases that contradict my overall analysis. However, I cannot respond to arguments based on anecdote[14] or to survey analyses that are so methodologically flawed that they are essentially meaningless. Furthermore, what I am discussing here is causality. If one thing causes another, it may also be the case that the direction of causality may be reversed. For example, the demand for a product is in part intrinsic and is in part driven by advertising—which doesn't just provide information to a consumer but also, ideally, creates a demand. This is a basic problem of marketing. Is it enough to simply identify and serve the market, or can a market for a product be created? The general rule of thumb is that it is easier to serve an existing market than to create a new one. A market for a product not in demand is usually nonexistent for good reason. Therefore, it would be reasonable to assume that, on balance, the market for feature motion pictures is driven by intrinsic demand rather than by a demand created by advertising (or the films themselves). In truth, marketing is a combination of the two, but the tendency toward serving an existing demand or adopting a tried-and-true formula is particularly pervasive in the film industry, where industry executives must attract millions of dollars of investment in commercial films that each have basically a one-shot, two-week window for success.[15]

My contentions are that film content is market driven and that the personal profile of filmgoers is unique enough to drive film content in a direction that may seem out of the ordinary (especially to the religious conservative). More specifically, I argue that the audience for movies is significantly more socially liberal and less religious than the norm and that filmmakers make movies intended to satisfy the intrinsic demands of that audience.

Furthermore, there are some practical reasons that cultural conservatives, older people, and families with children don't go to the movies. This I call the *crowding-out effect*. There is only so much time in the day. Older people have restricted mobility, and religious people or families with children are busy doing other things. The film industry is less anxious to serve this market because it is a less-lucrative market. While this situation may have changed to a certain extent due to the expanded market of American cinema, with the advent of VCRs, pay-per-view, and cable television, the main audience for American film is still foreign, younger, and more culturally liberal. Hollywood industry executives aren't changing their tune, not because they are out of touch, but because they are in touch in a way that only the market can enforce. Furthermore, there really isn't much of a prospect for a huge expansion of the production of films for cultural conservatives because they are the type of people who for some very understandable reasons don't go to the movies.

POLITICAL AFFILIATION AND FILM ATTENDANCE

The data presented here are the results of the Georgia State University/*Atlanta Journal Constitution* poll that includes several questions concerning movie viewing and attendance. The Georgia State poll was conducted by the Georgia State University Policy Research Center in the spring of 1997. It was a periodic telephone survey of voting-age Georgia residents. The results of this random sample were then weighted according to the 1990 census to compensate for distortions in the sample owing to the fact that more women responded and that fewer blacks had telephones. Thus, the answers of different groups are weighted to control for their over- or underresponse rate. This is a pretty standard survey research technique that is the norm on almost any large-scale poll.[16] There were 800 respondents to this survey.

It should be noted that children (people below the age of eighteen) were not interviewed in this survey, and yet there is pretty good evidence to suggest that teenagers in particular are frequent moviegoers. The problem is that it is difficult to survey people below the age of consent. Parents tend to object to the practice of strangers asking their children personal questions. Thus, this survey is not entirely representative of the population of moviegoers. Consider, however, that movie distributors suffer the same problem in doing their own marketing studies. They can survey children at the theater simply by seeing who attends, but in terms of doing broader comparative surveys of the population they are "flying blind." That may be one of the reasons that children's programming (not just in the movies but on the television as well) may be so scarce and is sometimes so inappropriate. Producers of children's entertainment have little information to go on and thus either make mistakes (by screening inappropriate material) or avoid the market altogether. As far as this survey is concerned, it is inaccurate in a representative way. That may sound like an oxymoron, but in fact in using these data we are working off the same kind of information available to the producers of entertainment themselves.

If film content is really market driven and if the audience for feature motion pictures is more culturally liberal than the norm, then film content will reflect a point of view that is more culturally liberal than the norm. One way to measure political attitudes is to look at response rates by party affiliation. Party labels are generally used as a surrogate for complex ideological beliefs. For example, for a candidate to identify as a Republican or Democrat tells the potential voter a substantial amount about the positions that will be adopted by the candidate if elected to office.

On the Georgia State poll 32 percent of respondents self-identified as Democrats, 24 percent as Republicans, 33 percent as independents, with 10 percent of the sample professing no partisan identification.[17] This is close to the national norm, where Democrats still hold a plurality but with the number of self-identified independents rising markedly. Respondents were asked about their attitudes in regard to a number of policy questions. In general, in accordance with the framework derived by Powers and colleagues, Democrats tended to be more culturally and economically liberal; independents tended to be more culturally liberal but economically conservative; and Republicans tended to be both culturally and economically conservative. Accordingly, if films are made to accommodate the sensibilities of the largest segment of the population, we would expect theater attendance to be virtually indistinguishable between Democrats and independents, while Republican theater attendance will be substantially less.

Respondents were asked the following question:

How often do you watch feature motion pictures?
Less than once a month
1–2 times a month
1–2 times a week
More than 2 times a week

If film content is basically market driven, movie producers will not care whether their audiences are Republican or Democrat, black or white, Martian or human, as long as they pay to see a film. Theater attendance is computed in terms of number of films viewed (or paid admissions). Not only are total paid admissions important to the film industry, but also just as important is the consumer who goes to the movies more frequently. Film content should be geared toward the frequent moviegoer, especially if the frequency of film attendance by a few far outstrips the less-frequent attendance of the many. In this survey, there are 255 Democrats, 197 Republicans, 264 independents, and 84 nonidentifiers. If we cross-tabulate film attendance by party identification, we find the following viewing habits:

Less than 1 film a month:
Democrats: 23 percent
Independents: 20 percent
Republicans: 20 percent
Nonidentifiers: 29 percent
1–2 films a month:
Democrats: 47 percent
Independents: 54 percent
Republicans: 61 percent
Nonidentifiers: 48 percent
1–2 films a week:
Democrats: 19 percent
Independents: 18 percent
Republicans: 15 percent
Nonidentifiers: 10 percent
More than 2 films a week:
Democrats: 9 percent
Independents: 7 percent
Republicans: 3 percent
Nonidentifiers: 12 percent

It can be estimated that those who watch less than 1 film a month, on average, see 6 films a year; those who see films 1–2 times a month see 18 films a year; those who see films 1–2 times a week see 72 films a year; and those who see films more than

Table 3.1.   Number of Films Viewed in a Single Year, by Partisan Identification
($n = 807$)

Movie Attendance	Partisan Identification			
	Democrats	*Independents*	*Republicans*	*Nonidentifiers*
less than once a month	352	236	317	151
1–2 a month	2,157	1,950	2,899	726
1–2 a week	3,488	3,421	2,128	604
more than twice a week	3,304	2,661	851	1,452
Total	9,301	8,268	6,195	2,933
Per capita	36	31	31	35

SOURCE: Georgia State/*Atlanta Journal Constitution* poll, 1997.

2 times a week see 144 films a year. If we multiply the number of party identifiers by the number of films they will view in a year, we arrive at the results in table 3.1.

Several things stand out in the results. First, the most frequent per capita filmgoers are Democrats and the apolitical. And although the percentage of Republican film viewing is not all that different from those of the other groups, because there are so many more independents and Democrats, every Democrat/independent/apolitical viewer is "worth" three Republicans to the filmmaker. It is not remarkable, therefore, that film content is geared toward cultural liberals.

The obvious response to these survey results is that Republicans don't go to the movies because they have nothing to see. As noted, however, it is much safer in a financial sense for a producer to serve an existing market than to create a new one. Certainly, marketing firms that work for the film studios have gotten pretty much the same results as the survey did. Consequently, the safest bet for financiers is to serve an existing audience. There are usually some valid reasons that a market for a particular product does not exist, which leads to our next analysis. Primarily because of the crowding-out effect, cultural conservatives (many of whom are Republicans) have other things to do when it comes to their spare time and are therefore less likely to go to the movies. Specifically, because religious people are otherwise occupied, particularly on the weekends, they will be less likely to go to the movies. We would assume for people who are serious about their religion that no amount of content change in the movies is going to make them shortchange their church activities in favor of going to the movies.

In the Georgia State poll, respondents were asked whether they attended church

Once a week
2–3 times a month
Several times a year
Less than 3 times a year

In all, 798 participants responded to this question. The results in percentage terms were that

39 percent attend church at least once a week ($n = 314$)
22 percent attend church 2–3 times a month ($n = 175$)
16 percent attend church several times a year ($n = 126$)
23 percent rarely or never go to church ($n = 183$)

If we cross-tabulate church attendance with movie attendance, we would expect an inverse relationship—the more people go to church, the less they go to the movies. Again the results are expressed in terms of movies viewed (admissions paid). After all, if film content is market driven, filmmakers will go where the money is—the frequent filmgoers.

As expected, per capita movie-viewing rates among churchgoers are much lower than they are among people who don't go to church. (See table 3.2.) While the absolute number of people who regularly attend church and go to the movies is higher than those who don't go to church (and the movies), it is unlikely that filmmakers would look at these results and resolve to go after the churchgoing market. It is much more likely that producers of films will conclude that the existing market is more expandable than the relatively untapped churchgoing audience. This is a judgment call. Certainly, there is a chance that the churchgoing audience can be tapped by filmmakers to a greater extent. However, it is going to take more than a scolding from Michael Medved or Bob Dole to make a publicly traded corporation finance those sorts of films based on this sort of evidence. Investment in films for religious audiences will have to be made as a matter of faith—something better left to the religious community that has a lot of financial resources and talent to make their own films—as Mel Gibson has done. But for businesspeople there is nothing in these numbers to indicate that they are directing their efforts in the wrong, unprofitable way.

Finally, it may well be the case that cultural liberals, besides being higher per capita filmgoers, are also more profitable for filmmakers. There are a number of ways that people can go to the movies. They can go to the local cineplex, or they can watch films at home on commercial television, subscription cable, pay-per-view, or on their VCRs and DVDs. For the film industry, the most lucrative audience by far is the one that pays full admission at a first-run movie house.[18] In a typical distribution deal, the distributor receives up to 80 percent (the theater owner, 20 percent) of the admissions

Table 3.2. Church Attendance and Number of Films Viewed in a Single Year ($n = 807$)

Movie Attendance	Church Attendance			
	1 < a Week	*2–3 a Month*	*Several Times a Year*	*3 > a Year*
less than once a month	527	239	96	192
2–3 times a month	2,872	1,723	1,436	574
1–2 times a week	3,447	2,298	2,298	2,872
more than twice a week	2,298	1,149	1,149	3,447
Total	9,144	5,409	4,979	7,085
Per capita	29	31	39	39

SOURCE: Georgia State/*Atlanta Journal Constitution* poll, 1997.

Table 3.3.   Number of Feature Films Viewed in a Theater in a Single Year, by Political Party (*n* = 179)

Movie Attendance	Partisan Identification			
	Democrats	Independents	Republicans	Apolitical
less than once a month	0	0	0	0
1–2 a month	612	972	630	144
1–2 a week	864	1,152	432	144
more than twice a week	576	720	0	144
Total	2,052	2,844	1,062	432
Per capita	41	69	14	36

SOURCE: Georgia State/*Atlanta Journal Constitution* poll, 1997.

revenue for the first two weeks that a film is screened. The distributor "take" begins to decline after that on a sliding scale. That makes high-gross box office features extremely profitable for the distributor (and long-running features extremely profitable for the theater owner). In the Georgia State survey, respondents were also asked where they preferred to watch feature films. Of 800 respondents, 183, or 23 percent, said that they preferred to watch feature films at a movie theater whereas 298, 37 percent, a plurality of respondents, prefer to watch films on their VCRs or DVD players at home. When those results are cross-tabulated by political party, we find the following:

The most lucrative audiences for feature films are independents, Democrats, and the apolitical, in that order. Republicans are so far behind that their share of the market is virtually meaningless. (See table 3.3.) Again, it is no wonder that feature films are made for cultural liberals.

FILM CONTENT AND THE MARKET: SOCIETAL CONCERNS

If film content is market driven, it will tend to reflect rather than drive societal attitudes. In other words, film content will tend to lag behind changes in public opinion. Because of the vagaries of public opinion polling (especially in terms of political attitudes) and evaluating film content, this is a difficult relationship to illustrate. Nevertheless, in certain areas of film content—specifically in regard to crime, punishment of crime, and fear of crime, real and imagined—there is some fairly reliable public opinion data. In addition, Powers and colleagues have performed a careful content analysis of top-grossing films, including a category that examines the amount of violence, criminal violence, behavior of the police, and the disposition of criminal actions in the courts. They come to the conclusion, in accordance with the central theme of their book, that Hollywood is out of touch with its market.

Surveying the extent of crime and violence in popular movies, we can confirm what seems obvious to many: The world according to Hollywood has become much more violent and dangerous over the past twenty-five years. This condition establishes a backdrop against which not only police, but also other characters, seek to accomplish their objectives. *The surroundings are contrivances of Hollywood.*[19] (original emphasis)

Table 3.4.   Movie Violence Perpetrated by or Inflicted on Major Characters

Major Characters	1946–1965	1966–1975	1976–1990
Committing crimes	27%	46%	38%
Resorting to violence	19	38	34
Becoming crime victims	34	39	50

SOURCE: Stephen Powers, David J. Rothman, and Stanley Rothman, *Hollywood's America: Social and Political Themes in Motion Pictures* (Boulder, Colo.: Westview, 1996).

It may be true, as the authors suggest, that the world as a dangerous place is a Hollywood "contrivance." However, it is much more likely that increases in crime rates in the movies are a reflection of either reality or a public contrivance. Powers and colleagues divide the period of 1946–1990 into three unequal periods: 1946–1965, 1966–1975, 1976–1990. This is an odd contrivance in and of itself. Nevertheless, using their own numbers, the authors contradict themselves.

According to FBI uniform crime reports, the rate of assaults (simple and aggravated combined) nearly doubled between 1946 and 1966 (from 0.67 percent to 1.1 percent per 1,000). While murder rates remained rather steady during that period (about .05 percent), robbery increased about 20 percent, and theft more than doubled (6 percent to 14.5 percent). This environment of increasing crime was hardly a Hollywood contrivance. It was a reality. Furthermore, after 1966 crime rates exploded, murder rates almost doubled between 1966 and 1973 (.05 percent to .09 percent); assaults increased another 60 percent; theft was up 60 percent as well; and robbery rates more than doubled. This was hardly a contrivance as well. Crime rates continued to climb until 1981 and then began a modest decline. Between 1981 and 1990, robbery declined about 22 percent, and assault declined about 7 percent. A cursory scan of table 3.4 suggests that the movies, according to Powers and colleagues' own figures, reflected this modest decline in the crime rate. In fact, given the relationship between changing rates of film violence and the actual crime rate from this perspective, it is remarkable how closely film crime rates track/follow actual crime rates. But, then again, if film content is market driven, it should come as no surprise that feature films reflect both the concerns and the reality of the moviegoing public.

Now, it is also true that while rates of increase and decrease in crime are accurately reflected in the movies, overall rates of violence and crime have always been well in excess of the norm in Hollywood movies. This is probably due to the "rubbernecking" aspect of Hollywood cinema. Even during the days of the production code, Hollywood presented the public with a skewed vision of American life. How many people who went to the movies actually came in contact with people such as Scarface (Al Capone)? Very few. But the movies, to them, represented a window into worlds that they could never know (and, in fact, that may not have existed). Popular films are cathartic. They allow the viewer to experience the thrills of the chase without the dangers. It is often said in television journalism, "If it bleeds, it leads." So it is with motion pictures. They will always be "larger than life." Women will be prettier. Story endings will be more pat. And the world will be more exciting and less mundane. But as the public's tastes change, so will the movies. Starting at an existing base of film content that was never an actual reflection of reality, films will nevertheless continue to reflect changes in the reality and concerns of the public.

Finally, Powers and coauthors show that the victimization of film characters increased steadily during the period of their survey while crimes committed actually dropped. This is not an accurate reflection of the reality of crime rates that declined modestly after 1981. Is this a Hollywood or public contrivance?

Between 1974 and 1994, according to a Roper Center survey, the percentage of the public that named "crime and lawlessness" as one of the "two or three items [it is] personally . . . most concerned about today" steadily increased from 30 percent to 54 percent—this despite the fact that crime rates began a steady decline after 1981. Whether crime rates were actually dropping or not, most of the public felt increasingly insecure. Again, even though actual crime rates were dropping, between 1981 and 1996 the percentage of respondents who felt they were "very safe" in their neighborhood dropped steadily from 44 percent to 29 percent. While this increased feeling of insecurity may have been a contrivance, it wasn't Hollywood's contrivance. The public was indeed feeling more insecure in this period, regardless of the fact that crime rates were dropping.[20]

To be fair, movie violence may drive insecurity at the same time as insecurity drives movie violence. The two aspects of communication are interrelated. As we shall see in the next chapter, establishing a direct causal relationship between media content and behavior is quite difficult if not impossible. While there is some fairly reliable evidence to suggest that specific groups are influenced by what they see on the television or movie screen, these groups are in the minority. It is not clear what the strength or direction of that causal relationship is in regard to the majority. So while there may be some truth to the argument that Hollywood is corrupting the morals of our youth, the question is, how great the corruption, whether the influence works in the opposite way in the opposite direction, and whether we should compromise our other principles, such as the protection of personal liberties, in order to ameliorate what may be a relatively minor problem. In this chapter, I examine film content as an effect of the audience for movies and the proclivities of the filmmakers. In the chapter to follow, I examine this issue of film as a cause of behavior rather than an effect. In other words, I answer the question, to what extent are movies the cause of certain behaviors or the influence on certain attitudes?

Feature Film: *The Postman* (1997)

Why do some films succeed while others fail? There may be many reasons, and if anyone knew for certain in advance whether a film was destined for success, he or she would be a candidate for a lucrative position in the marketing business indeed. In the following review, I choose one of the greatest flops in recent motion picture history: The Postman.

There can be lots of problems with films: bad acting, poor production, or a bad script. Films can fail in the market because they are released at the wrong time of year or because they come against a smash megahit that siphons off revenues (although a rising tide of moviegoing sometimes lifts all boats). Often, studio executives who don't believe in the marketability of a film will simply fail to promote it. And in the film reviewed here, the plotline is so implausible and obtuse that in retrospect we can see that it was bound to fail.

The Postman. *Courtesy of M.P. & T.V. Photo Archive.*

If you haven't seen this film you are not alone. This turgid and overblown potboiler didn't do a lot of business. In fact, in its first weekend at the box office, it did only $5 million (of its $80 million production cost), and it didn't fare much better after that. In recognition of its dubious achievements, *The Postman* received the not-so-coveted Razzie Award, given annually by the Golden Raspberry Award Foundation to the worst film of the year. *The Postman* practically swept the awards. Besides receiving the Worst Picture Award, Kevin Costner, in a rare double achievement, was voted both Worst Actor and Worst Director for his work on the film. The film also garnered the Worst Score and Worst Screenplay awards.

Why was this film so badly regarded? Why did the audience and Hollywood have such a visceral negative reaction to this film? The production values were first-class, and I think the acting was acceptable, the criticisms of Costner notwithstanding. Certainly, he did no worse in this film than he did in the widely acclaimed *Dances with Wolves* (1990), for which he was nominated for Academy Awards as actor and director.

I think this is an example of one of those films that has a plotline that people just won't buy. In a nutshell, for the many of you who haven't seen it, the plot of this film goes something like this. In the aftermath of World War III, a drifter, played by Kevin Costner, happens upon the wreck of a U.S. Postal Service truck. Costner dons the uniform of the postal worker and through a series of plotline contrivances takes it upon himself to restore the postal service as the basis of a new American government. The suggestion implicit in this plotline is that a governmental institution as basic as the postal service is an essential component in the fabric of a free, democratic society.

You know something, that's true—about the post office I mean. The largest civilian employer in the federal government is the U.S. Postal Service. The postal service is the agency of the government with which we have the most frequent contact. The post office is the only governmental agency mentioned specifically in the U.S. Constitution (article 1, section 8). The post office was a particular brainchild of Benjamin Franklin, who believed that a reliable postal system was essential for national commerce and defense.

We like to make jokes about the post office. In our vocabulary, "going postal" means to go crazy, grab a gun, and shoot your coworkers—which is why the plotline of this movie won't sell. The only line the postal service can play in a plotline is as a punch line. To treat it seriously, as an object of essence and admiration, goes against the grain of popular culture. It may be true that the post office is essential to a civilized society, but to make that case is to be preachy and obtusely humorless. That's why this film did so badly. It's just not funny in the way that it's supposed to be funny.

Don't agree? What do you think?

EXERCISE

Pick a major feature film that has been a commercial disaster. Analyze why it did so poorly in relation to its target population of moviegoers. Why was this film made in the first place?

NOTES

1. While there are many definitions of "art," the key distinction between art and product, from the perspective of many, lies in the motives of the creator. This point of view is well summarized by one author, who writes, "While the concept of art in industrial civilizations has broadened to an extraordinary degree in terms of medium and content, it has, at least implicitly, narrowed in terms of use, function, and meaning, a narrowing of the relation of art to its context. This is the concept of art as being purely for esthetic contemplation, art for art's sake, pure art, and the necessity of the uselessness of an object to be called 'art.'" Evelyn Payne Hatcher, *Art as Culture: An Introduction to the Anthropology of Art*, 2nd ed. (Westport, Conn.: Bergin & Garvey, 1999), 8–9.

2. Douglas Kellner, "Film, Politics, and Ideology. Reflections on Hollywood Film in the Age of Reagan," *Velvet Light Trap* 27 (1991): 9–24.

3. David F. Prindle, *Risky Business: The Political Economy of Hollywood* (Boulder, Colo.: Westview, 1993), 90.

4. Prindle, *Risky Business*, 98. Prindle notes that Hollywood "would still be a liberal community even if it contained no Jews" (99).

5. Patricia Evans, "Jews in American Cinema," in *Political Companion to American Film*, ed. Gary Crowdus (Chicago: Lakeview Press, 1994), 223.

6. See Steven Alan Carr, *Hollywood and Anti-Semitism: A Cultural History up to World War II* (Cambridge: Cambridge University Press, 2001), particularly chap. 9.

7. John W. Cones, *The Feature Film Distribution Deal: A Critical Analysis of the Single Most Important Film Industry Agreement* (Carbondale: Southern Illinois University Press, 1997), 46.

8. John E. Moser, "'Gigantic Engines of Propaganda': The 1941 Senate Investigation of Hollywood," *Historian* 63, no. 4 (2001): 731, www.questia.com/ (accessed December 1, 2004).

9. For a discussion of this, see Kevin MacDonald, *Separation and Its Discontents: Toward an Evolutionary Theory of Anti-Semitism*, ed. Seymour W. Itzkoff (Westport, Conn.: Praeger, 1998), particularly 52–59. For an example of the conservative media's focus on the political activities of Barbara Streisand, see "Streisand Chimes in on Iraq Politics," *Fox News Online*, September 27, 2002, www.foxnews.com/story/0,2933,64200,00.html (accessed December 1, 2004).

10. Powers, Rothman, and Rothman, *Hollywood's America*, 252–53. For a more recent version of this study with the same basic results, emphasizing among other things the overrepresentation of Jews in the "cultural elite," see Stanley Rothman and Amy E. Black, "Media and Business Elites: Still in Conflict," *Public Interest*, no. 143 (Spring 2001): 72, www.questia.com/ (accessed December 1, 2004).

11. Martin Scorsese and Michael Henry Wilson, *A Personal Journey with Martin Scorsese through American Movies* (New York: Hyperion, 1997), 20.

12. Michael Medved, *Hollywood vs. America* (New York: Harper Collins, 1993).

13. For a thorough discussion of the groupthink phenomenon, see Irving L. Janis, *Groupthink*, 2nd ed. (Boston: Houghton Mifflin, 1983).

14. "*Anecdotal evidence* is evidence stemming from a single, often unreliable source which is used in an argument as if it had been scientifically or statistically proven. The person using anecdotal evidence may or may not be aware of the fact that, by doing so, they are generalizing." *Wikipedia Online Encyclopedia*, "Anecdote," http://en.wikipedia.org/wiki/Anecdote (accessed December 6, 2004).

15. See Michael Bywater, "They're Not Selling Movies to You, They're Selling You to the Movies," *New Statesman*, February 14, 1997, www.questia.com/ (accessed December 6, 2004).

16. As an aside, the results that support my hypotheses are even stronger in the unweighted survey.

17. There has been a substantial shift toward Republican Party identification in Georgia in the last few years since this survey was taken. Whether that has changed movie attendance patterns in the state is a matter for further research.

18. This may be changing. See Edward Jay Epstein, "Hollywood's Profits, Demystified: The Real El Dorado Is TV," *Slate*, August 8, 2005 (accessed August 24, 2005). While it may be true that the greatest profit center for Hollywood has become television licensing, on a per capita basis, the first-run ticket purchaser is still the most lucrative movie patron. According to the industry's own figures, in 2004 ticket sales did not cover the costs of making films. However, it is hard to separate the box office attendance for a film from its marketability in

other venues. The licensing fee extracted for a film shown on television is a function of the film's perceived popularity, which is in turn driven by box office receipts. Thus, to say that box office receipts don't cover the cost of a film shifts the costs of production onto the theatrical release side of the industry and credits the profits to the licensing side of the industry. See the Motion Picture Association of America, *2004 Consolidated Television Sales Report,* table 1, www.edwardjayepstein.com/TVnumbers.htm (accessed August 24, 2005).

19. Powers, Rothman, and Rothman, *Hollywood's America,* 104.

20. The media (particularly the journalistic media) may bear some responsibility. Some evidence suggests that television news coverage that emphasizes crime and gore has colored the public's perception of risk in the world. On this topic, see Shanto Inyengar, *Is Anyone Responsible? How Television Frames Political Issues* (Chicago: University of Chicago Press, 1994).

SUGGESTED READING

Balio, Tino, ed. *The American Film Industry.* 2nd ed. Madison: University of Wisconsin Press, 1985.

Cones, John W. *The Feature Film Distribution Deal: A Critical Analysis of the Single Most Important Film Industry Agreement.* Carbondale: Southern Illinois University Press, 1997.

Lefcourt, Peter, and Laura J. Shapiro, eds. *The First Time I Got Paid for It—Writers' Tales from the Hollywood Trenches.* New York: Public Affairs, 2000.

Litman, Barry R. *The Motion Picture Mega-Industry.* Boston: Allyn and Bacon, 1998.

Parenti, Michael. *Make-Believe Media: The Politics of Entertainment.* New York: St. Martin's Press, 1991.

Powers, Stephen, David J. Rothman, and Stanley Rothman. *Hollywood's America: Social and Political Themes in Motion Pictures.* Boulder, Colo.: Westview, 1996.

Prindle, David. *Risky Business: The Political Economy of Hollywood.* Boulder: Westview, 1993.

Rafter, Nicole. *Shots in the Mirror: Crime Films and Society.* Oxford: Oxford University Press, 2000.

4

Film Content: Cause or Effect?

In this chapter, I examine the issue of causality. In a book on the relationship between film and politics, it is important to study the issue of causality at two levels. First, if it can be demonstrated that film and, in a larger sense, the media create some kind of undesirable behavior, then media content becomes a cause for political action. Calls for censorship, boycotts, or voluntary industry controls would have little meaning if there were no direct relationship between media depictions and behavior. At another level, the issue of causality is also important to the central theme of this book, that media and film content is a reflection of the sensibilities of at least some segments of our society. In chapter 3, I present evidence to the effect that the most lucrative audience for films is generally less political and more socially liberal than those who don't go to the movies. Furthermore, movie content, in terms of violence, tracks prevailing crime rates fairly well. Film content has been sensitive to public attitudes toward crime, even reflecting an unjustified spike in public insecurity in the 1980s. But to say that one factor (film violence) tracks another (the crime rate) is one thing; to say that one factor *causes* another is a more difficult proposition to support. Thus, in this chapter, I examine the relationship between film content and actual behavior, with a critical eye both to the potential and need for media censorship and toward the power of films to literally move an audience.

It appears to many that the body count in movies contributes to crime rates or that relaxed sexual attitudes on film drive increases in teenage pregnancy rates. As one set of authors sums it up,

> In research on aggressive behavior, it is generally believed that exposure to violent images such as those typically found in horrid fiction is capable of producing certain short-term responses through activation of cognitive structures semantically related to hostile action. In the same way that byproducts of priming can impact the development of social perceptions, activation of various cognitive structures may also influence displayed social behavior. Following exposure to materials with violent images or expressions, additional aggressive thoughts, scripts, and schema can be primed.[1]

But in this charge is a number of assumptions and alternative explanations that need to be examined. Also, it is quite unlikely that cause and effect in this case is simply unidirectional or not influenced by other intervening variables.[2]

First, the influence of movies on socialization and behavior is probably the least significant of any of the entertainment media, and the entertainment media are probably not a terribly important influence on the behavior of individuals in general.[3] The fact is that many studies of socialization, political and otherwise, suggest that the most significant variable in determining media influence is reinforcement, or the repeated and intense exposure to an influence. Furthermore, age and maturity seem to be determinant factors as well.[4] The more mature the individual, the less likely the exposure is to have a lasting impact on an individual's beliefs or behavior.

Because age and duration of exposure are such important variables, feature films are an unlikely source of many socialized behaviors and beliefs, if for no other reason than that moviegoing is a discrete experience. While viewing a film may be an intense experience, it is not a long-lasting one. Furthermore, the context of viewing a film, the movie theater, cannot be mistaken for anything but make-believe. In addition, while television shows such as the news can be watched continuously over long periods or video games played for hours on end, it is uncommon for a filmgoer, even an enthusiastic one, to see a film more than a couple of times. Finally, the rating system, albeit imperfect and spottily enforced, does at least keep the youngest children out of adult films. It is true that films can be rented on video by almost anyone and that there is no way to limit the viewing of the rented film, but the fact remains that serial consumption of media is more likely to occur via the television, the CD music player, or the video game. Finally, while in the relatively distant past, feature films were the most prominent form of media entertainment, in the modern context, films are but one of many competing forms of entertainment. To single films out as harmful or even influential in any meaningful way is to ignore the multitude of other, stronger influences on behavior. Thus, today, feature films are among the least powerful agents of media socialization.

To the extent that films have any influence at all on the socialization of children and young adults, they seem to reinforce existing beliefs. In a recent survey, a researcher found that among young adults ($N = 709$) those who were already predisposed toward conservative ideology were repelled by what they perceived as liberal attitudes in feature films and that the only effect a film had on those youngsters was, if anything, to harden their conservative predisposition. By the same token, young people who were predisposed toward liberal beliefs were repelled by film messages that they perceived as being objectionable, such as violence against women, but were otherwise unaffected by the liberal lifestyle characteristics portrayed in films.[5]

Therefore, because children generally have their most sustained and profound contact with their parents, the home is the most important influence on a child's socialization. Other institutions besides the family that may influence a child's socialization are school, church, peers, and the media, probably in that order of importance. Despite some notable instances where a link was made between a particular movie and a particular event, the connection is so tenuous and so many other factors are at work that it would be impossible to draw a direct causal connection. For example, the gunmen in the tragic Columbine High School shootings were said to have modeled their crime after an incident portrayed in the movie *The Basketball Diaries* (1995). However, so many other factors were involved—the perpetrators' being bullied in school, their circumvention of gun laws, their being influenced by other media (such as violent video games)—that to pin the blame on any one factor would be impossible. In fact, for lack of evidence, federal courts in a couple of cases dismissed lawsuits filed against the film producers and video game distributors by the parents of some of the victims of Columbine and another school shooting in Kentucky.[6]

There are always exceptions to any general rule. Certain individuals, no matter what their age, are so immature or disturbed as to be susceptible to violent or antisocial behavior portrayed in film. However, it is hard to act on such an assumption. What restrictions should we place on the content of film to prevent the rare incident, and would it make any difference anyhow? How can we predict what a disturbed individual will do when exposed to even the most innocuous film message or plot variation taken out of context? What, if any, is the predictable causal relationship between film and behavior?

The answer to this question is not as obvious as it may seem. Some politicians and pundits are fond of arguing that movies and the media in general are a terrible influence on American society.[7] However, implicit in this statement are a number of assumptions that need to be addressed, primarily related to the issue of causality. The nature of causality is always difficult to outline in the social context. To demonstrate, for example, that violent movies cause violent behavior is fraught with methodological peril.

First of all is the question of the direction of causality. To say that one thing causes another is to go beyond a simple correlation. The sun rises and the rooster crows: the relationship is close and consistent, but to say that the rooster's crowing causes the sun to rise is a jump in logic and is inaccurate as well. Thus, the statement that movie violence causes actual violence is a statement that assumes a relationship that is not supported by mere correlation. Nevertheless, it is an empirical, testable proposition. In the last chapter, I argue that because the film industry is a business in a free market, the market generally drives film content. Thus, the content of film more likely reflects our society (or, more accurately, the tastes of the audience for movies) than the other way around.

Second, and just as difficult to demonstrate, is the degree and nature of causality within a given context. It is not enough to argue that because the incidence of violence coincides with the release of a violent film, that one thing causes another. In the parlance of the methodologist, the relationship could be totally spurious.[8] Causation in this relationship implies that in the absence of violent movies, violent behavior would be less likely. However, since film viewing is such a universal experience and has been so for most of this century, it is difficult to know what would have happened in the absence of film. Nevertheless, we can examine this proposition by looking at things from a comparative perspective. Is violence less prominent in societies where American films are not screened, or was violence less evident before the advent of the movies?

In this century, the three greatest genocides committed were by regimes in states where American movies were heavily censored or strictly forbidden. Hitler's Germany, Stalin's Russia, and Pol Pot's Cambodia were hardly influenced by American film. The same can generally be said for states where the slaughter of citizens was more or less sanctioned by the government—for example, in the former Yugoslavia, Malawi, Red China, Afghanistan, Syria, and so on. Even the most cursory examination of the list of states involved in wholesale slaughter of civilians indicates that the operative factor leading to violence in those countries may be the absence of democratic rule or some other factor, not the screening of *Taxi Driver* (1976). Furthermore, it is difficult to argue that before the advent of film society was a less-violent place. How many assaults, rapes, and murders went unreported in the South before the end of slavery? The fact that we now define the killing of a black man in Mississippi as murder doesn't necessarily mean that there are more murders per capita now in Mississippi than there were one hundred years ago. The murders now are just reported more often.

But what I am referring to here is mainly organized violence. What about the influence of film on criminal interpersonal violence? The United States has the highest incarceration rate and one of the highest crime rates in the developed world. Crime rates are lower in virtually every other developed country, whether the media is severely restricted or not. Thus, at least from the comparative perspective, the presence of a free and unfettered media seems to make no difference in the rate of crime.

In fact, free media may actually be associated with a lower rate of criminality and violence. It should be noted that many authoritarian states have rates of crime lower than that of the United States—Iran and Singapore, for instance. The crime rate in either society, however, is not a good indicator of the amount of violence it experiences. Singapore has been described as "Disneyland with a death penalty"—a state in which the peace maintained is the peace of the authoritarian state. Iran is a "peaceful" place where the state has issued an execution order for the author Salman Rushdie that could best be described as an officially sanctioned contract for murder.

Another way to use the comparative approach to test the proposition that film violence causes actual violence is to look at crime from the regional perspective. It is fairly clear that criminal violence varies greatly within the United States from one locality to another. To demonstrate a definite link between film violence and real violence, we would have to show that, all things being equal, moviegoing is much more common in the poorer neighborhoods of Watts (California), East Saint Louis, or the South Bronx, which happen to have higher-than-average rates of crime. Besides the fact that there are virtually no movie theaters in those locales, this argument may suggest that poverty leads to crime (and the other way around) but not that movies lead to crime.

Nevertheless, besides violent crime, films may stimulate other types of interpersonal behavior that is objectionable—for example, in the United States, the decreasing age at which teens engage in sexual activity or the frequency with which they engage in sex. In sum, 34 percent of women become pregnant before the age of twenty, with some four million new cases of sexually transmitted diseases among teens estimated each year.[9] Results in this regard, however, are mixed. In the last decade, rates of teen pregnancy, abortion, birth rates, and sexual activity have been on the decline.[10] Also, in the 1990s the ages at which children were arrested for violent crimes and the vicious character of those crimes seemed to be changing for the worse.[11] But that trend has begun to reverse as well.[12] Something is clearly going on in our society in regard to the violent and sexual behavior of our youth. However, to say that the media is the cause is a stretch. At the very least, if there is a connection, then the media must be given credit for the good as well as blame for the bad. Furthermore, there is certainly a plethora of alternative, plausible explanations for the undesirable behavior of the young—such as the ready availability of guns, the higher rates of poverty among the young, and the economic necessity of having both parents work outside the home.

CAUSE OR EFFECT: MOVIES AND THE BEHAVIORAL APPROACH

The question of whether film content drives human behavior or not is a prime target for investigation by behavioral scientists. Consequently, there are literally volumes of research on the topic of media content and behavior. As noted, however, it is not enough to simply point out a simultaneous increase in actual violence and on-screen violence and then declare that movies cause violence. My having a cup of coffee every morning certainly does not cause the sun to rise every morning—likewise for movies and violence. The former does not cause the latter. In fact, in a previous chapter, I present evidence to suggest that public attitudes drive film content and not the other way around—which is a theory that is supported not only by the evidence presented here but also by pretty much everything we know about classical economics.

First, it is important to state the obvious. A significant amount of evidence suggests a kind of relationship between media violence and aggressive behavior. In a statement before a subcommittee of the Senate Judiciary Committee in October 1984, John P. Murray, testifying on behalf of the American Psychological Association, pretty much summed up the massive body of evidence in regard to the relationship between television violence and behavior:

> The first question raised the issue of whether viewers of televised violence are more aggressive than other people. On the basis of research evidence, I conclude that the answer to this question is emphatically yes. Children and adults who more frequently watch violent programs tend to hold attitudes and values which favor the use of aggression to resolve conflicts. They also tend to behave more aggressively. That does not necessarily mean that television causes this aggression but at least these studies show that there is a link between the two.
>
> The second question is: "Does television violence produce aggressive behavior?" The answer to this question, again, seems to be yes—based on studies conducted both in

laboratories and in naturalistic settings observing preschool children, school age young-sters, college students, and adults. The experimental evidence seems to support the notion that viewing violence does lead to aggressive behavior in these settings and that there seems to be a long-term relationship between viewing violence and behaving aggressively.[13]

Nothing that I can find in more recent studies seems to undermine the basic premise of this statement that people who are predisposed toward violence tend to watch violent programming and that the viewing of that programming tends to reinforce existing tendencies.[14]

Here is where the controversy begins. There is a wide-ranging and lively debate over media violence and cause and effect. On the one hand is the unusual combination of social conservatives and some groups on the Left who blame much of the degeneration of society (as they see it) on the media messages—in particular, those received by our children. Whether these beliefs are held as an article of faith and are part of a larger, illiberal worldview is an open question. Would it matter to some critics of the media what the scientific evidence says about the relationship between media messages and violence? From the perspective of some social conservatives, media messages that are not guided by the Bible or some similar dogma are by their nature unholy whether they have some kind of causal influence or not. This is a point that cannot be debated here (in fact, it can't be "debated"; religious beliefs are held as an article of faith and are thus not subject to question). Rather, in this chapter we are more interested in examining the issue of cause and effect from the scientific perspective.

There is in the field of the social sciences an intramural debate over the value of looking at society from the behavioral perspective as opposed to the structural perspective. This refers to the fact that behaviorists start from the premise that the sum of society's parts (individuals) are equal to its whole, whereas structuralists believe that the whole is greater than and different from its parts. More simply put, according to behaviorialists—who come mainly out of the field of psychology (although the subfield of social psychology is a bridge to the structuralist school)— if a phenomenon can be observed at the individual level, then that behavior will presumably register at the societal level as well. Thus, if it can be demonstrated that individuals respond with actual violence to viewing violence on-screen, then we can assume that film violence leads to actual violence. This seems like a pretty commonsense approach to looking at human behavior. However, it is, when examined more closely, a flawed and even preposterous point of view.

Structuralists (also known as institutionalists) believe that behavior is largely a function of setting. In other words, a person's behavior results from societal pressure. A husband remains faithful to his wife because of the constraints imposed by the institution of marriage. He may remain faithful because the Bible tells him so, and he believes that he will be punished by God if he cheats on his wife. Or he may come to believe that by remaining faithful to his wife, he well serves society and his family. Or he may remain faithful to his wife because he loves her and prefers her to other women. Or other women may find a married man to be a less attractive partner and so on. The least likely explanation for his faithfulness is that the act of marriage leads to a physical diminution of sexual desire for other women. The act of marriage mediates and redirects those desires. Thus, if a study of married men was to show that most husbands still lusted after other women (a result that would be quite likely), we still could not assume that men would be generally unfaithful to their wives. The institutional explanation for the tendency of husbands to remain faithful to their wives is probably more accurate.

The structural explanation is probably more accurate in other settings as well. People act, dress, and behave in ways that are dictated by their circumstances. This is not to say that people never act inappropriately; rather, it can be said that inappropriate behavior is a mistake committed by a normally rational person, the irrational response of an irrational person, and/or the result of some other, mediating factors. So it is with violence and other undesirable behaviors. We all may have a certain capacity toward violence. In general, however, the institutions of society, such as the family, religion, and the law, mediate our tendency toward violence.

Much of the argument in favor of some sort of restriction of film and television content relies heavily on the research of behavioral scientists.[15] At the same time, however, much of the criticism of film content suffers from what methodologists would call the *ecological fallacy*, or the unjustified assumption that the sum of the whole is equal to its parts. The argument that movie violence causes societal violence may fail simply because the societal constraints on violence, such as the law, the family, and morality, may well override any predisposition that a person has toward violence that has been stimulated by watching a violent film.

Just as it is true that most studies examining the link between media violence and aggressive behavior have supported that link, it is also true that the relationships demonstrated are fairly weak (albeit statistically significant). The person influenced by violent film content is also influenced by a myriad of other internal and external factors, such as societal constraints and personal inhibitions. Thus, if the link could be tested in the larger macrosense, then, all things being equal, there would be vir-tually no significant demonstrable link between societal violence and media violence. Remember that in the analysis in the previous chapter, movie violence lags societal violence and not the other way around. Therefore, the direction of causality at the societal level, where it really matters, is in the opposite direction than the one assumed by those who on the basis of behavioral research make the mistake of ignoring the ecological fallacy. At worst, media influence is a reinforcement of existing behavioral tendencies. But those tendencies, in most cases, are more than compensated for by societal and other pressures (discussed later). In other words, even though it is possible for behaviorialists to demonstrate that there exists a relationship between media vio-lence and aggressive behavior, these studies do not indicate that crime is a result—the isolated instance of John Hinckley (who attempted to assassinate President Ronald Reagan) and other copycat crimes notwithstanding.

Furthermore, we would have to assume that just as media-depicted acts of vio-lence stimulate corresponding behavior, so too do media-depicted acts of heroism, generosity, kindness, and love. Certainly, those who argue that violence and sex in the movies have pernicious effects on society because they influence behavior would also have to take into account the positive influence of graphic screen generosity and kindness. This fact, the good messages of film, would have a countervailing effect on screen violence at both the individual and the societal level that would offset much or all of the damage.

There has been so much research done on the relationship between screen and actual violence that it is now possible to summarize these results through meta-analyses. A meta-analysis is a collection and integration of any number of studies on the same general topic that controls for differences and samples. In one such meta-analysis, Susan Hearold summarizes the results of some 230 studies on the relationship between televised and actual violence. Her study produced three important findings: first, the more fantastic the setting of the violence depicted (cartoon violence, for instance), the weaker the relationship between viewing and actual violence; second, programs designed to produce prosocial behaviors had a stronger effect on positive behaviors than violent programs had on negative behaviors; and, third, the relationship between media and actual violence was stronger for males in their adolescent years than it was for comparatively aged females. Thus, it seems that positive messages and context mediate and in fact can trump the message of broadcast violence.[16]

In another, newer meta-analysis, Haejung Paik and George Comstock summarize the results of 217 studies.[17] While their results are quite similar to those of Hearold, the authors also found that the strength of the relationship between depicted and actual violence was over twice as strong when produced in the laboratory as opposed to that demonstrated in more naturalistic settings. Thus, laboratory results are misleading if for no other reason than the fact that they overstate the relationship between screened and actual violence.

Nevertheless, there are quite a few studies in both laboratory and naturalistic settings that show a distinct relationship between viewed and actual violence among children. In 1963 psychologist Leonard Eron began to follow the development of a group of children from one small New York village. In that study, he evaluates television-viewing habits, family settings, peer evaluations, and other relevant environmental data. In following the maturation of these children across time, he found a distinct relationship between television-viewing habits at age eight, violent behavior at age eighteen, and criminal behavior at age thirty.[18] This study has lots of potential methodological problems, yet there still seems to be plenty of evidence to show at least some relationship between viewing violence and perpetrating actual violence.[19]

Presumably then, the most impressionable segment of the population, children, is the most vulnerable to the messages sent to them through the media. These children are "most impressionable," meaning that because of their youth and inexperience they are to a certain extent "blank slates" that can be imprinted by what they see in real life or fiction. If that experience involves the use of violence for the resolution of conflicts, children will then absorb that lesson, which in turn will be reinforced by the programming they choose to watch and so forth. For adults, particularly those who are not predisposed toward violence, they will choose not to watch violent programming, which in turn will not reinforce any violent tendencies that they already have.

What all this suggests is that we have to be careful about corrupting our youth. In fact, everything from voluntary movie-rating codes to the Federal Communications Commission's regulating children's programming to the recently adopted V-Chip has been an effort to protect children and probably the rest of us from violent programming.

But to go beyond regulating the media to protect children is not only of questionable constitutionality; it is of questionable value. As stated, media audiences tend to be self-selecting. People who want to watch violence will watch violence. Even if we censor the content of adult cinema or television to control for violence, what do we do about other violent programming in the media? Can we order news organizations to stop reporting on violent crime or war on the supposition that such reporting encourages violent behavior? Should we restrict covering the imposition of the death penalty—a wildly popular example of the public's penchant to solve problems through violence? Should news organizations be restricted in their coverage of violence in Iraq, Bosnia, or Cambodia? Should Hamlet, a play that ends in a bloodbath, be performed for adults only?

What these examinations of over four hundred studies show is that there is really very little actual scientific evidence to support popular and widely held assumptions about the effects of media on violence at the societal level. This is not to say that the evidence is fairly solid at the individual level that media depictions influence behavior. But at the societal level, the evidence is not yet there.[20] In fact the opposite may be true. According to at least one researcher,

> Claims that the persistently high levels of violence in mass media, mostly television, are largely responsible for violence in society represent narrow views of very large issues. These narrow views overlook essential elements of both phenomena—violence and media. Direct models of interpersonal violence in families and in the community probably give rise to more violent behavior than indirect models in media. Disinhibitory and provocative aspects of media probably do as much or more to trigger violent behavior than violent narratives and violent actions. Comprehensive meta-analysis indicates that prosocial messages on television can have greater effects on behavior than antisocial messages. These data support the contention that mass media can play a strong and positive role in alleviating some of the distress of victims of community violence, and in redirecting the behavior of some of its perpetrators so as to protect the children.[21]

This contradiction, between the perceived and real role of media effects at the macrolevel, suggests that most "evidence" that purports to demonstrate a relationship between media, particularly film media, and undesired behaviors is probably science with an agenda. And for those studies that do purport to establish a relationship between entertainment media and undesired behaviors, media scholar David Gauntlett cautions us to be just as worried about the pernicious influence of media effects studies as we are about the effects of media.[22] He suggests that we look for any of ten possible flaws in studies that purport to support a causal relationship between media and undesirable behaviors:

Researchers attack the problem based on faulty but generally accepted assumptions. If researchers assume that there is a relationship between media and behavior and then study the relationship between media and behavior, they are making an unjustified assumption. For example, if we assume that marijuana smoking leads to heroin addition (since most heroin addicts have smoked marijuana), then we might be tempted to look for links between marijuana smoking and heroin use without considering that most marijuana smokers don't graduate to heroin. Without taking this last fact into consideration, we may establish a relationship between marijuana and heroin use that is completely spurious.

Researchers treat children as blank slates. To say that media influences children is one thing, but to assume that media *causes* children to act in a particular way is a jump in logic. Children can and do discern on their own right from wrong. That means they can withstand certain types of messages (even mixed ones) without any harm. General assumptions to the effect that children cannot decipher and discard certain types of messages have to at least be qualified.

Researchers have an ideological axe to grind. Any study not subject to rigorous professional peer review is likely to be biased at best and flawed at worst.

Researchers fail to define what they are studying. To say that media violence causes violence begs the question of what type of behaviors researchers are trying to explain. There is violence in crime, violence in war, psychological cruelty, doing violence to the truth, violence officially sanctioned by the state, spanking children, beating wives, and so on. What actions are related to what consequences?

Results of studies in a laboratory may not be transferable to the world at large. As noted, meta-analyses suggest that laboratory experiments tend to exaggerate effects. Subjects are often subject to stimuli that they wouldn't encounter in the real world (they are shown films, for example, that they wouldn't normally go to see) and are then asked to react to situations that they wouldn't encounter in real life. It is difficult, if not impossible, to extrapolate from that kind of test what people will do in real life, not to mention within the context of society as a whole.

The methodology of media effects studies can be profoundly flawed. While there are many problems with these studies, such as the ecological fallacy, the main problem (as stressed) is the use of correlations to impute causality. Just because two events co-vary does not support a causal relationship. Professional researchers would probably not make these kinds of mistakes (and still get their work published), but nonprofessionals in support of a particular point of view can misinterpret and misapply academic research.

The definition of undesirable behaviors serves a particular ideological perspective. Incidents such as the Rodney King beating can be viewed by different people and, in fact, different communities in different ways. If in a study of media effects, undesirable violence or sexual activities, or political or lifestyle choices, are narrowly defined to proscribe some behaviors and allow for others, then there may be researcher bias. To say that sexual relations outside marriage is a depiction of an undesirable behavior is to make an ethical statement, but such an ethical judgment cannot be made within the context of a scientific experiment without compromising the results. Apparently, for many people sex outside of marriage is not immoral, which brings us to our next point.

Researcher selection bias takes on the aspect of a public censor. A viewer may not care for televised wrestling matches. A viewer may not agree with certain political opinions. If that viewer defines, for the purposes of a study of media effects, some kind of show or behavior as being undesirable, then the researcher sets oneself up as a public censor. As noted, self-described conservatives are more likely to object to media content. They themselves are not influenced by that content. But if their dissatisfaction results in public policy or regulations that delimit the media behaviors or messages they don't like, then they are in effect acting as public censors.

Studies of media effects are not grounded in theory. To say that one thing causes another is not to say why one thing causes another. We may be able to show that media violence has an effect on children, but the more interesting question may be *why*. If, for example, children who are most likely to be affected by media messages are those who come from broken homes, the answer may not be to shield all children from certain types of programming but to encourage better parenting at home. But in doing research that is not well grounded in theory, "we may be kicking the dog because the cat scratched the furniture."

Research does not attempt to understand the meanings of the media. Most of us can divine the subtle meaning in complex story plots, even if those stories contain what might be seen, when taken out of context, as disgusting or despicable behavior. A number of studies have shown that audiences are able to discern nuanced meanings from subtle plotlines.[23] And thank goodness they can. What would literature and entertainment be without the author's being able to assume this ability on the part of the audience?

It is crucial to this discussion of cause and effect to expand on this last point—that is, to demonstrate that even if there are messages or events in film that, when taken out of context, are hard to understand or tolerate, most of us (adults) are capable of making up our own minds.

VIOLENT PROGRAMMING IN CONTEXT

The fact is that we live in a violent world and a violent society. We have plenty of opportunities beyond the cinema or entertainment television to view violence— football and boxing, for example. We also have many legitimate outlets for engaging in and celebrating violent behavior. The cinema or television are certainly not the only, and probably not even the primary, sources of violence in our society.

The suggestion here is that there is not even a consensus as to what constitutes "violence" in the meaning of film critics. Most of us would agree that under some circumstances violence is an acceptable option. In time of war, in the application of the death penalty for murder, or in the pursuit of self-defense, the use of violence is sanctioned by society. Sometimes the violence in films is even presented in such a way as to be emulated. In *Sands of Iwo Jima* (1949) lots of people are killed, most of them Japanese, and within the context of the film that is acceptable. Even when the main character, played by John Wayne, is killed, the death is a heroic one, to be emulated. Were we to evaluate the film's violence in context, most of us would regard it as acceptable violence as opposed to unacceptable violence. If we were to apply that standard, one that regards the "eye of the beholder," we would almost certainly find that films are a lot less violent than what we are led to believe.

Let us consider some of the many types of film violence. *Braveheart* (1995), for example, has lots of violence, almost all of which is placed in the appropriate context. English atrocities are dutifully recorded to put the Scottish rebellion into context. How could the viewer identify with the Scottish rebellion without feeling the sense of rage of the occupied toward the occupier? Furthermore, the battle scenes that feature some of the best kill scenes in film history capture the brutality, confusion, and heroism of hand-to-hand combat.

Other films demonstrate "cartoon" violence. *RoboCop* (1987) has, in my opinion, the best kill scene in history. A bad guy is doused with toxic waste, and as he begins to melt, he is hit by a car that explodes him like a bowl of Jell-O. His remains are then wiped off the car with the windshield wipers. Now that's cinema! It is hard to imagine that any adult with even a shred of sanity would take this scene seriously, much less go out and imitate it. However, within the context of this film, which is remarkably good, this sort of violence has internal consistency, so to speak.

Violence that is unjustified, however, is not uncommon in the modern cinema. The production code used to dictate that no act of evil, including the use of violence, could go unpunished. Now that the production code is no longer in effect, it is true that an act of unjustified violence can go unpunished with or without implications. Nevertheless, this sort of thing goes on a lot less often in the movies than we think. If for no other reason than that unpunished or nonconsequential violence is a hanging plotline, the "bad" type of violence is pretty rare. Furthermore, most of the bad type of violence is the result of brain-dead plot development or muddled thinking that went into the writing of films, such as that of *Starship Troopers* (1997). Therefore, unjustified violence, as rare as it is, is probably more an act of omission rather than commission.

Context also includes the film-viewing environment. Up until now, we have generally conflated television and the cinema. Because the Federal Communications Commission (FCC) licenses the broadcast media, television has been subject to an extraordinary amount of scrutiny based on the premise that through the licensing process, program content can be regulated. Although the FCC has demonstrated a certain reluctance to censor the television media, it has imposed a number of regulations on commercial television and radio to control content. The same cannot be said for feature motion pictures. There is no FCC for motion pictures, and despite a voluntary, self-imposed, and sometimes self-enforced rating code and despite the attempts by local communities to control the exhibition of certain films (mainly those rated NC-17) through zoning regulation, the motion picture industry is generally unrestricted in its content.

This lack of regulation means several things for the relationship between film violence and aggressive behavior. Television viewing is much more ubiquitous. The average television viewer may watch as much as forty hours a week of television, while even a frequent filmgoer, who is in the minority, will probably spend somewhat fewer than ten hours a week viewing movies. Thus, the cumulative effect of movie content will likely be less substantial if for no other reason than that for the average viewer the amount of time spent viewing movies is less than that spent viewing television. Furthermore, to go to the movies requires more of an effort than simply sitting down in front of a television set. To a large extent, film viewers are probably more selective about the films they are willing to pay to see. Children aren't even allowed into many adult-themed movies. And, as we have seen, those who are already predisposed toward violence will tend to go to violent films. Thus, the negative effect of film violence is somewhat mitigated by the structure of the theatergoing experience.

Of course, the theater experience is also more expansive. Films viewed in a theater are more all-encompassing. Presumably, then, any effect that film content has on behavior will be enhanced by the intimacy of the moviegoing experience. Furthermore, film content falls under none of the restrictions imposed by the FCC on television content. Thus, films can be tremendously graphic and shocking.

Consequently, we are generally at a loss as to how to predict, much less act on, the information that purports how some films may motivate some individuals to violence. The behavioral studies in this regard, as numerous as they are, are as equally hazy. John Hinckley watched *Taxi Driver* at least fifteen times before deciding to attempt to assassinate President Reagan in order to impress Jodie Foster. However, at the Hinckley trial the prosecution's chief psychiatrist, Park Dietz, suggested that Hinckley probably didn't realize the movie's import to his motivations until he explored the issue in sessions with a psychiatrist while preparing for his trial.[24] If even Hinckley didn't know what motivated him to act, how can we? Furthermore, we have no idea how many others were obsessed with, and identified with, Travis Bickle (the main character in *Taxi Driver*) without trying to assassinate the president.

CONCLUSION

In this chapter, I examine the relationship between film content and societal behavior from the perspective of a social scientist rather than a psychologist. In an earlier chapter, I present evidence to the effect that societal attitudes are much more of a determinant of film content than the other way around. This conclusion contradicts much of the criticism of film content that has emanated from conservative (and leftist) political circles. For those from the political Right this conclusion means that to attack movies and their producers for their content is to miss the point. The causal relationship between film content and behavior is much more likely from the bottom up (audience demand to the producer) than from the top down (producer bias to the audience). But for the conservatives to blame filmmakers for doing what comes natural to businesspeople and then to suggest that because one ethnic group or another is "overrepresented" in Hollywood and thus the cause of a distortion is to miss the point in a rather ugly way. Both the patron who views feature films and the capitalist system that translates that demand into product may be in need of reform. In another business, Protestants or Catholics would do the same thing to serve their customers, or they wouldn't be in the business for long. For conservatives the options are not all that daunting. If they think that films made for primarily religious audiences will make money, there is a whole wide world of filmmaking for them to explore on their own nickel (as Mel Gibson has done with great success). But to ask businesspeople to carry the word without compensation is un-American. Such a policy might be more appropriate in Iran.

For those from the Left who criticize film content for being too much in the service of the economic elite, pretty much the same response can be reiterated.[25] The public consumes what it wants to consume. The viewing public may be misguided in wanting to be entertained by films that trumpet the benefits of American democracy and its capitalist economy, but that is their choice. The Left has the same access to the economy as anyone else. Independent filmmakers can make and market their products on a shoestring—and make a bundle provided that there is an audience for their product. For example, consider the success of Michael Moore's production *Fahrenheit 9/11* (2004) which as of this writing (2005) has grossed $119 million with a production budget of $6 million.[26] While this may somewhat overstate actual access to the market, it is worth a try. Is the shortage of progressive films a function of the capitalist system that suppresses dissent, or is it the failure of the political Left to put its money where its mouth is? Parenthetically, the Hollywood production crowd cannot be classified as part of this political Left. Hollywood may be a big source of funding for the Democratic Party, but that does not mean it nor the Democratic Party is socialist. This attempt to lump the Democratic Party with the socialist Left is largely false and is McCarthy-ite demagoguery of the worst kind.

Finally, I have taken issue with behaviorialists or, more to the point, those who misuse behavioral studies to support their political agenda. The behavioral approach is limited to studying phenomena at the individual level. Influences on the individual, however, may not translate into large-scale influences on society. Furthermore, film violence needs to be viewed in context. While media violence may have an influence on aggressive behavior, so do other messages, many of which are countervailing.[27]

Much of what we see in movies is also an affirmation of what is good and wholesome in America. Thus, it would make no sense to argue that the same degenerate Hollywood culture that produced *It's a Wonderful Life* (1946) and *Mr. Smith Goes to Washington* (1939), films touted as reflections of mainstream America, also produced *Natural Born Killers* (1994) and *Casino* (1995), films that have been described as being degenerate. Either the culture of Hollywood has changed, or the films it produces reflect both the good and the bad in society.

What we have here is not so much a controversy about whether violent films cause actual violence or not. I argue that what we have here is no more than a matter of taste. But it is not enough for some to argue that many films and television shows are in bad taste. Because there are those in society who wish to censor films that are in bad taste and because they know that the First Amendment stands in their way, they have tried to invent a case for the negative public health consequences of lousy films. But, in the end, lousy films are just that, lousy. We should be alarmed that people are so undemanding of the shows and movies they watch that they tolerate so much of the drivel. But that dynamic has more to say about the tastes of the public than it does about the degeneracy of Hollywood.

In the next chapter, I discuss what a bad film is—not what I think a bad film is (except for the purposes of illustration), but what for the individual viewer can be a standard for declaring a film good or bad. In this era of the third monopoly, the chances of walking into the wrong film are substantially higher than what they have been in the past. As I have said, this is both a good news and a bad news story. There is a lot to see out there, and there is a lot of trash. Use the next chapter, as you will improve your chances of enjoying the movies.

Feature Film: *Taxi Driver* (1976)

Besides being regarded as one of the best films of all time—ranking forty-third in the Internet Movie Database's top 250—this movie is also famous for having supposedly inspired John Hinckley to shoot president Ronald Reagan. If ever there is an example of the clash of First Amendment freedoms and the public good, this is it. Does the artistic value of films such as this and their audience appeal outweigh the potential harm? If not, what should we as a society do about it?

You have probably heard that this film supposedly inspired John Hinckley to shoot President Ronald Reagan. That is a tragedy for many reasons, probably the least of which is that the event sullies the reputation of a fine filmmaker and a fine film.

This is a film about a feeling. It may seem to be a film about a person, Travis Bickle, a disaffected Vietnam veteran who now works as a taxi driver. But rather, this is a film about alienation. Some people become so estranged from society that they cease to function as normal human beings. In this film, Bickle, as portrayed by Robert De Niro, practically writhes with pain. And the thing that seems to eat at him most is his gnawing loneliness. He is no longer capable of ordinary human contact. While that feeling is hard to describe, Martin Scorsese (the director) and De Niro capture that loneliness beautifully. Ultimately, Bickle's frustration with his existence explodes in a paroxysm of violence. After first failing to shoot the presidential candidate for whom the object of his affection works (Betsy, played by Cybill Shepherd), he ultimately shoots his way into a brothel and frees from the bondage of

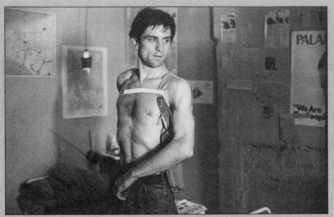

Taxi Driver. *Photo by Josh Weiner. Courtesy of M.P. & T.V. Photo Archive.*

childhood prostitution the other object of his affection (Iris, played by Jodie Foster). While we are never completely sure why he goes this route of violence, it makes sense within the context of the film. He has to do something, or he will implode. It just so happens that the thing that he manages to do is generally for the good. But by the end of the film we are never entirely sure that he isn't a ticking time bomb ready to go off again, this time for something bad.

The violence in this film is horrendous. And that may have set John Hinckley off. I rather suspect, however, that the seduction scene is probably more to blame in which Harvey Keitel, playing a pimp, seduces young Iris. The scene is at the same time mesmerizing and in many ways just as horrifying as the violence even though the consummation takes place offscreen. Despite the scene's emotional impact and the ethereal performances of Foster and Keitel, I don't recall that it made me want to shoot the president.

Besides Hinckley's crime, I wonder what other behaviors the film inspired. Did someone go nuts and try to get better mental health benefits at the Veterans Administration? Did somebody go insane and try to get more stringent gun laws passed? Did somebody go off their rocker and try to stop the international trade in child prostitutes? Well, probably not. You have to be insane to be moved to action by this movie. Or maybe this movie isn't influential enough.

Don't agree? What do you think?

EXERCISE

After watching a film, write down what prevailing social behaviors are depicted in the film. Are the behaviors within the context of the film treated positively or negatively or without comment? Do you agree with the overall philosophy of the film as reflected in the treatment of political issues, social relations, and violence? How much violence is in the film and how would you define it? Most important, do you think that the film has moved you to act in a way you normally wouldn't act?

NOTES

1. Ron Tamborini and Kristen Salomonson, "Horror's Effect on Social Perceptions and Behaviors," *Horror Films: Current Research on Audience Preferences and Reactions,* ed. James B. Weaver and Ron Tamborini (Mahwah, N.J.: Erlbaum, 1996), 186.

2. See E. Jo and L. Berkowitz, "A Priming Effect Analysis of Media Influences: An Update," in *Media Effects: Advances in Theory and Research,* ed. J. Bryant and D. Zillmann (Hillsdale, N.J.: Erlbaum, 1994), 43–61.

3. "We believe that a workable model [of socialization] should involve the exploration of complex environmental factors, internal and external to the child, within the interactive forces of cognitive, social, and physiological development. The goal facing developmental psychologists, then, is the description and explication of the interactive processes of socialization among simultaneously changing systems." Thomas D. Yawkey and James E. Johnson, eds., *Integrative Processes and Socialization: Early to Middle Childhood* (Hillsdale, N.J.: Erlbaum, 1988), 16.

4. See Jeffrey Jensen Arnett, "Adolescents' Uses of Media for Self-Socialization," *Journal of Youth and Adolescence* 24, no. 5 (1995): 519–33.

5. See David J. Jackson, *Entertainment and Politics: The Influence of Pop Culture on Young Adult Political Socialization* (New York: Lang, 2002), chap. 4.

6. *Sanders v. Acclaim Entertainment Inc.*, 188 F. Supp. 2d 1264 (D. Colo. 2002); *James v. Meow Media Inc.* (02-740); *James v. Meow Media Inc.*, 300 F.3d 683, 696 (6th Cir. 2002).

7. See, for instance, Senator Joe Lieberman, "Crude, Rude, and Lewd," *Blueprint,* September 1, 2000, www.ndol.org/ndol_ci.cfm?contentid=1955&kaid=115&subid=145 (accessed December 11, 2004).

8. A statement that is "plausible but false," "specious reasoning." HyperDictionary.com, "Spurious," www.hyperdictionary.com/dictionary/spurious (accessed December 11, 2004).

9. Kaiser Family Foundation, "Teen Sexual Activity Fact Sheet," January 2005, www.kff.org/youthhivstds/3040-02.cfm (accessed August 20, 2005).

10. Centers for Disease Control and Prevention, "Teenagers in the United States: Sexual Activity, Contraceptive Use, and Childbearing, 2002," December 2004, www.cdc.gov/nchs/data/series/sr_23/sr23_024.pdf (accessed August 20, 2005).

11. U.S. Department of Justice, "Trends in Juvenile Violent Crime," March 1996, www.ojp.usdoj.gov/bjs/pub/pdf/tjvfox.pdf (accessed August 20, 2005).

12. National Institutes of Health, "Teen Birth Rate Down, Youth Less Likely to Be Involved in Violent Crimes: Kids More Likely to Be Overweight," July 16, 2004, www.nichd.nih.gov/new/releases/americas_children.cfm (accessed August 20, 2005). Would the media also be held responsible for teen weight gain?

13. Senate Subcommittee on Juvenile Justice, *Oversight on Alleged Media Violence as It May Affect Children,* 98th Cong., 2nd sess., 1985, 47.

14. See Faith McLellan, "Do Violent Movies Make Violent Children?" *Lancet* 359, no. 9305 (2002): 502; Brad J. Bushman and Craig A. Anderson, "Media Violence and the American

Public: Scientific Facts versus Media Misinformation," *American Psychologist* 56, nos. 6–7 (June–July 2001): 477–89; J. Garbarino, "Violent Children: Where Do We Point the Finger of Blame?" *Archives of Pediatric Adolescent Medicine* 155 (2001): 13–14.

15. See, for example, Committee on Public Education, American Academy of Pediatrics, "Media Violence," *Pediatrics* 108, no. 5 (November 2001): 1222–26.

16. Susan Hearold, "A Synthesis of 1043 Effects of Television on Social Behavior," in *Public Communication and Behavior*, vol. 1, ed. G. Comstock (Orlando, Fla.: Academic, 1986), 65–133.

17. Haejung Paik and George Comstock, "The Effects of Television Violence on Antisocial Behavior: A Meta-analysis," *Communication Research* 21 (1994): 515–46.

18. L. D. Eron, "Parent-Child Interaction, Television Violence and Aggression of Children," *American Psychologist* 27 (1982): 197–211.

19. For another careful study on children and effects of televised violence, see A. H. Stein and L. K. Friedrich, "Television Content and Young Children's Behavior," in *Television and Social Behavior*, vol. 2, ed. J. P. Murray, E. A. Rubinstein, and G. A. Comstock (Washington, D.C.: U.S. Government Printing Office, 1972), 202–317.

20. Nevertheless, in November 2004, 62 percent of those in the general public who were surveyed believed that "Hollywood was lowering moral standards." "*CBS News/New York Times* Poll," http://pollingreport.com/media.htm#Content (accessed December 13, 2004), conducted November 18–21, 2004; $N = 885$ adults nationwide; margin of error ± 3.

21. B. Z. Friedlander, "Community Violence, Children's Development, and Mass Media: In Pursuit of New Insights, New Goals, and New Strategies," *Psychiatry* 56, no. 1 (February 1993): 66.

22. See David Gauntlett, "The Worrying Effects of Media Effects Studies," in *Ill Effects: The Media/Violence Debate*, ed. Martin Barker and Julian Petley (London: Routledge Press, 1988), 47–62.

23. See Annette Hill, *Shocking Entertainment: Viewer Response to Violent Movies* (London: John Libby Media, 1997).

24. Reported in Wayne Wilson and Randy Hunter, "Movie-Inspired Violence," *Psychological Reports* 53 (1983): 435–41.

25. For a complete rendition of the Left's attack on the corporatization of the media, see George L. Gerbner and Hamid L. Mowlana, eds., *Invisible Crises: What Conglomerate Control of Media Means for America and the World* (Boulder, Colo.: Westview, 1996).

26. Internet Movie Database, "Business Data for Fahrenheit 9/11," www.imdb.com/title/ tt0361596/business (accessed December 14, 2004).

27. An excellent book on this topic of the ecological fallacy of traditional psychology is Edward S. Reed, *Encountering the World: Toward an Ecological Psychology* (New York: Oxford University Press, 1996), particularly 18–19.

SUGGESTED READING

Barker, Martin, and Julian Petley, eds. *Ill Effects: The Media/Violence Debate*. London: Routledge Press, 1988.

Crigler, Ann N., ed. *The Psychology of Political Communication*. Ann Arbor: University of Michigan Press, 1996.

Gauntlett, David. *Video Critical: Children, the Environment, and Media Power.* Luton, Eng.: John Libbey Media, 1997.

Gerbner, George L., and Hamid L. Mowlana, eds. *Invisible Crises: What Conglomerate Control of Media Means for America and the World.* Boulder, Colo.: Westview, 1996.

Jackson, David J. *Entertainment and Politics: The Influence of Pop Culture on Young Adult Political Socialization.* New York: Lang, 2002.

Moy, Patricia, and Michael Pfau. *With Malice Toward All? The Media and Public Confidence in Democratic Institutions.* Westport, Conn.: Praeger, 2000.

5

Film Criticism: What Is a Bad Movie?

Most people go to the movies for one specific reason—to be entertained. But beyond that, the moviegoing experience is a personal one. Most professional film critics evaluate movies according to a rather specific set of criteria—the qualities of filmmaking as a craft. Production qualities, plot development, and acting are the primary standards by which most film critics measure the quality of a film. But those form only one set of standards for evaluating a film, which is certainly the case when considering the fact that some of the greatest box office successes have been critical failures—and the other way around. The whole *Smokey and the Bandit* (1977) series comes to mind. Apparently, there is a large audience for these films even when film critics warn viewers that they are going to the theater to see bad movies. Nevertheless, audiences are entertained.

And entertainment value seems to be an important standard by which to measure the quality of a movie. Apparently, there is something entertaining about a car-chase formula that hasn't escaped Hollywood executives. And even though critics find most car chases after the defining car chases in *Bullitt* (1968) and *The French Connection* (1971) to be hackneyed and boring, the public can't seem to get enough. Audience members find it entertaining, and, the truth be told, it is.

When there is a car wreck on the freeway during rush hour, traffic can be backed up for miles. Before the wreck is cleared and the bodies are carted off, drivers can't help but slow down just to take a look. Rubbernecking is a human trait. A morbid curiosity is not an indication that we are monsters or moral degenerates just because we take an interest in the macabre, the gruesome, or the antisocial. Even social moralists probably slow down and take a look at an accident scene. In fact, as suggested in previous chapters, much of the criticism of the modern media's parading themselves as being concerned for the moral and cultural sensibilities of the masses is, in reality, a thinly veiled contempt for the tastes of the average movie patron. Much of the junk science that purports to prove that media messages lead to society-wide misbehavior is simply part of a larger political agenda of one group or another.

Mobster films, horror films, and slasher films have been the commercial staple of Hollywood since the beginning. By the standard of simple entertainment, these types of films are like roller-coaster rides: they take us out of our everyday humdrum existence and give us a window into something that we never witness in person—a mob hit, a face melt, a barroom brawl, or a car chase (in which no one gets hurt). And the popularity of those genres probably means little more than that—a little metaphorical rubbernecking.

Professional film critics are possibly rubberneckers of a sort as well. But when they go to the movies, car wrecks or natural disasters do not entertain them. They are looking for something different and are thus measuring a film by a different standard. What they are looking for is something they haven't seen before—and what a tough audience they must be. After watching five or six films a week for years, professional film critics must have seen just about everything at least once. Therefore, what probably thrills professional critics is originality. They are quick to praise the small independent production, the foreign import, or the directorial efforts of a promising newcomer (witness the critics' over-the-top reaction to Sophia Coppola's *Lost in Translation*). This is not to say that these films are not noteworthy—for the film scholar, they are probably the raison d'être—but the critic's seal of approval isn't always a ticket to enjoyment.

By contrast, what a "bad" film is to a professional critic is the sequel, the remake, the big-budget production that must recoup its investment by appealing to the lowest common denominator, and the niche film designed to appeal to a specific segment of the public—car-racing buffs, for example.

It now becomes clear that there are several standards by which to measure the quality of a film.[1] First is the artistic/aesthetic standard. As noted, commercial films are mostly product, not art. Nevertheless, some filmmakers, whether because of their skills or their clout, are able to make films that are more art than product. But this is probably the exception to the rule. Film scholars make a distinction between two types of directors: technicians and auteurs. For the technician, scripts are a kind of architectural plan for a film; the film is constructed from the script. And while the films of the technician may be competently constructed or even elegantly crafted, they hardly represent an independent vision that reflects the aesthetics of the director. Auteurs, on the other hand, create a distinct vision; they have a distinct style regardless of the script. That the auteur allows his or her personal vision to dominate the film, irrespective of the demands of the market, makes the film of the auteur an art form.[2] It is hard to know how many auteurs fail in the market—probably more than we would think—simply because their films never achieve enough commercial success to be widely screened. But in some exceptional circumstances, the public takes a shine to the work of an auteur and gets to experience creative magic in the local cineplex. Some of the noted auteurs of the American film industry are Alfred Hitchcock, Orson Welles, Sam Fuller, Nicholas Ray, Fritz Lang, John Ford, Stanley Kubrick, and Woody Allen. Each one of these directors produced a film that has a notable style, a feel, and even signature conventions, such as Hitchcock's habit of appearing once on-screen in all his films.

As dominant as the American film industry has been, there have probably been as many or more foreign filmmakers who could be considered auteurs, including Sergei Eisenstein (Soviet Russian), Jean-Luc Godard (French), Werner Herzog (German), Federico Fellini (Italian), Pedro Almodovar (Spanish), and Ingmar Bergman (Swedish), just to name a few. Perhaps the reason that so many foreign directors are auteurs is that they are often relatively free from the demands of the market. Many, if not most, of these foreign filmmakers were subsidized in one way or another by their respective governments.

So it seems that by taking the market, if even partially, out of the filmmaking equation, there may be a greater likelihood that the films produced are more likely to be art than product. Even fascist totalitarian regimes, which have utterly and completely controlled their film industries, have nurtured brilliant filmmaking, such as Leni Riefenstahl's *Triumph of the Will* (1934) or Eisenstein's *Potemkin* (1925). By the same token, during Hollywood's golden age of cinema, or what is termed in previous chapters the "second monopoly" of American cinema, many fine films were produced simply because the moguls wanted them produced as a kind of homage to their vanity. But even so, auteur filmmakers such as Charlie Chaplin and Orson Welles were either harassed or driven out of the industry by the Hollywood power structure of the golden era.

Today in the rough-and-tumble market of filmmaking corporatization, film auteurs still exist, but their films are produced for relatively limited release. Modern American film auteurs include the Coen brothers (Joel and Ethan), Woody Allen, David Mamet, and Robert Altman, among others. Any film they make is worth a look—if you can find it. Most art films in the modern era don't make it out of the larger markets, and, even when they do, they are generally shown on a limited number of screens for a limited period. Most of the films may also become available on DVD or VHS—again if you can find them and if it's worth the trouble to view a film on the vastly inferior appliances available to most of us at home as opposed to the vastly preferable in-theater screening.

Another standard by which to measure the quality of a film is by its technical merit—how well have the moviemakers employed their craft? This category of criticism encompasses everything from acting to direction, special effects, and script continuity. Script continuity is the degree to which a film maintains its internal consistency. It may not make sense in the real world for dinosaurs to be wandering an island off the coast of Costa Rica, as they do in *Jurassic Park* (1993), but within the context of that film, it makes perfect sense. But even the finest films often lack the detail of plot continuity.

For example, there are some serious problems with the script of the recently released and critically acclaimed *Mystic River* (2003). This film is wonderfully acted and meticulously shot, but the story line is full of holes that could better be described as plotline culs-de-sac. Case in point, a story thread that runs through the movie is the troubled relationship between the character played by Kevin Bacon and the character's wife. Perfectly good scenes in the film are derailed by a series of strange phone calls between these two characters, which in the end lead to nowhere. In another scene, toward the end of the film, Sean Penn's character and his character's wife, played by Laura Linney, have an encounter in which Linney plays Lady Macbeth to Penn's King Macbeth. Apparently, she is the one pulling the strings behind the scenes. But since this exchange comes at the end of the film, out of context and out of nowhere, it explains exactly nothing and motivates no more a reaction among the film's audience than a scratching of the head.

The fact is that in terms of craft American films produced for general release are probably the most technically proficient films in the world. Even the worst American commercial film rarely falls below the threshold of at least being technically competent. And when it's really done well, modern filmmaking is a marvel.

What is less likely to be competent is the thought that is put into a film. This is probably the case for five reasons. First, while filmmakers are well trained in the craft of making movies, they may have neglected the obligatory liberal arts education, courses in philosophy, literature, and politics that would help their films make better sense.

Second, because of the trend toward outsourcing the production of a film, there is no single intelligence guiding its production. Financiers may want the film to do and say one thing; writers something else; directors another thing; and editors may envision yet another message entirely. The outsourcing of film production has led to the release of many a commercial film that is a visually stunning, magnificently acted, unmitigated mess. One of the more prominent recent examples is Martin Scorsese's *Gangs of New York* (2002). This film is incomprehensible from beginning to end. It is more like a series of tableaus held together by a variety of grunting, thumping, and grinding noises. The acting is as good as it can be, given that there is no plot. But one thing that can't be faulted about this film is that it is visually stunning. The script, however, appears to have been passed around like a Thanksgiving turkey.

Third is the problem of plagiarism, which includes copies, remakes, and sequels. For example, *La Femme Nikita* (1991), an excellent French action film, was remade in the United States as *Point of No Return* (1993). There is nothing wrong with rehashing an old idea. After all, there is always a terrible shortage of really good plotlines. Besides, great literature usually revolves around some of the enduring questions of life—love, hate, sacrifice, and so on—which need to be rehashed. However, the American version of *La Femme Nikita* was an exact copy of the French movie, but in English. Why not just dub the film in English? There was nothing original about this film.

Fourth is the problem of script gimmicks. In that respect, the recently released *The Jackal* (1997) is one of the worst films ever made. Start with the fact that this film is a remake of one of the best thrillers ever produced, *The Day of the Jackal* (1973), and it is all downhill from there. The film doesn't make sense from beginning to end. But besides the fact that the film suffers in comparison to its predecessor, *The Jackal* harbors a little gimmick that deserves special note. At some point in the plot—and that is to use the term loosely—Bruce Willis, a macho actor playing a macho role, assumes the cover of a homosexual to accomplish some amorphous goal. We are treated to a pickup scene in a gay bar, the entire purpose of which is to have Bruce Willis kiss another man on the lips. I watched this film in Greenwich Village, so nobody really reacted. This sort of thing happens there all the time. I can only imagine the gasp that arose in the average suburban multiplex. I guess the filmmakers accomplished their goal—another original way to shock the audience and without expensive special effects (an added bonus). This little incident, however, had nothing to do with the plot. It is little more than having a microphone boom slip into the top of the frame. It is unprofessional, crass commercialism of the worst kind. At best, it is simply a distraction, and at worst it is an insult to the viewer's intelligence.

Finally, there is the siren song of special effects. Many a film has been dashed against the shoal of special effects. What technicians can do these days on film is remarkable. All one needs to do is to take a look at Stanley Kubrick's *2001: A Space Odyssey* (1968) and compare it to *Blade Runner* (1982) and then to *The Matrix Reloaded* (2003) to see how far we have come in the production of special effects. But these special effects do not come without a price.

Special effects cost money, to be sure, but at some point they cost the story as well. Despite several justifications, special effects—although downright distracting—cost so much that they can't be cut from the film. Imagine if in the final edit of a film, the director were to suggest that a million-dollar special effect be deleted. What would be the producer's reaction? A million-dollar investment is just too valuable to sacrifice for a mere story line. The result is a film such as *X2* (reviewed at the end of chapter 2); *Star Wars: Episode II—Attack of the Clones* (2002); or the Bruce Willis vehicle *The Fifth Element* (1997), which is visually stunning, technologically advanced, and pretty much impossible to understand. At least when David Lynch makes an incomprehensible film, *Mulholland Drive* (2001) for example, he probably does so intentionally. But these are really technical problems with a script. Since most of us don't live in the film world and are not professional film buffs, the standards listed here are of some value but aren't particularly useful to the average filmgoer. Most of us go for the story. Assuming that most commercial filmmaking is at least technically competent, the success or failure of a film with a general audience lies in the script. The primary consideration in this regard is the entertainment value of a film. A lot of mediocre films are financial successes because they give the public something that it wants—thrills, awesome special effects, car chases, steamy love scenes, the right stars, and so on. Entertainment is certainly important, and we shouldn't give that standard short shrift, but whether films are entertaining or not is really not the subject of this book. Furthermore, it may be that in providing entertainment the industry may be subtly degrading society. That is certainly the argument made by ideologues on both ends of the political spectrum. Even if the audience does not realize it, films contain plotlines and messages that may be historically inaccurate, morally questionable, or downright subversive. Since, as we have seen, many people get their information about the world from the entertainment media (talk radio, for instance), the hidden meanings of films may be reinforcing ideas or behaviors that do have a public policy impact. Certainly, Arnold Schwarzenegger's election to the governorship of California is related is some way to the fantasy persona that he cultivated in his film roles.

Take, for instance, the film *Batman* (and to a lesser extent the sequels). The modern remake of *Batman* is in many ways a work of art. The world created by director Tim Burton, a master of this sort of aesthetic sensitivity, is meticulously designed to connote Gotham City's ominous sense of malevolence. The cast is great—any film with Jack Nicholson is worth taking a look at—and the story is fine. This is all true except for the fact that the Batman story has a somewhat questionable provenance.[3]

When the *Batman* comic strip was first introduced in the 1930s (at about the same time as the aptly named *Superman* strip), the United States was in a depression. The world was dominated by totalitarian regimes. It was not entirely clear that democracy would, or should, survive. After all, if the Great Depression demonstrated anything, it demonstrated that democratic governments appeared powerless to take care of their citizens. In the time before the war, fascism began to gain a limited appeal in the United States and other industrialized democracies. Some of this flirtation with fascism manifested itself in the popular culture of the day. For example, in 1933 publisher William Randolph Hearst financed and cowrote a modestly successful film titled *Gabriel over the White House*. The plot of the film, which involves the replacement of a democratically elected president with a more "suitable" leader, is unmistakably fascist.[4]

The *Batman* comic strip is born of the same ilk. In the Batman story, the democratically elected government of Gotham City is supine. The government is unable to exert control and is corrupt to the core in any event. Consequently, the city is being taken over by criminals. The citizens of Gotham are no longer able to move about independently for fear of falling victim to crime. Indeed, the wealthy orphan Bruce Wayne lost his parents to just this kind of street violence. He decides to avenge himself against the criminals (i.e., their class), who have taken his parents and his city. So he dons strange body armor and a mask, develops all sorts of technical crime-fighting aids, and adopts the symbol of the bat. He then goes to town in his spare time and arrests and often punishes "bad" people. Fortunately, he never makes a mistake and never punishes the wrong guy—hence no need for constitutional rights nor the niceties of law. Once he cleans the city of its bad people, he returns to his mansion. Of course, the city can always call on him again in its time of need (which is apparently pretty often) by projecting the symbol of the bat onto the clouds.

This is a flat-out fascist solution for the problems that ail democratic society. It is probably not the case, however, that by screening this film we are going to turn out a generation of Hitler youth. After all, at least in the West, fascism is an ideological museum piece. Democracy is now ascendant. And so whatever messages of the *Batman* series that may have resonated in the psyche of the 1930s are merely entertainment today. But that doesn't mean that we don't have our own present demons that need to be exorcised through popular entertainment.

Let's take, for instance, the *Dirty Harry* (1971) series. In the 1970s there was a substantial rise in the crime rate. Public concern over that increase was reflected in the entertainment media of the time, through higher body counts and rates of victimization in dramatic television series and the movies. The *Dirty Harry* movies were enormously popular in their day because they provided a kind of cathartic release for moviegoers who had a fear of crime but also believed that the government's response was inadequate. The problem is that the *Dirty Harry* solution for crime, while satisfying to the audience, is hardly the way to run a society governed by the rule of law.

In the film, Clint Eastwood playing Harry Callahan is judge, jury, and executioner. It is not to besmirch the fine career of Eastwood to say that his portrayal of Inspector Callahan is subversive—subversive in the sense that his portrayal may undermine support for the rule of law. It is not his fault. When he had an opportunity to make his own film, *The Unforgiven*, Eastwood depicted violence, the consequences thereof, and the role of the law marvelously—well deserving of the Academy Award that film and director received. But as Dirty Harry, Clint Eastwood plays fast and loose with the U.S. Constitution, which makes this in some sense a bad film. In *Dirty Harry*, Callahan makes no secret of his contempt for the law and for the bureaucrats and the courts that enforce it. At least he is up front about his beliefs.

A much more dangerous and subtle play to the darker side of the public's appetite for vengeance occurs in the enormously popular film *The Untouchables* (1987). In what is otherwise a gripping and exciting film occurs one of the oddest and most contradictory moments in American film history. Kevin Costner, playing the prototypical G-man and straight shooter Eliot Ness, murders a suspect in custody. It is an act that is so out of character, such a cheap sop to the visceral emotions of the audience, such an easy way out for the filmmakers that it virtually ruins the film. The suspect who is killed, Frank Nitti, is no doubt a bad guy and deserves what he gets, but that is not the point. If the point of the film is the age-old struggle between good and evil, law and lawlessness, the murder of a suspect already subdued, no matter what he is accused of doing, muddies the waters. Eliot Ness is no longer as straight as he seems. While he is better than the man he kills, he is not much better. He's just a hit man for the government. Who will stand up for justice if not Eliot Ness?[5]

In the 1980s the women's liberation movement became a prominent part of America's social scene. In trying to cash in on this political movement, filmmakers attempted to create film plots and roles more sensitive to the plight of women. One such film was *Working Girl* (1988), starring Melanie Griffith, Sigourney Weaver, and Harrison Ford. It is sometimes the case that filmmakers try to do the right thing but get it wrong. *Working Girl* is such a film.

In it, a secretary from a working-class neighborhood on Staten Island (played by the always radiant Griffith) tries to break into the ranks of the junior executive in her Wall Street brokerage house. However, her way is blocked by sexist men and by a particularly predatory female boss (played by Weaver). The film is supposed to be about how, through hard work and pluck, this woman manages to gain the first rung on the ladder to her ascent to the top. This is a modern Horatio Alger tale with a twist. In this story, the protagonist is a woman, giving the film the veneer of a contemporary story about a woman's liberation.

Why is this a bad film? The production values and acting are first class, but the problems start with the main plot and encompass the entire outline of the film. While hard work and pluck are supposed to be rewarded in our capitalist system, in this film they are nothing of the sort. In the beginning of the story we find that no matter how hard she tries, how many night school classes she attends, Griffith, viewed by her coworkers as merely a voluptuous secretary, is never taken seriously. Her multiple attempts to move to the level of management trainee are constantly rebuffed by the personnel office. Finally, in desperation, while her boss is out of town, she assumes the role of her supervisor and manages through this subterfuge to work out a big deal and bed a handsome dealmaker from another firm (played by Ford). The problem with all this is that it has nothing to do with capitalism or with women's liberation. The main character, Tess (Griffith), gets ahead through cheating the system and the judicious use of her lovely body. If anything, this film is an advertisement for socialism because, stripped to its core, the message of the film is that the only way for Tess to get ahead is to cheat and sleep her way to the top.

And what a "top" it is. In the last scene of the movie, Tess succeeds in getting her own office as a management trainee. This accomplishment seems dubious. One gets the sense that being a junior executive in this firm is just like being a glorified secretary. As if to reinforce that point, as the credits role and the music swells (a lovely inspirational tune sung by Carly Simon), the camera pulls back from the building in which Tess's office, put in perspective, resembles a cell in a beehive. This last scene delivers a punch like a knockout blow. This is what she fought for, so that she could have her own secretary and have someone else get the coffee? In a magnanimous gesture, Tess makes it clear to her new secretary that she'll get her own coffee. This probably means that Tess will be a "good" boss—sort of like a good slave master. Nevertheless, the reality is that the secretary is still in the "pool." But, then again, so is Tess herself.

If there were a sequel to this movie, my guess would be that Tess, after having spent the best years of her life slaving away for the company, will be laid off in a cost-saving measure before her pension vests. After all, her supervisors will reason, she was promoted because she slept with and married the character played by Ford, which brings us to the ludicrous and insulting way in which women (and working-class people, in general) are treated in this film.

When the evil witch (Weaver) is vanquished, in a parting shot she is told to get her "bony ass" out of the building, as if the character played by Weaver really cares what some CEO thinks of her ass. Can't women just be evil in their own right? Do they have to be demeaned as well? Look at it from another perspective. Would John Wayne shoot someone and then comment on the size of his victim's penis?

As for the working people, the way this film treats them is an abomination. Joan Cusack and Alec Baldwin, cast in roles as Tess's best friend and boyfriend, play their roles as drunken louts from Staten Island, incapable of expressing or even having an intelligent thought. I suppose this is a plot device necessary to convince the denser of us that what Tess is doing to achieve a higher level of dronedom is worth it. The alternative to a luxury apartment on the Upper East Side is a life of drinking, whoring, and wearing bad clothing. This in fact may be the way that producers see the world, but it is patently untrue and insulting to working men and women, most of whom have a life worth living.

Far from being a paean to women's liberation and capitalistic justice, this film would resonate well in the former Soviet Union. *Working Girl* could be interpreted to mean that if the only way that working people can get ahead in a capitalist system is to cheat, steal, and lie (in more ways than one) their way to the top, then maybe the capitalist system should be overthrown once and for all. Other films of this "liberationist" ilk include *Pretty Woman* (1990), where the protagonist solves her problems by marrying money; *Thelma and Louise* (1991), where the heroes of this female buddy flick solve their problems by killing themselves; and *Striptease* (1996), the only film in history inspired by a cosmetic surgical procedure, Demi Moore's breast enhancement.

In the 1990s the whole role of government came under attack. The Republicans won control of Congress in 1994 for the first time in forty years, largely by running against the corruption of the Democratically controlled Congress and, in general, against the corruption of an overly intrusive and corrupt government. Popular entertainment, too, fed these claims. In supplying stories and protagonists who highlighted the sinister side of government, some films reinforced these beliefs. For example, two enormously popular films of the 1990s were *The Firm* (1993) and *The Client* (1994), both based on novels by best-selling author John Grisham.

For those who haven't seen the movie *The Firm*, it is about a supposedly brilliant young Harvard-trained lawyer (Tom Cruise) who gets a job with a Memphis law firm and whose job it is to help its clients avoid and evade paying taxes (tax avoidance is legal; tax evasion is illegal). Unbeknownst to our hero, the firm's main client is really the Chicago mob, and the firm is really responsible for helping it launder its ill-gotten gains through the Cayman Islands. Our hero soon discovers this fact. He also finds that anyone in the firm who objects to this practice is murdered. At the same time, our hero is approached by the FBI, which is also aware of what is really going on, and he is asked to serve in an undercover role as an FBI informant. This is where the film takes a strange turn.

Instead of leaping at the opportunity to serve the cause of justice and fight the Mafia (and, in the process, to clear his name), our hero rebuffs the FBI. Why? Because of some completely fallacious and self-centered reasoning about his future as a lawyer. Somehow, he reasons, if he turns state's evidence, he will violate his sacred client–lawyer relationship (with the mob?) and have his license to practice revoked. Even if there were a risk that his license would be revoked (no matter how remote) or that he would be cooperating at some personal risk, it seems probable that he has the obligation as an officer of the court, and as all citizens do, to cooperate with the authorities in their investigation of capital crimes. How would he (the "hero") feel if someone else refused to testify or cooperate with the police in the investigation of a crime of which he was the victim? Instead, he keeps his salary, his fancy house, and his car and decides to investigate the firm on his own for some purpose that is not entirely clear. At the very least, he should resign immediately upon learning what sort of things the firm is up to.

The rest of the film is devoted to the story of his narrow escape and personal triumph. In the course of this adventure, he manages to blackmail the government (that is "us" if you believe that we live in a democracy) into releasing from prison his brother, a convicted murderer (one wonders how the victim's relatives feel about that), and extorting $750,000 of our taxpayer money from the FBI. This is not to mention that he betrays his wife, betrays his firm, and manages to protect the Mafia all at the same time. And this guy is a hero? Only in the 1990s could such behavior be considered heroic. In contrast to the protagonist in *The Firm*, consider the role of Jimmy Stewart as an FBI agent in *The FBI Story* (1959). In that movie the FBI is portrayed as an elite crime-fighting unit with dedicated heroic agents— not as it is in *The Firm* as some sort of hybrid between the Keystone Cops and the gestapo. Clearly, attitudes concerning governmental institutions have changed. Why most other people didn't have the same general reaction as I did to *The Firm* can only be attributable to some broad general components of our American political ideology that some politicians so skillfully managed to exploit in the politics of the 1990s.[6]

In fairness to Grisham, he did not write the scripts for *The Firm* and *The Client*. Furthermore, in a later movie based on a Grisham novel, *The Rainmaker* (1997), the gist of the story is that the institutions of society prevail in delivering justice. However, it should be noted that *The Rainmaker* was much less a commercial success than was *The Firm* or *The Client*, which may tell us something about the public's appetite for stories about the success of governmental institutions. Although filmgoers may be more socially liberal, it is not clear that they are more politically liberal.

In the discussion of judging a film, we can apply another standard by which to measure the quality of a film aside from its entertainment value or technical quality. The films examined in this chapter are viewed from the sociopolitical perspective. Up to now, we have outlined the standards used by professional film critics to measure the quality of a film, but it is also the case that film reviewers and the public can view a film from an ideological perspective. To capture the spectrum of opinions on the quality of films from the ideological perspective, it is essential that we understand the broad outlines of American political thought.

AMERICAN POLITICAL IDEOLOGY AND AMERICAN FILM

It may come as a surprise to some that American political ideology is generally regarded as being relatively homogeneous.[7] In comparison to the range of political thought in other countries—such as France, Germany, Italy, or practically any other Western democracy—the range of American political thought is relatively narrow. In the United States, we have no large-scale fascist or socialist movements. There are no political groups in support of a return to monarchy or dictatorial control. In the United States, most of us share two core beliefs: a belief in political democracy and one in free market economics.

Given the spirited and sometimes nasty tone of American politics, it is hard to believe that there is less political difference between John Kerry and George W. Bush than among the party leaders on the ends of the political spectrum in almost any other country. However, when Bush and Kerry debate industrial regulation, tax cuts, or health care reform, they discuss "how much and for whom" rather than what fundamental changes need to be made in the political process or how we should construct our economic system.[8] This is not to say that one side can't charge the other with being socialist or authoritarian; after all, it is the job of politicians to highlight their differences with their opponents but in an unfavorable light for the latter. But beneath the veneer of spirited political competition in the United States, there is a core of consensus. Again, this is not to discredit the substantial differences between the parties and candidates in the United States. However, these differences for the most part take place within a common consensus.[9]

In what is to follow, I identify six ideological types that exist within the American consensus. Then, for the purposes of comparative contrast, I outline two ideological perspectives that are outside the American consensus. A description of the socialist and the fascist views will give us some idea of reactions to American film abroad.[10] Finally, I choose a current controversial film, *The Passion of the Christ* (2004), and display critiques of it from each of the American ideological perspectives. As the reader, identify your own point of view, or portions of your point of view, from the list.

First, we need to discuss the American consensus in a little more detail. It is quite remarkable that as culturally diverse as our population is, we are so politically homogeneous. The reason is that most Americans have in their family background the shared experience of flight, or as I described it in chapter 1, the immigrant experience. This experience has at the same time both a leveling effect and the effect of producing a nation of individualists. Save for Native Americans, no American has any more of a claim to being an American than anyone else. Furthermore, the immigrant experience has the effect of inculcating us with a healthy fear of government. After all, most immigrants have fled oppressive governments or social regimes. Thus, Americans are basically egalitarians and largely individualists, and most would therefore agree that the government that governs best governs least.

There are times, however, when we need a government. In times of war, for example, a government organizes an army for defense. Most of us would also agree that the court system, the police, and other basic functions of government, such as the building of roads and other infrastructure improvements, are essential. But the devil is in the details. How much should government do and how should we pay for it? What are the legitimate rights of individuals and what kinds of behaviors should be restrained? These are the baselines of debate in American politics. To settle these issues, we rely on a representative democracy. Democratic rule makes the most sense for our individualist state because through democracy the restrictions that the government imposes are basically restrictions that we place on ourselves. Consequently, there is a consensual agreement in the United States concerning the legitimacy of democratic governance. Furthermore, because we are individualists or life entrepreneurs, we tend to believe in free market economics, where each individual can make or break him- or herself in the rough-and-tumble of the market. Thus, an outline of the American consensus. But as I have said, the devil is in the details. The following are some of the more prominent divisions of American politics.

Six Ideological Types within the American Consensus

Libertarian. Libertarians believe that the government that governs best governs least—period. Libertarians promote the minimal state with the only absolute guiding principle being the absolute respect for property rights. Libertarians define property rights rather broadly to include not just a person's right to obtain and possess property but also the property rights that one has in one's own body. Thus, libertarians oppose the expropriation of property in all forms, including taxation, theft, and assault. To the extent that government exists, it does so to protect the property rights of the individual. In terms of public policy, libertarians oppose most forms of taxation, zoning restrictions, firearm bans, drug laws, and government activities beyond the police function and national defense.[11] While most Americans are libertarians to some extent, they reject in one way or another the absolutism of the libertarian. Thus, while most Americans believe that the government that governs best governs least, they do so with a few provisos.

Welfare liberals. Welfare liberals also believe that the government that governs best governs least. However, it is often the case that individuals find themselves in circumstances in which the government should help them out.[12] Children, the disabled, the sick, the aged, and the infirm are generally at a disadvantage through no fault of their own. Children, for instance, can't choose their parents. Sickness and the ill effects of aging are unavoidable. Consequently, welfare liberals support government programs to provide for public schools, public hospitals, aid to the indigent, public health, and other components of a social safety net. These liberals are generally tolerant of social differences, behaviors, and other religious practices. However, they do not tolerate unfair discrimination, defined as that made on the basis of race, gender, or political conviction.

Of course, the problem with welfare liberalism is in deciding who is genuinely at a disadvantage. Is the smoker to blame for his heart disease, the overeater for her diabetes? At what point should children be responsible for themselves? These are questions that dog the welfare liberal ideology and are often raised by those in our society called *conservatives.*[13]

Secular conservatives. Secular conservatives, as well, believe that the government that governs best governs least. However, there are times that government ought to intervene in order to facilitate the market or preserve the existing order of society. The government can often help the market be more efficient by providing an adequate infrastructure. Consequently, conservatives, along with liberals, support public education, public health, road building, some forms of trade regulation, and a strong national defense. Where they disagree with liberals is on the issues of *why* and *how much*. Conservatives support social programs as an investment and therefore hold those programs to an investment standard. When policies such as public education begin to show a diminished return, conservatives tend to lose interest and begin to promote their privatization. Because conservatives hold these programs to an efficiency standard rather than a rights standard, as liberals do, conservatives are less willing to be expansive in public spending to cover all possible needs. Therefore, secular conservatives disagree with welfare liberals on the size and scope of the welfare state.

Unlike libertarians, however, conservatives do not believe that anything goes in terms of behavior. Certain standards and traditions need to be upheld if only to protect the smooth, working order of society. For example, conservatives support harsh antidrug penalties because, from their position, drug abuse leads to crime and wasted lives. Conservatives generally oppose gay marriage and civil unions because of the perceived threat that such relationships pose to traditional notions of child rearing, the nuclear family, and the allocation of public benefits.

The problem with the secular conservative position is that if social programs are held to an efficiency standard, many individuals in need fall through the cracks. School vouchers may help a middle-class child move into a private school, but as school vouchers are generally proposed, they won't be enough to get a poor child into a private school. Thus, the efficiency standard tends to be class biased. A decline in funding for facilities such as public housing, transportation, hospitals, and schools tends to weigh most heavily on the poor. The question liberals then pose is, Are housing, health, nutrition, and basic education a right or a privilege?

Religious conservatives. Like the others, religious conservatives believe that the government that governs best governs least. However, if the government acts in a way that contradicts religious doctrine or if the government doesn't act at all when the moral order of society is threatened, they want the government to intervene. Religious conservatives agree in many ways with both liberals and conservatives. They agree with conservatives on most social and economic issues, and, in a general sense, they agree with liberals on the importance of social programs to provide for children, the sick, and the indigent. However, the Bible, the Koran, and the Torah guide their beliefs in the promotion of government action.[14] Because these books, in the opinion of religious conservatives, are literally the word of God, they cannot compromise on issues where the secular government and the religious texts contradict. Consequently, religious conservatives reject the notion that there should be in government a separation of church and state. Furthermore, they believe that government should subsidize religious organizations as being the primary suppliers of social benefits. Therefore, religious conservatives don't disagree with liberals on the need for alms for the poor; they disagree on how those services should be supplied.

While religious conservatives generally support a free market economy, they would do so with some provisos. The problem for religious conservatives is that the market is neither moral nor immoral—it is amoral. So, when there is a market for abortion on demand, pornography, liquor, and gambling, religious conservatives support government intervention to close these markets. Religious conservatives do not measure programs by an efficiency standard, as do secular conservatives; they do not measure programs by a rights standard, as do liberals; they measure programs by a Biblical standard. Programs that do not meet that standard are by definition a violation of the word of God and must be opposed.

Of course, secular conservatives object to the religious conservatives' rejection of the efficiency standard. Furthermore, secular conservatives may have a problem with religious conservatives who oppose teaching science in school or who impose arcane restrictions on gambling and alcohol. Liberals, for their part, don't believe that religious organizations have the resources to adequately supply social services on their own. Furthermore, liberals believe that religious organizations are discriminatory and thus not the way that government funds should be distributed in a democracy.

It should be noted that not all religious people are conservatives. A significant segment of the religious community is liberal. Its members believe in the secularization of politics and that the holy books can be read to mean that a much more activist government is in order.

Religious liberals. Religious liberals are more likely to support the separation of church and state, as they are more tolerant of diverse lifestyles and practices. They tend to side with welfare liberals when it comes to providing for the welfare state. They believe as do welfare liberals that health care, schooling, food, and housing are rights, not privileges. They arrive at this conclusion in their reading of the Bible.

Green Party. Finally, there is a relatively new phenomenon in American politics: the Green Party. The Green Party was born of the environmental movement. Greens borrow much of their ideology from the ancient religions that saw the human race as simply being part of a whole. It is then the responsibility of the human race to live in harmony with nature. If that means doing without personal automobiles, nuclear power, or the globalization of trade, then so be it. In many ways, the Green Party is both the most unusual and the most traditional political movement in the United States. Greens do not necessarily believe that the government that governs best governs least. They can see that in many cases collective action, sometimes through government and sometimes through private organization, is a better way than the market to achieve society's goals. In this sense, they share something in common with the socialists. On the other hand, the Green Party is the most traditional of American political movements, as they draw much of their inspiration from the Native American religions that predate Western settlement of North America.[15]

The problem with the Green movement from both the liberal and the conservative political perspective is its rejection of free market capitalism. From the religious perspective, the Green movement is troublesome in the sense that Greens seem to reject traditional notions of religion. Thus, the Green movement is really, for now, outside the mainstream of American politics. But there is a chance that in the future Greens will widen their agenda and appeal enough to become a major player in American politics.

Two Ideological Perspectives Outside
the American Consensus

Socialism. One of the most common smears in American political discourse is to label an opponent a socialist (that to label someone a socialist in our country is a smear is remarkable in and of itself). Yet there are few true socialists in the United States and no real socialist movement. Socialist movements, however, are strong and alive abroad. Therefore, we should consider their reaction to American culture, if only to understand the attitudes of many abroad toward the United States.

True, socialists also believe that the government that governs best governs least. The ultimate goal for the socialist is the withering away of the state. In that socialist utopia, there would be no need for government because states would have no need to go to war against one another, and for individuals it would be "from each according to his ability, to each according to his needs." In the meantime, however, socialists believe that the source of many of the world's problems is a function of the capitalist system. Capitalism, according to the socialist, is inherently exploitative. To maintain this exploitative system—that is, workers being exploited by the owners of the means of production—states are forced to subdue other states and subdue their own workers. Capitalists do so in a number of ways. Because they own the media, they use propaganda to maintain their control and cover up their crimes. By and large socialists reject religion as "the opiate of the masses." Capitalists use religion to pacify exploited workers. And finally, if worse comes to worst, capitalists use force.[16]

This is not part of the American debate. No leading candidate for political office in the United States proposes state ownership of the means of production (although there have been some calls for nationalized health care in the style of the Canadian system, although Canada is hardly a socialist state). The problem with socialism is that it may be wildly inefficient. Capitalists cannot see how centralized planners can outperform the market in the distribution of goods. Furthermore, individualists cannot see why they should sacrifice their own ambitions for the good of society or for the good of people at large. Thus, socialism has not found and is unlikely to find much of a following in the United States.

Socialist, however, is not the only smear used in the rhetoric of politics. Another label bandied about in the United States is *fascist.*

Fascism. Fascism did not die with Adolph Hitler. It is alive and well all over the world, but it hasn't had much of a presence in the United States since before World War II. Fascists believe that there is a natural hierarchy in society, that in society there are the strong and there are the weak. According to the fascist, it is the role and indeed the obligation of the strong to rule the weak. Of course, the problem with this prescriptive order is determining who is the strong and who is the weak. The fascist invariably self-identifies as the strong and identifies the "other" as the weak.[17] Liberals and conservatives reject fascism, among other reasons, because fascism rejects democracy; religious conservatives and liberals reject fascism, among other reasons, because of its total and complete rejection of traditional religion. There are no significant fascist political movements in the United States, nor are there likely to be because of the United States' core political belief in essential egalitarianism.

Each of these ideologies and their variants looks at the world through a unique set of lenses. In the following section, I take as an example a recent controversial film, and I examine how the film is seen from each of the political perspectives discussed here, save for that of the Green Party and including that of the Jewish and the black perspective.

IDEOLOGY AND *THE PASSION OF THE CHRIST*

It is clear by now that *The Passion of the Christ*, an enormously controversial film produced by actor Mel Gibson, is a huge financial success. The film was produced for the rather paltry sum of $30 million and has to date (2005) grossed more than $600 million,[18] a huge success by any standard. The film has provoked a tremendous amount of controversy due to its interpretation of the Bible, its violent content, and its medieval approach to the Christian religion. It has also become a metaphor for the spectrum of American political debate.

Before we examine this film from the perspectives of the aforementioned ideologies, let's first consider the standard movie review. Roger Ebert of the *Chicago Sun-Times* writes,

> Is the film "good" or "great?" I imagine each person's reaction (visceral, theological, artistic) will differ. I was moved by the depth of feeling, by the skill of the actors and technicians, by their desire to see this project through no matter what. To discuss individual performances, such as James Caviezel's heroic depiction of the ordeal, is almost beside the point. This isn't a movie about performances, although it has powerful ones, or about technique, although it is awesome, or about cinematography (although Caleb Deschanel paints with an artist's eye), or music (although John Debney supports the content without distracting from it).[19]

Ebert applauds the artistry and the passion of the filmmakers without passing judgment on its content. This is one standard of evaluation to be sure, but it can also be used as a standard to praise *The Triumph of the Will* (1934), Leni Riefenstahl's celebration of the Nazi Party. Do film reviewers owe us more? Do we want them getting out of their expertise, the film business, to comment on something that they probably know little more about than we do?

Typical of a critique from the far Left is J. Hoberman's review in the *Village Voice*:

> Sitting through the film's garishly staged suffering, one might well ponder the millions of people—victims of crusades, inquisitions, colonial conquests, the slave trade, political terror, and genocide—who have been tortured and killed in Christ's name.[20]

Hoberman focuses not on the artistry of the film but on the destructive consequences of religious passion. His standard for criticizing this film is the effect that *The Passion* may have on those who watch it.

A typical, mainstream welfare liberal response to this film is from David Ansen, writing for *Newsweek* magazine:

> It's the sadism, not the alleged anti-Semitism, that is most striking. (For the record, I don't think Gibson is anti-Semitic; but those inclined toward bigotry could easily find fuel for their fire here.) There's always been a pronounced streak of sadomasochism and martyrdom running through Gibson's movies, both as an actor and as a filmmaker. The Oscar-winning "Braveheart" reveled in decapitations and disembowelments, not to mention the spectacle of Gibson himself, as the Scottish warrior hero, impaled on a cross. In "Mad Max," the "Lethal Weapon" movies, "Ransom" and "Signs" (where he's a cleric who's lost his faith), the Gibson hero is pummeled and persecuted, driven to suicidal extremes. From these pop passion plays to the Passion itself is a logical progression; it gives rise to the suspicion that on some unconscious level "The Passion of the Christ" is, for Gibson, autobiography.[21]

Ansen is clearly concerned about this film's potential to produce a bigoted response. But rather than critique Gibson as a member of a group (radical religious conservatives), Ansen focuses on Gibson's individual responsibility. Ansen suggests that the passion in this film is Gibson's passion and that, more than anything else, this film may reflect the fact that Gibson is more than a little crazy. This review is fine as far as it goes, but it begs the obvious. Millions of people have bought into Gibson's passion. What may be a personal statement apparently resonates with millions of people. The ideas expressed in *The Passion* are more generally shared than what Ansen is willing to admit. In some sense, then, Ansen is in denial.

From the secular conservative perspective, *New York Times* columnist David Brooks's comments are illustrative:

> The flap over Gibson's movie reminds us that religion can be a dangerous thing. It can be coarsened into gore and bloodshed and used to foment hatred. But we're not living in Afghanistan under the Taliban. Our general problem is not that we're too dogmatic. Our more common problems come from the other end of the continuum. Americans in the 21st century are more likely to be divorced from any sense of a creedal order, ignorant of the moral traditions that have come down to us through the ages and detached from the sense that we all owe obligations to a higher authority.
>
> Sure, let's get angry at Mel Gibson if he deserves it. But let's not forget that the really corrosive cultural forces come in the form of the easygoing narcissism that surrounds us every day.[22]

Brooks's comments are from what could be called the "kids these days don't believe in anything" school of thought. Brooks is clearly uncomfortable with the religiosity of Gibson's film, but he can't resist getting in a dig at liberals, who, in his opinion, have contributed to the moral degradation of modern society. Secular conservatives are concerned about the breakdown of the traditional social order. However, they are also concerned that replacing our civil society with a religious society, one may go too far in the other direction. We have seen what the imposition of fundamentalist religious beliefs has done (or hasn't done) for the economic and social development of Saudi Arabia and Iran.

A good example of a conservative religious reaction to *The Passion* comes in a column written by Robert Novak:

> At the heart of the dispute over "The Passion" is freedom of expression. Liberals who defended the right to exhibit Martin Scorsese's "The Last Temptation of Christ," which deeply offended orthodox Christians, now demand censorship of "The Passion of Christ." As a result, Abe Foxman [head of the Jewish Anti-Defamation League] and his allies have risked stirring religious tensions over a work of art.[23]

Novak sees criticism as censorship. However, to criticize is not to censor. Pundits on both ends of the political spectrum often use this riff, equating criticism to censorship, to intimidate their opponents. However, Novak goes one step further. There is an implicit threat in his suggestion that criticism of the film may stir up "religious tensions." Religious conservatives are more sensitive to criticism than are other groups because they believe that they are acting according to the will of God. Therefore, to criticize the activities of religious conservatives is to criticize God.

Religious liberals, however, have a totally different reaction to this film. Monsignor Lorenzo Albacete is a Catholic theologian, author, lecturer, and former president of the Pontifical Catholic University of Puerto Rico. Writing in the *New Republic*, he suggests,

> I found Gibson's film to be, at some level, powerful. But his reduction of the passion and death of Jesus to an emotionally wrenching story is problematic. What is one supposed to do about this story? Cry? Be inspired to make sure things like that don't happen again? Why not seek revenge (as anti-Semites throughout the ages have done)? None of these is the intended purpose of this narrative. To separate the facts of the passion from their proper context is to open the door to unchecked religious emotionalism. This is what worries me about Gibson's film.[24]

Albacete is clearly concerned about the ramifications of the release of a religious film that incites so much passion without so much direction. Over the years, passion plays have often incited Christians to riot, committing atrocities against local Jewish communities. While only 8 percent of Americans believe that Jews are responsible for the death of Christ, that belief is more widely held in the rest of the world and could grow larger as the result of this film.[25]

Many Jews do feel threatened by a film that can be interpreted by some to blame the Jewish people for the death of Jesus. After all, Jews have been persecuted for centuries by Christians who accuse them of deicide. Leon Wieseltier, writing for the *New Republic*, voices these concerns when he writes,

> *The Passion of The Christ* is an unwitting incitement to secularism, because it leaves you desperate to escape its standpoint, to find another way of regarding the horror that you have just observed. This is unfair to, well, Christianity, since Christianity is not a cult

of Gibsonesque gore. But there is a religion toward which Gibson's movie is even more unfair than it is to its own. In its representation of its Jewish characters, *The Passion of the Christ* is without any doubt an anti-Semitic movie, and anybody who says otherwise knows nothing, or chooses to know nothing, about the visual history of anti-Semitism, in art and in film. What is so shocking about Gibson's Jews is how unreconstructed they are in their stereotypical appearances and actions. These are not merely anti-Semitic images; these are classically anti-Semitic images. In this regard, Gibson is most certainly a traditionalist.[26]

One wonders how Christians would react were their ministers and religion depicted in the same way that Gibson portrayed Jews and Judaism in *The Passion*. Wieseltier is pointing out that in his decision on how to portray the Jews and emphasize some parts of the New Testament over others, Gibson depicts Judaism in a negative light and reinforces negative stereotypes of Jews. Whether Gibson is anti-Semitic or not is beside the point. He has the right to his opinion. But if the film he makes is anti-Semitic, that's a different matter. Gibson may not be anti-Semitic, but his insensitivity to the roots of bigotry is manifest.

And it's not just Jews who complain about Gibson's depiction of Jesus. James Hill, writing for *Black Entertainment Television*, writes,

> It is troubling that even in 2004, a director would go so far as to use solely Aramaic and Latin languages in order to ensure a historically accurate film, and yet still hire mostly White actors to play people who were anything but what scholarship suggests. Despite Gibson's efforts to hide lead actor Caviezel's European heritage behind a prosthetic nose and digitally darkened eyes, Jesus and the majority of the cast comes off looking like all the other theatrical productions of Jesus' life—Whitewashed.[27]

African Americans have often criticized the film industry for whitewashing its productions. There is some controversial scholarship to the effect that Jesus was black. Whether that is true or not, it is certainly the case that African Americans have been historically underrepresented in the production and casting of Hollywood films.

Hill sees this film from a perspective based on his ethnicity, which brings me back to my original point. The conversation about film is often the conversation about politics. In this section, we see how almost every major political perspective in the United States has weighed in on the quality of this film. Is *The Passion of the Christ* a bad film? Well, as they say in politics, "Where you sit is where you stand."

Feature Film: *Working Girl* (1988)

As we have seen, even films that are on the surface devoid of political content can promote, ignore, or distort certain political beliefs. In a bit of a departure from the standard movie review, I have chosen to analyze one particular film, Working Girl, *from several different ideological perspectives.*

Working Girl. *Courtesy of M.P. & T.V. Photo Archive.*

To reprise, Tess McGill, played by Melanie Griffith, is a secretary for a Wall Street financial firm who tries to get ahead in her job by working hard and by not just a little deception. As we have already discussed the plot of this film extensively, let's now examine it from various political perspectives.

Libertarian

This is a movie about reality, not what we would like reality to be. Tess is at a disadvantage because she is discriminated against. Get over it. Discrimination is a fact in our society and is simply one of the natural barriers that one needs to overcome in order to get ahead. Outlawing discrimination is like outlawing gravity. To get ahead, Tess breaks the rules. But who is hurt by her deception? No one and that is the standard we should use in evaluating the morality of her actions. In fact, we are all better off for the increased efficiency in our economy brought about by free, unfettered economic transactions, such as that demonstrated in the plot through the purchase of radio stations by Trask Enterprises. In the end, because of her hard work and pluck, Tess succeeds. Isn't that the way it ought to be?

Welfare liberal

Tess is confronted by unfair discrimination. There is no reason that just because she is a woman and she comes from humble beginnings, she can't perform the same job at the same level of efficiency as the men do in her office (and the one woman at the corporate management level, portrayed by Sigourney Weaver). That is what I mean by *unfair* discrimination. Fortunately, there are laws against discrimination on the basis of gender. Rather than take matters into her own hands (and thereby delegitimize her behavior), she should hire a good litigation attorney and sue the company for illegal discrimination on the basis of gender. In doing so, not only will she help herself, but she will help her fellow workers, who are beset by a pervasive atmosphere of sex discrimination.

Secular conservative

In some sense, Tess should be applauded for her efforts to get ahead. We have provided for her a good education and an infrastructure in support of business that is second to none. Clearly, she and her company have benefited from the limited assistance that government provides to promote business. Tess, however, thinks the world owes her a living. When the company she works for refuses to grant her a promotion, rather than look for work somewhere else or display the patience necessary to get a reward for work well done, she decides to cheat and scheme her way to the top. I have got to wonder why she hasn't yet been promoted. Could it be that an employee who uses the company's keyboard to disrupt the stock ticker in the middle of a trading session is not seen by the company as management material? In other words, isn't she at fault for the fix she's in? Clearly, she looks in a mirror and sees that she dresses like a clown and talks like longshoreman. Should the company be expected to promote her before she cleans up her own act?

Religious conservative

Tess is on a dead-end path. Her ignorance of God and his word makes her life meaningless. In the end, when she faces the judgment of the Lord, she will have nothing to show for her life but a legacy of sin and money. The pursuit of money of and for itself is a sin. The fact that she cheats, lies, steals, and has immoral sexual intercourse compounds that sin. In the end, were she to find the Lord, she would receive all of the sustenance that she needs. She would lead a good and generous life and would be rewarded in the end in the kingdom of heaven. This film sets a terrible example for our youth. At the very least, the film should be marketed with a warning label interpreting and highlighting the degeneracy of this film as being promoted by a bunch of Hollywood liberals.

African American

Where are all the black faces in this and all the movies we have seen? The fact that Hollywood hires blacks neither in front of nor behind the camera breeds racism. Audiences for this and other movies never see blacks in positions of responsibility, nor are they told of the discrimination that is still rampant in our society. Therefore, the racial problems of this country become invisible to the European majority, and racism persists.

Fascist

Tess has the will to power. She is obviously born to rule. Liberal society's rules exist to protect the position of the degenerate upper classes. The fact that Tess breaks the rules to get ahead is simply nature taking its course. If people like Katherine (Tess's boss), who achieve their position of responsibility by virtue of birth, are allowed to continue to rule, the state will eventually perish. Therefore, what Tess does in this film is not only essential; it is right.

Socialist

Tess is on the path to oblivion. As a worker, she expends all her energy to "get ahead," which, in the end, means moving from a desk out in the open to a closet that passes as an office. Her reward is to be able to lord it over her secretary. But is this petty exploitation a true reward? Does she realize her true potential? Does her climbing over the backs of other workers make anyone better off (except the bourgeoisie)? No. Tess must recognize that the corruption she sees in her office is endemic to the capitalistic system. To know that and to still participate in it is to be part of the problem, not the solution. What she needs to do is to organize and educate other workers to rise up against the oppression of the capitalist state. Then she will be truly free.

Don't agree? What do you think?

EXERCISE

Interpret a current top-grossing film from five different American political perspectives: libertarian, welfare liberal, secular conservative, religious conservative, and religious liberal. See if you can identify your own personal political philosophy in the way that you analyze film.

NOTES

1. For a good discussion of film criticism, see Warren Buckland, *Film Studies* (London: Hodder and Stoughton, 2003), particularly chap. 6.

2. See Andrew Tudor, *Theories of Film* (New York: Viking, 1974), 121–24, for a discussion of the director as auteur.

3. For an excellent discussion of the sociological meaning of the comics, see Arthur Asa Berger, *The Comic-Stripped American: What Dick Tracy, Blondie, Daddy Warbucks, and Charlie Brown Tell Us about Ourselves* (New York: Walker, 1973); on Batman in particular, see 160–71.

4. John E. O'Connor and Phillip C. Rollins, eds., *The American Presidency in Film and History* (Lexington: University of Kentucky Press, 2003).

5. For an examination of vigilantism in comparative perspective, see H. Jon Rosenbaum and Peter C. Sederberg, "Vigilantism: An Analysis of Establishment Violence," *Comparative Politics* 6, no. 4 (July 1974): 541–70.

6. For a full-length review of these films, see Daniel P. Franklin, "A Day at the Movies: 'The Client' Breeds Anarchy," *Atlanta Journal-Constitution*, August 4, 1994, A15.

7. The classic exposition of this point is made by Samuel Huntington in *American Politics: The Promise of Disharmony* (Cambridge, Mass.: Belknap, 1981), 230–31; or Louis Hartz in *The Liberal Tradition in America: An Interpretation of American Political Thought since the Revolution* (New York: Vintage, 1955). For a further discussion and partial refutation of this point, see Rogers M. Smith, "The 'American Creed' and American Identity: The Limits of Liberal Citizenship in the United States," *Western Political Quarterly* 41, no. 2 (June 1988): 225–51.

8. For a more complete rendition of this argument, see Theodore J. Lowi, *The End of Liberalism*, 2nd ed. (New York: Norton, 1979).

9. For more on this, see Russell Hardin, *Liberalism, Constitutionalism, and Democracy* (Oxford: Oxford University, 1999).

10. For a book-length discussion of these ideologies, see Terrance Ball and Richard Dagger, *Political Ideologies and the Democratic Ideal*, 5th ed. (New York: Pearson-Longman, 2003).

11. For a good exposition of the libertarian ethic, see Robert Nozick, *Anarchy, State, and Utopia* (New York: Basic, 1974), especially chap. 7.

12. For a prominent justification of the welfare liberal state, see John Rawls, *A Theory of Justice* (Cambridge, Mass.: Harvard University Press, 1971).

13. See Clarence Y. H. Lo, "Countermovements and Conservative Movements in the Contemporary U.S." *Annual Review of Sociology* 8 (1982): 107–34.

14. Geoffrey C. Layman and Edward G. Carmines, "Cultural Conflict in American Politics: Religious Traditionalism, Postmaterialism, and U.S. Political Behavior," *Journal of Politics* 59, no. 3 (August 1997): 751–77; Geoffrey C. Layman, "Religion and Political Behavior in the United States: The Impact of Beliefs, Affiliations, and Commitment from 1980 to 1994," *Public Opinion Quarterly* 61, no. 2 (Summer 1997): 288–316; Kirk W. Elifson and C. Kirk Hadaway, "Prayer in Public Schools: When Church and State Collide," *Public Opinion Quarterly* 49, no. 3 (Autumn 1985): 317–29.

15. From the Green Party platform, "Green politics is an ecological approach to politics that links social and ecological problems. Ecology studies the relationships among organisms and their environment. Political ecology brings human institutions and ideologies into this holistic perspective. We find that the same institutions and ideas that cause the exploitation and oppression of humans also cause the degradation and destruction of the environment. Both are rooted in a hierarchical, exploitative, and alienated social system that systematically produces human oppression and ecological destruction. For the Greens, therefore, the fights against racism, sexism, class exploitation, bureaucratic domination, war, and all other forms of social domination and violence are central to the movement for an ecologically sustainable society. In order to harmonize society with nature, we must harmonize human with human" (www.greenparty.org/Platform.html; accessed December 23, 2004).

16. There are many versions of socialist thought; the description here is drawn mainly from Karl Marx, *The Communist Manifesto*, in *The Marx-Engels Reader*, ed. Robert C. Tucker, 2nd ed. (New York: Norton, 1978): 469–500.

17. For more on this, see Kevin Passmore, *Fascism: A Very Short Introduction* (Oxford: Oxford University Press, 2002).

18. Box Office Mojo, *The Passion of the Christ* (2004), www.boxofficemojo.com/movies/?id=passionofthechrist.htm (accessed December 23, 2004).

19. Roger Ebert, "Current Reviews: *The Passion of the Christ*," *Chicago Sun-Times*, February 24, 2004, www.suntimes.com/output/ebert1/cst-ftr-passion24.html

20. J. Hoberman, "Flogged to Death," *Village Voice*, February 25–March 2, 2004, www.villagevoice.com/film/0408,hoberman,51305,20.html (accessed August 4, 2005).

21. David Ansen, "So What's the Good News? The Debate over 'The Passion' May Be Less Harsh Than the Film," *Newsweek*, March 2004, www.msnbc.msn.com/id/4338528/ (accessed August 4, 2005).

22. David Brooks, "Hooked on Heaven Lite," New York Times, March 9, 2004, A25, www.nytimes.com/2004/03/09/opinion/09BROO.html?n=Top%2fOpinion%2fEditorials%20and%20Op%2dEd%2fOp%2dEd%2fColumnists%2fDavid%20Brooks (accessed August 4, 2005).

23. Robert Novak, "The Passion of Christ," November 3, 2003, www.townhall.com/columnists/robertnovak/rn20031103.shtml (accessed August 4, 2005).

24. Msgr. Lorenzo Albacete, "Facts of Life," *New Republic*, March 5, 2004, www.tnr.com/doc.mhtml?i=express&s=albacete030504 (accessed August 4, 2005).

25. "*ABC News PrimeTime* Poll," www.pollingreport.com/religion.htm (accessed August 4, 2005), conducted February 6–10, 2004; $N = 1,011$ adults nationwide; margin of error $\pm$ 3.

26. Leon Wieseltier, "Mel Gibson's Lethal Weapon: The Worship of Blood," *New Republic*, February 26, 2004, https://ssl.tnr.com/p/docsub.mhtml?i=20040308&s=wieseltier030804 (accessed August 4, 2005).

27. James Hill, "'Christ' Only Preaches to the Choir," *BET.com*, http://www.bet.com/Entertainment/Archives/BET.com+-+_Christ_+Only+Preaches+to+the+Choir+303.htm (accessed August 4, 2005).

SUGGESTED READING

Ball, Terrance, and Richard Dagger. *Political Ideologies and the Democratic Ideal.* 5th ed. New York: Pearson-Longman, 2003.

Bordwell, David. *Making Meaning: Inference and Rhetoric in the Interpretation of Cinema.* Cambridge: Harvard University Press, 1989.

Buckland, Warren. *Film Studies.* London: Hodder and Stoughton, 2003.

Corrigan, Timothy. *A Short Guide to Writing about Film.* 4th ed. New York: Harper Collins, 2000.

Elsaesser, Thomas, and Warren Buckland. *Studying Contemporary American Film: A Guide to Movie Analysis.* New York: Oxford University Press, 2002.

J. Haberski, Raymond. *It's Only a Movie: Films and Critics in American Culture.* Lexington: Kentucky University Press, 2001.

Metz, Christian. *Film Language: A Semiotics of the Cinema.* New York: Oxford University Press, 1974.

6

Why They Don't Make Them Like They Used To

Why are films so different today from those of the past? There are really three main areas of development in the evolution of commercial film that have had a profound effect on the content of film: technological developments, changes in the market, and the evolution of American political culture. Each of the changes has had a varying impact on the sociopolitical content of film. Let us consider each of these changes in turn and its potential for future impact.

TECHNOLOGY

Until now, three major technological developments have characterized the evolution of the American film industry. As discussed in chapter 1, first is the development of a mechanical pull-down device that allowed for the conversion of still photography to motion pictures. Second is the invention of capabilities to record sound right onto the film stock itself, allowing for the efficient and improved synchronization of sound and motion in motion pictures. Surprisingly, those two technological advances, introduced at the turn of the twentieth century and in the 1920s respectively, have been up to now the most important developments in film technology in the last one hundred years. Most films today are still shot on photographic film stock, with cameras that are in many ways mechanically similar to the cameras used by D. W. Griffith in shooting *Birth of a Nation*. Third is the introduction of computer-generated special effects. But even before the advent of the computer, Hollywood had been able to produce some remarkable special effects—in the fantasy film *Jason and the Argonauts* (1963), for example. Nowadays, however, special effects are even more spectacular, cheaper, and easier to produce because of the advent of computer technology.

Of course, the question is, how important really are these technological developments to the content of commercial films? This question really has two answers. On the one hand, technological developments have probably less effect on the nature of films than what one would think. In film, to paraphrase Shakespeare, the play is still the thing. At another level, however, technological developments present and future can change the content of film because they change the economics of film. Digital photography and computer-generated special effects will have an increasing effect on who can make movies, how those films will be distributed, and what decisions filmmakers will make in the production of film.

For many of those who are middle-aged, one of the fondest memories of youth is that of gathering around the television set to see the annual screening of *The Wizard of Oz* (1939). Even never having seen *The Wizard of Oz* in a movie theater, I still find the experience of seeing the film transporting. Nevertheless, most commercial films don't translate well to television, and it is not just because of commercial interruptions, the censorship euphemistically called "editing for content," and the fact that wide-angle photography will not fit onto most television screens (resulting in the development of "letterbox" presentations of films, which may be necessary but is still distracting).

We now have a chance to view movies on the Turner Movie Channel, premium cable, or on VCRs and DVDs without commercial interruptions, yet sometimes something gets lost in the translation. It turns out that the film industry did not have to worry all that much about the advent of television. Up to now, either television doesn't compete with film, or it actually provides another outlet for Hollywood films. In fact, judging from much of the tripe that is aired on Showtime and HBO, cable television provides a second life for some of the worst, talentless, brain-dead filmmaking in America.

However, there is some really excellent television programming salted in among the dreck. For example, HBO recently aired *Brave New World* (1998), a made-for-television adaptation of the novel that, considering the complexity of the material they were dealing with, was a nicely produced piece. Showtime and HBO have also produced some of the most innovative television series ever produced and made-for-television movies that, ironically, now sit beside mainstream Hollywood films on the shelves at video stores. There are, in fact, some forms of dramatization that can be done better on television than on film. Plot and character development have always been superior in well-crafted television series. The cable channels in particular have taken this advantage to the next level in producing series such as *The Sopranos* and *Six Feet Under*.

And of particular interest to those of us who study the politics of film are the made-for-television "docudramas." Because of their relatively low cost (and high profitability compared to that of showing Hollywood films on air) and short lead times for production, networks have begun producing their own dramatizations of current events. Of course, there is a danger in re-creating historical events. It is often the case that writers and directors will have to exercise a certain degree of poetic license to produce a "clean" or entertaining plotline. And because a large proportion of the public gets its information from the entertainment media, docudramas can be misleading—not because they adopt a particular interpretation but because they are factually incorrect. This was the argument made by those who protested the recently produced docudrama *The Reagans* (2003). In writing dialogue for the former president, the filmmakers had the president make a number of controversial remarks. Despite the fact that this is hardly recent history, the policies of the Reagan administration are still being played out. Thus, the film became part of the national political debate (and was eventually withdrawn by CBS). The result has been more of a tendency on the part of the networks to shy away from current or near current political events in their stories to rely more on crime dramas, such as the *Elizabeth Smart Story* (2003), or the re-creation of ancient legends, such as the *Odyssey* (1997).[1]

Besides the occasional outstanding documentary, made-for-television movie, and television series, some movies also translate well to the small screen. Some people would argue that small films are well viewed on television—small action for the small screen. For example, *My Dinner with Andre* (1981), which is a filmed dialogue between two people at dinner, works well on television or the big screen. But so does *The Wizard of Oz.* Why the disparity? What makes a film work when viewed on any medium is most likely the story. *The Wizard of Oz* is a great story played on a soundstage with special effects no more elaborate than cutting from black-and-white to color, dressing a bunch of little people and monkeys in costumes, creating a cardboard cutout of Emerald City, and exploding some torches representing the Wizard himself. What makes the film work on any screen is the wonderful story, a stellar cast, some beautiful music, and the viewer's imagination. Although the film is visually stunning, it is so for its costumes and designs, not its special effects.

The fact is that no matter how realistic or spectacular the special effects, "the play's the thing." But in case after case, the modern film is driven onto the rocks of financial disaster by the siren song of special effects. A few years ago saw perhaps one of the worst films of the decade in *Lost in Space* (1998). *Lost in Space* is a feature-film adaptation of a modestly successful television series that ran for three seasons, from 1965 to 1968. From beginning to end, the film is one long series of explosions, flashes of light, and brilliant and amazing computer-generated special effects strung together with one of the most idiotic, incomprehensible, and inane film scripts in history.[2] Parenthetically, the film didn't make money.

Why did they do this? What were they thinking when they made this piece of trash? One gets the sense that the producers had to make a choice between spending on special effects and spending on script writing. They chose the former. Maybe they knew they had a lousy script and hoped to cover it up with a bunch of special effects. In any event, unless *The Wizard of Oz* were placed into the hands of a capable production company, the modern era would dictate that it come out as *Dorothy and the Tornado.* It would be a film that would feature terrific special effects at the expense of Judy Garland and a script. That is the destructiveness of modern technology: filmmakers, who are after all craftsmen and craftswomen, fall in love with the craft of filmmaking; they often don't think or maybe even care that much about their story.

This is not to say that great camera work or terrific special effects don't contribute mightily to the quality of a good film. This is to say that movies that start out with an excellent story and then are embellished by outstanding cinematography or special effects are a class of films that are simply not television worthy. For example, while

2001: A Space Odyssey is a great film on any screen, it is best in a theater. When I first saw it during its original release, I and, apparently, most people were blown away by the effects. Furthermore, the beauty of nature can't well be captured on the small screen in *Out of Africa* (1985) or *Little Big Man* (1970). But what makes these stories entertaining is not their cinematography but the ripping yarns around which their outstanding screenplays are constructed.

In the future, the next major technological step in filmmaking may be the move to digital technology, or the shooting, editing, and display of films on computer chips. Filmmakers still need to solve some major problems in making this technology economically viable. For anyone who has ever stored high-resolution photographs on a computer, the main problem of digital technology is easy to understand and can be summed up in one word: storage. High-quality images take up a lot of space. For example, a single high-resolution photograph occupies more storage space on a computer hard drive than the entire book you are now reading. To paraphrase James Monaco in *How to Read a Film*, with digital technology "a picture really is worth a thousand words."[3] Digital technology can be used to produce motion pictures, but because of storage-space demands, the effects produced through digital technology still have to be transferred to film or to videotape, with the corresponding loss of clarity.

Assuming that filmmakers overcome these technological problems—and they almost certainly will—the question becomes, what will the effects of digital-technology adaptation be to the making of film? Probably less than what one would expect. Filmmakers will explore the possibilities of digital art. For example, the line between animation and real-world cinematography will continue to blur, as it did in the recent Quentin Tarantino blood fest *Kill Bill: Vol. 1* (2003). Digital production certainly presents the possibility of expanding the art of cinema, but it is unlikely that digital production will supplant the story (and still be successful). IMAX films are spectacular novelty items, but the novelty will begin to grow thin without the addition of substance. Here again, the play is still the thing.

Finally, will the digital revolution democratize film production? By using the term *democratization*, I am asking, will the digital revolution make the tools of film production accessible to those people and groups who have not traditionally had voices in the filmmaking industry? The answer is yes and no. Yes, it is certainly the case that digital filmmaking will eventually become widely available, and, no, it still won't democratize film production. Baseball bats and gloves are widely available, but major-league baseball can still only be seen in a major-league ballpark. The introduction of video cameras did not spark a wave of people's films; word processors have not introduced us to more budding Shakespeares (at least that we know of). Filmmaking is still a specialized craft, and the lion's share of the cost of making a film is still in marketing, salaries, and distribution, the nontechnological aspects of film. Consequently, filmmaking may have new technology, but it still is an old art, and digital technology won't change that. The bottleneck of film production is in its marketing and distribution. Therefore, a much more likely source of change in the content of film will be the transformation of the film industry's political economy.

ECONOMICS

As discussed in previous chapters, part of the reason that movies are so different today is that the movie industry has gone through three eras of monopoly: the short-lived Edison trust, the golden era of Hollywood cinema, and now the corporatization of American film. Monopolies have a profound effect on film content because decisions made about the content of film in a monopoly are in large part the function of the eccentricities of the trust holders.

It should be noted, however, that even monopolies come under pressure to change and to alter their products. The best way to understand the evolution of a monopoly, and most institutions for that matter, is to reference the work of noted historian Arnold J. Toynbee. In his massive multivolume *A Study of History*, Toynbee came to the conclusion that the history of humankind advanced in a pattern that was both predictable and idiosyncratic. He termed that pattern "challenge and response." As he describes it,

> The effect of a cause is inevitable, invariable, and predictable. But the initiative that is taken by one or other of the live parties to an encounter is not a cause; it is a challenge. Its consequence is not an effect; it is a response. Challenge-and-response resembles cause-and-effect only in standing for a sequence of events. The character of the sequence is not the same. Unlike the effect of a cause, the response to a challenge is not predetermined, it is not necessarily uniform in all cases, and is therefore intrinsically unpredictable.[4]

According to Toynbee, excessive scientism in the social sciences has mislead us to believe that we can reliably predict the outcome of human history. However, because of the eccentricity of the actors' decisions and because of the decisions of others, according to Toynbee, it is impossible to predict in describing behavior whether an individual makes the right or wrong decision. Furthermore, even decisions that appeared to be right at the time have in the end proven disastrous. The example that Toynbee uses is the decision that the emperors of Rome made in building a system of roads, with the result being that "all roads lead to Rome." What was intended to be a public works project for the benefit of trade and defense eventually became a barbarian-invasion route that led to the sacking and collapse of Rome.

Toynbee was right in positing challenge and response as his vision of the pattern of history. Therefore, in examining the evolution of the film industry, we reference Toynbee when we recognize that the decisions made by the studio heads, writers, directors, and corporate CEOs are not the only decisions possible and that the effects of those decisions, even if they seem right at the time, can in the end prove to be mistaken.

Let's take for instance the rise and fall of the Edison trust. No one could ever accuse Thomas Edison of being a man with a lack of vision. And, yet, when it came to motion pictures, he appeared to have a blind spot. He never recognized the true potential of their mass exhibition. It appears that his judgment was clouded by his experience with one of his earlier inventions, the phonograph. The phonograph and its progeny was, and still is, used as a personal medium. For the most part, records, tapes, and now discs are essentially produced for private consumption. But films, as it turns out, are much better viewed in a theater. Edison never saw the difference, and his refusal to recognize the exhibition potential of films led him to eschew its development as a mass medium. Instead, he decided to build a monopoly of filmmaking based on the collusion of the film technology producers. This decision turned out to be a fatal mistake for two reasons. First, others recognized the potential of film, and they acted to subvert and elude the monopoly. Furthermore, Edison made his decision to form a monopoly in an era of reform when the government was actively trying to break up trusts.

Edison's miscalculation led to the transfer of filmmaking into the hands of a rather small, ethnically homogenous group of European Jewish immigrants who just so happened to be the marketers of the Edison trust product. It is merely an accident of history that the Jews invested so heavily in the arcade and theater business at the turn of the century. In another era, another group, with their own eccentricities, would have likely come to dominate the film industry. But as it was, first-generation Eastern European Jews came to dominate the industry, and they brought with them their own set of idiosyncrasies.

Having been in the minority in both the Old World and the New World and, in fact, throughout most of their history, Jews were particularly conscious of their conspicuous outsider status. As a result and in order to produce a marketable product, the Jews of Hollywood attempted to "out-American the Americans." The films of the golden era of Hollywood cinema rarely stray from the established dogma of American culture. It is ironic that the films of the golden era that are now praised by some for their wholesomeness were more often than not produced by men with an accent and with a set of religious practices foreign to most Americans. And, as if to remind Jews of their outsider status, Hollywood Jews had to clear their product through the self-appointed, Christian-dominated production board that oversaw the content of their films throughout almost all of the golden era.

Therefore, the content of the Hollywood-era films should be seen in part as the Hollywood moguls' response to the challenge of making films for the majority culture that were not only acceptable but inoffensive. In response, the moguls were a remarkable success. But they eventually faced a set of challenges for which they were not prepared and made a series of decisions that led to the end of the monopoly of the golden era.

Just as Edison had failed to see the potential of mass-marketed, full-length dramatic feature films, the moguls failed to adapt to the threat of television. In addition, they had to react to the revival of the European film industry after the war but in a way that would conform to the production code. Their reaction to these challenges were the release of big-budget biblical epics and the Cinerama spectaculars,[5] bedroom farces of the 1950s, along with the introduction of a new genre known as *film noir*, which managed to slip below the radar screen of the censors. But in the end, it wasn't enough. Losing audiences and hemorrhaging money, the moguls' movie empires collapsed, to be bought up piecemeal by corporate conglomerates and corporate raiders.

The movie business was then rebuilt to conform to the business model of a modern, publicly held corporation. The studios both expanded and contracted their business. They got into amusement parks, television production, music, and, in regard to cinema, the financing and distribution of films. For the most part, studios outsourced the actual production of films, as would any other modern manufacturing corporation, which has been the structure of the movie industry more or less to this day. The product is technically competent, more often than not pedestrian, but generally profitable. In some cases, films these days, even big-budget ones, can be excellent, and a whole sector of specialty films known as *indies* has sprung up in the industry to cater to niche audiences (though, in fact, indies are often financed or at least distributed by the majors). These films are often daring and sometimes excellent. Finally, the industry has adapted in fits and starts to new technologies that allow for the viewing of films in private, on videotape and DVDs. Nevertheless, there is always going to be the problem of film piracy, which, as bad as it is in the United States, is worse abroad. Indeed, in 1995, President Bill Clinton precipitated a confrontation with the People's Republic of China over intellectual property rights, including that over the piracy of American music and films.

What are going to be the new challenges to the American film industry, and how will it respond? Probably the most recent notable challenge to the film industry establishment has been the remarkable success of Mel Gibson's *The Passion of the Christ*. This film, which may personally net Gibson as much as $300 million, was privately financed, targeted at an audience that was thought to be unprofitable, and promoted in a most unusual way. By keeping the production as secret as possible leading up to its release and by refusing to show the film in prerelease screenings to anyone but a sympathetic audience, *The Passion* generated a firestorm of controversy that helped promote its release in no other comparable way. Whether intentional or not, all of this innovation can't fail to attract the notice of the corporate Hollywood moguls. Does this suggest a market for religious films or what some call medieval religious films? Has Mel Gibson shown us a new way to promote blockbuster motion pictures?

Hollywood's initial reaction to the success of *The Passion* was that of denial. For example, as noted movie critic Leonard Maltin suggests,

> The history of the box office of Hollywood is studded with one-shot success stories. . . . The bulk of its success has to come from people with deep religious convictions, but perhaps an equal number of moviegoers have gone simply to see what all the shouting's about, people who might not otherwise go to see a biblical film.[6]

Then there was the more predictable response. Television shows based on biblical themes were quickly aired. For example, the made-for-television movie *Judas* was shown by ABC in the aftermath of the release of *The Passion*. *Judas* had actually been filmed in 2001 but was pulled out of the vault for the release of *The Passion*. In addition, the networks recycled other biblical movies, including Martin Scorsese's *The Last Temptation of Christ* (1988), a film that is absolutely loathed by the audience targeted for *The Passion*. Finally, even *Life of Brian* (1979), Monty Python's hysterically funny send-up on the New Testament, was scheduled for a theatrical re-release in 2004.

But what is more interesting about the rollout of *The Passion* is the fact that this is an individually financed statement of what, in this case, is a set of personal convictions. Is it possible that other individuals and groups will see the potential in *The Passion* for financing films to promote their own points of view? What *The Passion* makes clear is that there is plenty of talent available to make a first-class film without the direct participation of the film industry. Furthermore, there is just a chance that such a film will make money. Will *The Passion* touch off a wave of nontraditionally financed films that are produced by those with an ax to grind? One possible vision for the future of the film industry is the use of the film medium for the promotion of political and religious points of view. The only potential problem with this scenario is the expense involved in producing a film. Gibson had the money to produce his film—do others have the resources to respond in kind?

Indeed, the election of 2004 spawned competing campaign films. Michael Moore's *Fahrenheit 911* (2004) was a biting critique of the Bush administration and its handling of the September 11, 2001, attacks on the World Trade Center. Supporters of President Bush responded with two films of their own: *Celsius 41.11: The Temperature at Which the Brain . . . Begins to Die* (2004) and *Stolen Honor: Wounds That Never Heal* (2004). In one way or another, both films were wildly successful. On a $6 million budget, Moore's film grossed over $120 million,[7] and while neither *Celsius 41.11* nor *Stolen Honor* were commercial successes, they generated a tremendous amount of publicity for the case criticizing Senator John Kerry's Vietnam War record. The success of these films, along with that of *The Passion*, demonstrate the enduring power of film as a tool of propaganda, with the bonus being that when marketed in the right way to the right audience, specialty films such as *Fahrenheit 911* can turn a substantial profit (though, there is a debate over whether this film can be classified as a documentary). We are certain to see more of these privately financed, politically motivated films produced in the future.

THE CULTURAL CONTEXT

When David Easton, a prominent political scientist, writes about political systems, he discusses the context in which a system operates. Rather than determine what kind of public policy a system will produce, context—historical, geographical, and cultural—delimits the response.[8] Certain ideas, concepts, and conventions fall outside the boundaries of a society's context. Regardless of the technological opportunities or limitations of films and despite the corporate structure of the film industry, certain stories are either appropriate or inappropriate given the time and place in which a film is produced. Nevertheless, some verities, as discussed in previous chapters, are based in American political culture so that American films of the past, even when viewed today, still have a certain ring of truth. In the following section, I discuss the evolution of film content. The list and discussion are by no means exhaustive, but what follow are films representative of their time.

Way Down East (1920)

In *Way Down East*, directed by D. W. Griffith, Lillian Gish plays Anna, a young girl born of modest means. She is forced to live with the family of her wealthy cousins, where she meets the dashing ladies' man Lennox Sanderson (Lowell Sherman). Sanderson cons the innocent Anna into thinking that he wants to marry her, and he stages a fake wedding to get her into bed. Of course, as is always the case in these sorts of things, a pregnancy results. Sanderson rejects Anna and reveals the false pretenses under which he seduced her. To make things worse, Anna's mother dies, and the baby is born with an illness to which it eventually succumbs. Anna is now penniless and alone, scorned as a wanton woman. Anna begins to wander the roads and comes upon the house of the Bartlett family. The Bartletts show compassion toward her and take her in, where she draws the attention of the Bartletts' son David (Richard Barthelmess). But as fate would have it, the Bartletts are neighbors of the Sandersons, the family of the man who seduced Anna. Eventually, the truth comes out that Anna was involved with another man, and David's father feels compelled to throw Anna out of his house. In despair, Anna tries to commit suicide by jumping onto an ice flow in the dead of winter. David comes to the rescue, proclaims his love for Anna, and they get married and live happily ever after.

When the movie business started, many of the earliest feature-length films were adapted from stage plays. *Way Down East* had been an enormously popular stage play in the late nineteenth century, so it was an obvious choice for film adaptation. Thus, the film is both familiar to modern sensibilities and foreign. First, the plot has an obvious religious allegory. Anna is a martyr to society's cruelty. But through the proper application of religious doctrine, forgiveness and generosity, she is redeemed to find a fulfilling life. The film is Victorian rather than Edwardian in its mores, meaning that the act of sex outside of marriage is considered taboo so that for some who view the film today, the customs of the film may seem remarkably strict and arcane.

However, are we really so different today? While there isn't the same social stigma associated with illegitimacy, don't we still condemn women who have children outside of wedlock—despite the fact that most teenage mothers are seduced by men much older than themselves? There is one major difference at least. In theory, we try to get the fathers to pay for their sins. However, the effort is less than fulsome: it is almost exclusively a civil matter, and the father still probably assumes less of a stigma for bearing an "illegitimate" child than does the mother. The economic consequence for the mother is substantially worse as well. In other words, despite the fact that *Way Down East* is a silent film and the characters dress and act a little different, how much have we really changed as a society? The major difference is that without the divine intervention of David Bartlett, many young women today are condemned to ride the ice flow over the falls.

All Quiet on the Western Front (1930)

This is probably the greatest antiwar film of all time. Based on a novel of the same name, written by Erich Maria Remarque (who had himself been a German soldier in the First World War), the film was well received both critically (winning the Academy Award for Best Picture) and financially. On a personal note, when I first saw this film, in the 1960s, it blew me away. I was raised on John Wayne and James Bond, and I had never seen or read anything but about the glory of war. *All Quiet on the Western Front* has an entirely different take on war, one to that point I had never seen.

In the film, Paul Baumer, a young German high school student (played by Lew Ayers), is persuaded by his respected professor to join the army and go to war. In the army he finds friendship and camaraderie but also the waste and horror of war. The film is filled with heartbreaking scenes as the audience begins to grasp the pointlessness of war. One of the most moving scenes of all is the one in which Paul has to spend the night in a foxhole with a French soldier he has just stabbed. As the man dies before him, Paul comes to realize the dreadfulness of what he has just done. The French soldier, he finds, has a family; he feels pain; he is another young man who just happens, by accident of birth, to speak another language, and Paul has killed him. It is important not to reveal the end of the film. If you haven't seen it, you should; after you do, you can in good conscience consider yourself a student of politics and film.

This film will appear to modern sensibilities as being quite unusual. Besides the production values of the time, the film is about a theme, the pointlessness of war, that is rarely explored today. There was a brief period in the aftermath of the Vietnam War when filmmakers took a shot at antiwar themes—*Apocalypse Now* and *Platoon* are two notable examples. But one gets the sense that those two films and others don't go as far in condemning war as did *All Quiet*. The battle scenes in *Apocalypse Now* and *Platoon* are thrilling and cathartic, as if they solve some problem. And the main critique of war in these films reflects the debate of the time over the Vietnam War, which questioned the leadership that led us into war and the conduct of the war but never really the use of war as a way to solve problems.

That is what makes *All Quiet on the Western Front* unique. In the aftermath of World War I and the apparent failure of the war to change the international system, it appeared to Americans that the purpose of all that bloodshed had been pointless, except to line the pockets of the manufacturers of arms (the so-called merchants of death) and to protect the colonial holdings of the victorious European powers. *All Quiet on the Western Front* even goes so far as to question the usefulness of nationalism—in this case German nationalism but nationalism nonetheless. And, as such, the film provides us with a unique window into its time, the isolationist period that led up to World War II. Perhaps, then, *All Quiet on the Western Front* is the most daring and original film discussed in this section. It really has very little to do with our modern sensibilities, but it is nevertheless a window into an unprecedented period of our past.

Sergeant York (1940)

This film is a different take on World War I, but it isn't really about World War I. It is metaphor for facing what at the time was a menacing threat, the rise of fascism in Europe and in Asia. The film was an enormous success with both the audience and the critics, winning two Academy Awards (including Best Actor for Gary Cooper), being nominated for nine others, and ending up as one of the one hundred top-grossing films of all time.

Alvin C. York (Cooper) is a backwoods Tennessee farmer who has been raised by the "good book" to believe that the killing of another man is wrong. He leads a simple life with his only aspiration to get a good piece of bottomland. To that end he scraps and scuffles and even tries to use his marvelous skill at shooting to win the money that he needs in order to buy the land. All of this setup is unusually long and detailed and is intended to provide us with context as the main act begins. When the United States enters World War I, York is drafted. As a conscientious objector, York appeals his induction into the army but to no avail.

At the basic training camp, York is a good soldier, liked and respected by his fellows but distrusted by his superiors, who see in his record that he tried to claim conscientious objector status. But there is one thing about York that everyone admires: his remarkable marksmanship. Because of his skill as a shooter and because of his natural talent as a leader, the captain of his company proposes to promote York to corporal. But the captain is concerned about York's reluctance to kill the enemy in battle. In what is one of the most surreal scenes in the movie, York and his captain debate the morality of killing. York relies on the Bible. "Thou shall not kill" is pretty unambiguous. The captain can't argue with that. So the captain gives York a book on American history to read—presumably to demonstrate that the United States, which is a good thing, was actually founded by violence, which in pursuit of a good thing is acceptable. He then sends York on leave to ponder his response.

York goes back to the Tennessee hills and reads the book on American history. In the end he comes to the conclusion that killing in the pursuit of the good is acceptable. This is a strange transformation for someone who is quite obviously a fundamentalist who believes in the literalism of the Bible. But as a plotline convention, it is the only way to justify what follows.

Cut away to France and the battlefield. York's company is assigned to assault a hilltop controlled by several German machine-gun nests. The casualties are appalling, and York is thrust into a position of command. On his own initiative, York, circling around the Germans, wipes out an entire German machine-gun nest and captures almost one hundred prisoners. The producers even use some comic relief in the battle scene when York makes a noise like a turkey, causing the Germans to pop up and be shot in turn. As the Americans march the Germans off to captivity, a German officer pulls out a pistol and shoots one of York's friends. The German is then shot in turn. This incident is a sop to German perfidy.

In the aftermath of the battle, York's captain asks York how he overcame his reluctance to kill his fellow man. York replies that he has come to the realization that you have to take lives to save lives, ironically a justification later to be used to defend the nuclear destruction of Hiroshima and Nagasaki. York is then awarded a lot of medals and gets the bottomland he always wanted.

Sergeant York reflects one side of a spirited debate in 1940–1941 over the advisability of getting involved in the war, which had just broken out in Europe the year before. Pacifism of the kind reflected in *All Quiet on the Western Front* was still quite widespread in the United States along with a strain of isolationism that was making it difficult for Franklin Roosevelt to assist the British and their allies in the war against the Germans. It may seem strange in the modern context to realize that until the attack on Pearl Harbor and before the German atrocities of World War II became widely known, there was both popular support for the German cause, even the fascist style of government, and widespread opposition to the war. *Sergeant York* is an answer to most of these objections. The film takes the pacifist message head on, and even the Germans are portrayed as evil.

While the names have changed, the subjects of modern films are not so different. After the war, the Russian and Chinese communists were the enemy, then the Arabs after that.[9] In order to keep current, Hollywood is always trying to capitalize on the enemy du jour. Sometimes the enemy is treated in metaphor. In *Star Wars* (1977) Darth Vader, wearing an exaggerated German helmet, represents an evil empire intent on ruling the universe on behalf of "the dark side." The analogy to the Cold War is inescapable, with a random Nazi reference thrown in. Even President Ronald Reagan referred to the Soviet Union as the evil empire.

What makes *Sergeant York* unusual is that rather than a film that reinforces existing beliefs or provides a cathartic release in seeing our enemies vanquished, the film is an advocate, a part of the political debate of its time. In general, the moguls stayed away from anything but the most superficial treatment of political controversies (see, for example, *Gentleman's Agreement*, 1947); or, when they did enter the political fray, it was through themes related to political slam dunks, such as prison reform in the South (*I Am a Fugitive from a Chain Gang*, 1932). In this case, however, the war in Europe was important enough in 1940 for the moguls—specifically, those of Warner Bros.—to take a chance on a film that advocated what at the time was a controversial point of view.

The Bridge on the River Kwai (1957)

The top-grossing films from the 1950s in order of box office receipts (controlled for inflation) are *The Ten Commandments* (1956), *Ben Hur* (1959), *Sleeping Beauty* (1959), *The Robe* (1953), *Around the World in 80 Days* (1956), *The Greatest Show on Earth* (1952), *Lady and the Tramp* (1955), *The Bridge on the River Kwai* (1957), *House of Wax* (1953), *Peter Pan* (1953), and *The Caine Mutiny* (1954). With the exception of the Disney cartoons, this is a pretty forgettable lineup. In the 1950s Hollywood operated under pressure from three sources: television, the revival of the European film industry, and the production code. To meet the challenge of the avant-garde, the tiny screen, and the code, Hollywood was forced to rely on technological gimmicks and biblical epics. *House of Wax* (1953), for example, was shot in 3-D, requiring patrons to wear plastic glasses. A number of terrific films were made in the 1950s, such as *The African Queen* (1951), *On the Waterfront* (1954), *North by Northwest* (1959), and a number of others, but they did little to forestall the collapse of the studio system. But probably the most memorable statement of the times was *The Bridge on the River Kwai*.

Of its eight Academy Award nominations, *The Bridge on the River Kwai* won seven, including Best Picture. It is also one of the top-grossing films of all time. In it, British colonel Nicholson (Alec Guinness, who won the Oscar for best actor) matches wits with Japanese prisoner-of-war camp commander Colonel Saito (Sessue Hayakawa). This is a film about a clash of cultures; it is also about duty and the obligation of soldiers in time of war. Colonel Nicholson is a by-the-book commander who, prisoner or not, is very much in command of his troops. Colonel Saito is a classic Japanese warrior. He cannot understand the lack of shame and the obstinacy, even in the face of death, of his nemesis Colonel Nicholson. Nicholson, for his part, has simply no interest in Colonel Saito's Japanese point of view. To Nicholson, there is the British army way of doing things and the wrong way of doing things. In the end, it is he who breaks Colonel Saito and not the other way around.

This film has a number of unusual plotlines, unusual in the sense that they deviate from the typical war film of the 1940s. For one thing, in a departure from typical Japanese stereotyping, Colonel Saito is treated as a rather sympathetic character. There is also the question of whether in the exercise of his sense of duty Colonel Nicholson is actually collaborating with the enemy. One of the most remarkable characters in this film is Commander Shears (William Holden). For his time, Shears is quite unlike the usual movie war hero and is in fact more of an antihero (presaging the characters portrayed in *MASH* [1970], a classic 1960s-era counterculture film). Shears is a common seaman who, when his ship is torpedoed off the coast of Thailand, assumes the identity of a naval officer in the hope of getting better treatment as a prisoner of war. He escapes the camp where he is held with Colonel Nicholson and maintains the fiction of his rank even after the British rescue him. When asked by the British to help guide them back into the jungle to blow up the bridge that Colonel Nicholson and his men are building, Shears demurs. Only when he is confronted with the fact that the British have discovered his ruse is he forced to "volunteer" to return to the river Kwai. But Shears is acting against type. He is not a coward; he is not a pacifist; for lack of a better word, he is a survivor. As Shears puts it, in addressing one of the gung-ho British commandos,

> You make me sick with your heroics. There's a stench of death about you. You carry it in your pack like the plague. Explosives and [suicide] pills—they go well together, don't they? And with you it's just one thing or the other: destroy a bridge or destroy yourself. This is just a game, this war! You and Colonel Nicholson, you're two of a kind, crazy with courage. For what? How to die like a gentleman . . . how to die by the rules . . . when the only important thing is how to live like a human being.[10]

After two world wars and Korea, maybe Americans had had enough. Maybe they were ready to accept this type of character. And in the end, when the bridge on the river Kwai lies in ruins and Colonel Nicholson, Colonel Saito, and Shears all are dead, the last words of the film, uttered by a cynical British doctor observing the scene, are "madness, sheer madness." *The Bridge on the River Kwai* is not your typical war film. In it we can see the stirrings of the 1960s.

Lonely Are the Brave (1962)

Unlike the other films discussed, *Lonely Are the Brave* did not do well at the box office. The studios limited release of the film, and while the film did well in Europe, it didn't have much success in the United States. This relatively modest film, shot in black and white, is now considered a classic. And if you can ignore period costumes and props, the film holds up well because it is based on a theme that was and still is basic to American politics.

The back story to the film is that it was written by Dalton Trumbo, who had been blacklisted by the Hollywood studios in the early 1950s for not naming names of fellow movie-industry employees who were suspected of being communists. From that point onward, Trumbo had not been permitted to submit scripts under his own name. So, at great financial cost to himself, he was forced to hire a front, a writer who submitted scripts written by Trumbo under another name.[11] Trumbo—who was a friend of Kirk Douglas, star of the film—was not even allowed to set foot on the grounds of a Hollywood studio during the latter half of the 1950s.

However, by the early 1960s Douglas and the producers of the film decided that the time had passed for the blacklist and that Trumbo deserved to have his name on the credits of the films he wrote. His first public attributions after the blacklist were for the enormously successful films *Spartacus* (1960) and *Exodus* (1960). Threatened boycotts of these films failed. Nevertheless, two years later the studios inexplicably limited the release of *Lonely Are the Brave.*

Lonely Are the Brave opens with a cowboy camp, a smoking campfire, a horse, and a wide-open plain. At first we get the impression that this is a typical Western set in the late nineteenth century, but then a jet flies overhead. Jack Burns is a cowboy from the old school. He doesn't have a driver's license, a social security card, a home, a car, or any of the accoutrements of modern life. He is constantly at odds with the modern world. When he runs into a barbed wire fence, he cuts it. When he runs into a highway, he crosses it on his horse, a dangerous proposition to all involved. He follows his own rules, which are not without morality, just not the rules followed by the rest of the world so that when he finds out that a friend has been thrown in jail for transporting illegal immigrants, Jack thinks nothing of getting into a barroom brawl to get himself into jail to visit and try to help his friend. That being done, he then decides to break the two of them out of jail and make a run for Mexico.

His friend Paul won't go. Paul has a family; he has responsibilities; and he can't live his life on the run. This is the central conflict of the film. On the one hand, we want the freedom enjoyed by Jack Burns to go where we want and do what we want. On the other hand, we have responsibilities that have their own compensations. By the same token, at the societal level, we want to have the freedom to do whatever we want, but because we live in a community, we are limited by the rights of others. There is a constant tension in the United States between our freedom and our responsibilities. Everything from the debate over taxes to the clash over the environmental movement is symptomatic of the conflict between the rights of the individual and the health of the community. Nowhere is this conflict more affecting than in the American West, where the disappearance of wilderness has destroyed a way of life. In that respect *Lonely Are the Brave* is an achingly poignant film that should resonate at some level with most Americans.

National Lampoon's Animal House (1978)

Without exaggeration, this film shaped a generation. It shaped a generation of films; it shaped a generation of comic actors; and to some extent, it shaped the youth generation of the 1980s. Let me say from the start that this film is funny—very funny. And on this point, I am not alone. *Animal House* is one of the fifty top-grossing films of all time, with box office receipts of almost $300 million (in 1998 dollars). It is also politically incorrect in practically every way imaginable. It is misogynistic, racist, anti-establishment, anti-intellectual, and about every other *anti* you can think of, but at the same time it's just a lot of fun.

For those of you from another planet, the film centers on the Delta house, a fraternity at mythical Faber College. The Delta house is the filthiest, raunchiest, most slovenly fraternity house on campus, and Dean Wormer means to close it down. Bluto (John Belushi), Otter (Tim Matheson), Boon (Peter Riegert), and Pinto (Tom Hulce) lead the Delta house through a series of hijinks that have become the rights of passage for many students in college, including a toga party, a road trip (spawning a movie of the same name), seducing the dean's wife (well, that doesn't quite qualify as a rite of passage), a food fight in the cafeteria, stealing a midterm exam, and a number of other lighthearted and, fortunately, relatively nonconsequential adventures. The picture ends in a paroxysm of cheerful destruction as the Delta house lays waste to the local town in retaliation for being placed on "double-secret probation" by the dean. As the credits role, we are informed that the misfits of the Delta house are the leaders of tomorrow, and in some sense that is true. The future is now.

Animal House is distinctive in its complete disregard for convention. In laying waste to the niceties of gender, ethnic, and other social relations, the movie not only makes it fun to flaunt conventional niceties; it makes it cool. A whole generation of moviegoers has developed through this movie and other influences contempt for civility, often sneered at as political correctness. They are, after all, free to do whatever they want. In that sense, there is a connection between *Animal House* and *Lonely Are the Brave.* Jack Burns and the boys at the Delta house have something in common when they flaunt authority. But the difference is that Burns flaunts authority on principle; the boys at the Delta house flaunt authority because it feels good. In that sense, the philosophy of the Delta house is nihilism.[12] Their only motivation to act is to feel good, so that when thinking and feeling become indistinguishable, as individuals they are little more than the sum of their appetites. In that sense, using the term *animal house* to describe the Delta house is probably right on the mark.

This sort of coarse humor has now become the discourse of American media entertainment. It is not just in the movies that this sort of *Animal House*–like, politically incorrect humor is on display. It is on television, too. For example, see the cartoon series *South Park*. In books, see the writings of P. J. O'Rourke. It has even entered our political realm as talk radio, which is mostly dominated by mainly secular conservative commentators and which owes much of its style to the kind of politically incorrect comedy rolled out in *Animal House*. In appropriating the humor of the Delta house, conservatives have made the ideology of Eisenhower, Nixon, Reagan, and Bush cool.

Raiders of the Lost Ark (1981)

In some ways, the 1980s resemble the 1950s in the sense that there is a disconnect between films that achieved financial success and films that achieved critical success. For the audience of the eighties, political commentary was out and escapism was in. Contrast the films of the era that achieved critical success with those that achieved financial success. On the critical side, Academy Award winners include *Ordinary People* (1980), *Chariots of Fire* (1981), *Gandhi* (1982), *Terms of Endearment* (1983), *Amadeus* (1984), *Out of Africa* (1985), *Platoon* (1986), *The Last Emperor* (1988), and *Driving Miss Daisy* (1989). These are some terrific films, but they are generally downers. In all but a couple, the main character dies in the end. That's not the kind of entertainment that excites when "it's morning in America."[13] On the other hand, the top-grossing films of the era were *E. T.* (1982), *The Empire Strikes Back* (1980), *Return of the Jedi* (1983), *Raiders of the Lost Ark* (1981), *Beverly Hills Cop* (1984), *Ghostbusters* (1984), *Batman* (1989), *Back to the Future* (1985), and *Tootsie* (1982). These are some pretty good films too, but with the exception of *Tootsie*, they are all in one way or another cartoons.

In *Raiders of the Lost Ark*, mild-mannered archeology professor Indiana Jones (Harrison Ford) dons his signature hat, grabs his bullwhip, and heads off to collect (steal) the artifacts of ancient civilizations. Nowadays, no self-respecting archeologist would despoil the site of an ancient civilization by removing its artifacts. But in the era that the film is set, leading up to World War II, Jones is in the business of collecting for his university's museum in the United States.

The film opens with Jones hacking his way through a South American jungle to retrieve a golden idol. What follows is about twenty minutes of death-defying, nonstop action and special effects that have become the signature of many a Steven Spielberg film. In the end, however, Jones is frustrated by his archrival Belloq, an evil French archeologist who steals the idol from him. Jones barely escapes with his life.

Jones is then enlisted by the U.S. government to search for the fabled ark of the covenant, which apparently bestows on those who posses it the power of God. U.S. intelligence services fear that the Nazis are close to finding the ark. The problem is that if they possess the ark, they will have the power to conquer the world. Indiana Jones accepts the mission and sets off on his quest. Along the way he meets up with Marian (played by Karen Allen), an old flame; a sadistic gestapo agent; an old Egyptian friend; various evildoers, including a monkey who turns out to be a Nazi spy; and, finally, his old nemesis Belloq. In the end, through a series of hair-raising adventures, Jones retrieves the ark; God smites the Nazis; and in the last scene, the ark, now stored in a crate, is carted off to a corner of a vast, government warehouse to be lost for another millennium.

This movie is a lot of fun, but it isn't Shakespeare. It has marvelous special effects, handsome characters, and lots of action, including some terrific "happy killing"[14] and the best "face melt" in motion picture history. In that sense, the film is analogous to its era, as the United States faced down the evil empire of the Soviet Union, a feat led by a handsome, swashbuckling president (himself a former actor) engaged in a variety of adventures, including the full-scale invasion of a small tropical island, Grenada.

President Reagan was a master of the art of the political spectacle. A spectacle is a staged event designed to elicit an emotional rather than an intellectual response.[15] In that sense, as pure entertainment, most movies are spectacle. So it is not too much of a stretch to suggest that, because of his skill in inducing an emotional response, former actor Ronald Reagan became our first movie president, one who in his days as an actor could have played Indiana Jones. The problem is that in the movies inducing an emotional response is entertaining; in a political system, inducing an emotional response (fear, anger, greed) is antidemocratic. After all, in a democracy, voters should have to think to vote. Therefore, in the sense that it was the ultimate spectacle, *Raiders of the Lost Ark* was a movie for its times.

Malcolm X (1992)

The remarkable thing about this picture is that it was made at all. To suggest in a previous era that a mainstream Hollywood film depicting the life of a Muslim African American activist who called for resistance "by any means necessary"[16] would get made and make money would be preposterous.[17] Civil rights issues had been treated in the past but mostly from the white political perspective or in a sort of idealized way from the black perspective that soft-sold the effects of discrimination. One can in some sense track the progression of civil rights through its movies—those of its era and those that predate it. First there was the minstrel show as depicted in *Show Boat* (1936, remade in 1951), where the music is lovely, where the dancing is great (*The Littlest Rebel*, 1935), but where stereotypes abound. Then there was the "they are just like us" school of films, represented by *The Defiant Ones* (1958), a film in which a black and a white convict are chained together and have to learn to get along. Then in the earliest days of the civil rights era, Hollywood took on more controversial issues, such as mixed-race marriages, as in *Guess Who's Coming to Dinner* (1967). Hollywood later wrote its own history of the civil rights movement in *Mississippi Burning* (1988), a film in which blacks and civil rights activists in general have remarkably little to do with the success of the civil rights movement. In fact, the protagonists in the film are two

FBI agents who presumably were taking time off from spying on Dr. Martin Luther King (on the orders of J. Edgar Hoover, director of the FBI) to finally enforce the law.[18] In *Driving Miss Daisy* (1989) the theme is that blacks have been discriminated against but so have many of us. The film is well done but walks a fine line of recalling the depiction of blacks from an earlier era.

In *Malcolm X* director Spike Lee takes civil rights conventions head on. In the opening scene, when he features the police beating of Rodney King, he implies that the issues of discrimination and racism in America are still very much a part of our nation's culture. He then proceeds to deliver a sympathetic, some would say idolizing, biography of one of the most polarizing figures in the middle part of the twentieth century. While there are mistakes of emphasis and those of fact, Lee's movie is not just a good film; it is an important film.[19] Probably, not many whites have read Malcolm X's autobiography. In viewing this film, they may get the only information they ever receive about Malcolm X and a major part of the civil rights movement. Our leaders are anxious to tout the nonviolent approach adopted by Dr. King, but in Malcolm's more strident politics, we get a sense of the rage in the black community that sometimes and in some segments exists right below the surface. In that sense, this movie is important because it somewhat accurately documents and much more accurately engenders the ethos of the civil rights era from the black perspective.

Parenthetically, Denzel Washington was marvelous in the role of Malcolm X. He didn't get the Academy Award for Best Actor, but he should have. Instead, he received the award for his work in the film *Training Day* (2001), which represents the latest stage in the evolution of black-white relations on-screen. In it, Washington portrays a crooked cop who plays villain to Ethan Hawke's hero. The fact that Washington happens to be black is of little significance to the plot. In that sense, *Training Day* is colorblind, and while we still struggle with issues of race in this country, that ethnicity is unremarkable in this film and others is an advance in and of itself.

CONCLUSION

Without the motivating force of the Nazi or Soviet threat and without the pressure put on the economy by the Great Depression and even in the aftermath of September 11, we have lost some of the shared feeling of community that comes with pursuit of a common cause. Thus, while the end of the Cold War and the economic boom of the 1990s are by any standard wonderful things, they come at a price—the loss of community. Consequently, movie plots based on a premise of self-sacrifice for the community—for someone other than our immediately families—seem a little silly in the modern context.

Take, for instance, the recently released film *The Man in the Iron Mask* (1998), which, all in all, is not a bad film. It is one of a plethora of makes, remakes, and spin-offs of the nineteenth-century novels of Alexandre Dumas. I was, however, a little disturbed by an underlying message of the film, that the four musketeers were largely motivated by a sense of loyalty to one another rather than to France. This was not my reading of the Alexandre Dumas novel so that when in the film D'Artagnan seems motivated by a love for his king (not necessarily the person but the office), I was pleasantly surprised by the subtle faithfulness of the movie plot to the novel (and to an eighteenth-century notion of patriotism). We come to find, however, that this is not the case at all. It turns out that the reason why D'Artagnan is so protective of the king is that in years past D'Artagnan had an affair with the queen mother and is in fact the king's father. Besides the fact that this plot device is preposterous, it's also a cop-out. Apparently, the scriptwriters either did not understand or could not conceive of a plotline that would permit D'Artagnan to be loyal to the king (no matter how rotten a person he was) for the simple reason that Louis was the king of France. The plot continues along in that vein, completely obscuring any notion of loyalty to something other than family and friends.

It turns out that I'm not the only one who thinks this way. Communitarians from the Right also get a sense that the United States is losing its sense of community. On June 24, 1998, the National Commission on Civic Renewal issued a report that suggested that the United States is becoming "a nation of spectators." The commission is cochaired by former education secretary and Republican morals czar William J. Bennett and former Democratic senator Sam Nunn (Georgia). The following statement best summarizes the report:

> Never have we had so many opportunities for participation, yet rarely have we felt so powerless. In a time that cries out for civic action, we are in danger of becoming a nation of spectators.

Among other things, the report recommends that the entertainment industry be held "as accountable for civic harm" as much as the tobacco industry is for physical harm.[20]

Our nation, to a certain degree, may have lost its sense of community. However, not all modern sensibilities are bad. Up until the early twentieth century, we tended to ignore the subservient position of women, minorities, and Native Americans. Accordingly, our society did indeed seem a gentler place at the time. Apparently, however, we only felt that way because some of the more egregious injustices in our society were being ignored. With the modern enlightenment brought about by the civil rights movement, we have come to recognize that at least some of our nation's success was built on a rotten foundation.

So why don't they make 'em like they used to? The answer is quite simple. They don't make 'em like they used to because they can't. In part this is true because the economics of the film industry is not what it was in its golden era—a monopoly. Filmmakers didn't have to respond to a captive market in the past in the same way that they respond to a free market now. A cynical public would not sit through a 1930s version of *Mr. Smith Goes to Washington*. What now passes for a realistic depiction of American politics is just as cynical and exaggerated as the original *Mr. Smith Goes to Washington* is in its own over-the-top patriotic way. Critics today would probably pan

Frank Capra's *Mr. Smith Goes to Washington* just as they have praised two of the most cynical movies ever produced about American politics: *Bulworth* (1998) and *Wag the Dog* (1997). For better and for worse, the public has a dynamic sense of what is real. No longer able or willing to depict the value of sacrifice to the community or to abide racist discrimination, the films of today reflect modern sensibilities both good and bad—as will the films of tomorrow.

Most films produced for general release are not great art. They reflect the simple reality that in order to recoup the enormous cost of an elaborate production, film studios must cater/pander to a low common denominator. This is not to mention the fact that since the lion's share of an American film's profits is derived in foreign release, modern high-budget filmmakers must be conscious of how their films will translate into Urdu, Chinese, or French. Such an economic imperative dictates that films in need of a large foreign gross contain more physical action, less dialogue, and scripts that are much less reflective of core—and sometimes, from the world's perspective, eccentric—American values. But what is particularly exciting about the current market is that not all blockbusters are expensive to make. Every once in a while, a low-budget film makes a breakthrough or is at least modestly successful, and that fact encourages the production of ever more ambitious films by independent production companies. Although many indies are not all that good, they are at least reflective of a dynamic, creative environment that will eventually produce films just as good as *Citizen Kane*. Therefore, we should be relatively optimistic about the future quality of American film.

Finally, it is quite remarkable how little modern technology has changed the character of film. A bad story is still a bad story no matter how many computer-generated graphics, long shots from a helicopter, car chases, face melts, high school cheerleaders in short skirts, or graphic sex acts it employs. Film is still, after all, a two-dimensional medium. Special effects can never compete with the Technicolor of the imagination. Nevertheless, there appears to be a niche for special effects–based films. *Twister*, a film without a plot that basically stars a special effect, ranks fifty-sixth among the top-grossing films of all time (adjusted for inflation).[21] That ranking probably means that we will have to endure ever more elaborate and mindless films of the same ilk. But then again, we don't have to go see them.

What this ultimately means is that they don't make 'em like they used to, and that is both a good-news and a bad-news story. The good news is that in the wide-ranging and dynamic market for films, there are many good, creative, and uplifting products to be consumed. Unfortunately, many of the good films are not very popular, and many of the bad ones are. But such is the nature of a free market. Should we aspire to control the market, say, by censoring or restricting the production of films, we won't just return to the days of the golden era; we will also be returning to the days when a vast assortment of topics of social import and historical significance were off-limits to film.

Nevertheless, there are those who attempt to censor films. The next chapter explores the general issue of film censorship. Each form of censorship brings with it a set of good, bad, and unintended effects. Thus, as an alternative to the free market, censorship probably isn't worth the effort and may in fact be downright dangerous.

Feature Film: *Mr. Smith Goes to Washington* (2004)

Both the good and the bad of our society are reflected in the content of our dramas—thus, the reason why they don't make 'em like they used to. The rights and wrongs of society have changed dramatically across time—and it is not just that we tolerate more violence and explicit sexual behavior in our films. Beyond simply graphic depictions, our modern dramas contain subtle (and not so subtle) distinctions that make it impossible to remake for popular consumption the great films of the past. To illustrate my point, for my feature film, I have rewritten Mr. Smith Goes to Washington *from a twenty-first-century perspective.*

Mr. Smith Goes to Washington. *Courtesy of M.P. & T.V. Photo Archive.*

Jefferson Smith (Josh Hartnett) is the lead guitarist in a fabulously successful rock band called the Boys Camp. He's just turned thirty-five and is having a midlife crisis. Somehow the fame and fortune aren't enough. He wants a new gig, so he decides that it would be cool to run for the U.S. Senate. Much to the surprise of the political pundits, he beats a skilled and well-financed opponent in the primary, and because of his basically unlimited financial resources, he trounces the candidate from the other party in the general election.

He buys a mansion in Georgetown and takes off for Washington in his private jet. He brings his roadies, along with the rest of his band, to act as his staff. He announces through his publicist that the goal of his first term in office will be to "rock the Capitol."

When he arrives in his office, he sees one lone secretary at work. Clarissa Sanders (Melissa Joan Hart) has worked on the Hill for a couple of different senators and knows the legislative process pretty well. She is a mousy-looking young woman with glasses, a shapeless dress, and frizzy hair. Since nobody in his troop knows anything about the legislative process or the Senate, Jeff keeps Clarrissa on to help him draft and pass his first piece of legislation, to change the national anthem from "The Star-Spangled Banner" to "Stairway to Heaven," by Led Zeppelin.

Of course the other, less-than-hip senators won't go for it. After all, they're, like, stuck in the twentieth century or something. Clarrissa thinks it's a joke, too, but at least it's a job. But after a while, Jeff's animal magnetism ignites something more elemental in her soul. For Jeff's part, he begins to see Clarrissa's inner beauty. At first, he treats her like any other groupie, but Clarrissa won't have any of it. She needs to know a guy before she will go to bed with him. So for the first time in years, finding that he actually has to woo a woman, Jeff begins to romance Clarrissa.

In the meantime, the rest of the senators get together and decide to teach this young upstart a lesson. The fact that he is a famous rock star means nothing to them, so they don't appoint him to any committees, and his legislation doesn't go anywhere. Eventually, they vow to kick him out of the Senate altogether, so a group of senators initiate an investigation into corruption in the rock world, in which Jeff is a prime target.

On the verge of being expelled from the Senate, Jeff takes to the floor to filibuster in favor of rock fans everywhere. He sings songs, writes lyrics, and, in general, performs on C-Span II as if it were another Jerry Lewis telethon. Rockers from all over the country crowd the Senate chamber. Concerts dedicated to Jeff are organized all over the country. At first, just R&B, blues, and country join in, but then come jazz groups and even symphony orchestras. The entire music community is united behind Jeff. Groupies line the rails of the Senate chamber, but Jeff has eyes only for Clarrissa (who has miraculously undergone a complete makeover).

Eventually, the power of rock wins over the country. The Senate folds under the pressure. The United States adopts "Stairway to Heaven" as its national anthem, and Jeff asks Clarrissa to be his main squeeze in the White House.

EXERCISE

Okay, sounds a bit silly, but why don't you pick a major feature film from the past and rewrite the plot according to the politics and the cultural sensibilities of the modern era.

NOTES

1. ShowBizData, "TV Companies Now Wary of Docudramas, Say Producers," November 20, 2003, www.showbizdata.com/contacts/picknews.cfm?ID=33994 (accessed August 4, 2005).

2. Added to the viewing experience of seeing *Lost in Space* was one of the most dreadful screenings of a film I have experienced outside of viewing super-eight films of my family's driving trip across the country. In its screening of *Lost in Space* the theater had the sound turned up so loud that it was unbearable. When I asked a theater employee to turn it down, I got a teenager who told me that he didn't know how. The popcorn was much too salty; the theater was filthy, as were the bathrooms—and this was the first showing of the day. It would be nice that, along with technological changes in making a film, improvements would also be made in the screening of films. Improvements in popcorn technology or bathroom cleanliness may be too much to hope for.

3. James Monaco, *How to Read a Film: Movies, Media, Multimedia*, 3rd ed. (New York: Oxford University Press, 2000), 525.

4. Arnold J. Toynbee, *A Study of History* (London: Oxford University Press, 1972), 97.

5. Cinerama was a film-display technique that attempted to re-create the full range of human vision. The technique involved the use of a giant concave viewing screen with three projection screens shot by three cameras. Cinerama debuted in 1952 in the travelogue *This Is Cinerama*, which ran for only thirteen weeks in one theater in New York City and was nonetheless the top-grossing film for the year. See Greg Kimble, "This Is Cinerama" *Cinema Technology*, December 2002, www.cineramaadventure.com/kimblearticle.htm (accessed August 23, 2005).

6. Reuters, "Repeat of 'The Passion' Seen as Leap of Faith," March 17, 2004, http://msnbc.msn.com/id/4550687 (accessed August 4, 2005).

7. Internet Movie Database, "News for Fahrenheit 9/11," www.imdb.com/title/tt0361596/business (accessed December 24, 2004).

8. David Easton, *A Systems Analysis of Political Life* (New York: Wiley, 1967), particularly chap. 7.

9. See Jack Shaheen, *Reel Bad Arabs: How Hollywood Vilifies a People* (New York: Interlink, 2001).

10. Internet Movie Database, "Memorable Quotes from *The Bridge on the River Kwai*," www.imdb.com/title/tt0050212/quotes (accessed August 4, 2005).

11. One of the screenplays that Trumbo wrote under a pseudonym actually won an Oscar: *The Brave One* (1956). Woody Allen starred in a film on just this subject, titled *The Front* (1976).

12. "Nihilism is the belief that all values are baseless and that nothing can be known or communicated. It is often associated with extreme pessimism and a radical skepticism that condemns existence. A true nihilist would believe in nothing, have no loyalties, and no purpose other than, perhaps, an impulse to destroy." Alan Pratt, "Nihilism," *Internet Encyclopedia of Philosophy*, www.utm.edu/research/iep/n/nihilism.htm (accessed August 7, 2005).

13. This was Ronald Reagan's catchphrase for his 1980 presidential campaign.

14. *Happy killing* is a term that can be used to describe cartoon killing or killing without consequence.

15. For a complete discussion of the idea of a presidential spectacle, see Bruce Miroff, "The Presidency and the Public: Leadership as Spectacle," in *The Presidency and the Political System*, ed. Michael Nelson, 3rd ed. (Washington, D.C.: CQ Press, 1990), 289–313; or Bruce Miroff,

Icons of Democracy: American Leaders as Heroes, Aristocrats, Dissenters, and Democrats (New York: Basic, 1993).

16. See Malcolm X's speech "Ballot or Bullets," April 3, 1964, www.americanrhetoric.com/speeches/malcolmxballot.htm (accessed August 4, 2005).

17. So-called *blaxploitation* ("black-exploitation") films—the most prominent example of which is *Shaft* (1971)—had been financially successful, but they were shot on small budgets and were of poor production quality.

18. For a good discussion of the historical inaccuracies of both fact and emphasis in this film, see William H. Chafe, "Mississippi Burning," in *Past Imperfect: History According to the Movies*, ed. Mark C. Carnes (New York: Henry Holt, 1996), 274–77.

19. On the inaccuracies of the film, see Clayborn Carson, "Malcolm X," in Carnes, *Past Imperfect*, 278–83.

20. Quoted in Associated Press, "Report: Civic Life Eroding in the U.S.," *New York Times*, June 24, 1998.

21. In the middle of the film, I went out for popcorn and found the longest line possible at the concession stand.

SUGGESTED READING

Carnes, Mark C., ed. *Past Imperfect: History According to the Movies*. New York: Henry Holt, 1996.

Gabler, Neal. *Life the Movie: How Entertainment Conquered Reality*. New York: Knopf, 1998.

Kauffmann, Stanley. *Regarding Film: Criticism and Comment*. Baltimore: Johns Hopkins University Press, 2001.

Miroff, Bruce. *Icons of Democracy: American Leaders as Heroes, Aristocrats, Dissenters, and Democrats*. New York: Basic, 1993.

Shaheen, Jack. *Reel Bad Arabs: How Hollywood Vilifies a People*. New York: Interlink, 2001.

7

Movies, Censorship, and the Law

Make no mistake about it, American films are censored now and always have been. When we talk about the advisability of film censorship, it is not a discussion of whether or not but how and how much. Films are censored in one of three ways: by the market, by the industry, or by the government. The real question in the debate over film censorship is what form of censorship should take place and under what circumstances. In this chapter I examine the pros and cons of, as well as the reality of, each form of censorship.

CENSORSHIP IN THE MARKET: BIAS AND BOYCOTTS

The market censors film in two ways: through the decisions that consumers make and through those that producers make. A vigorous debate centers on which influence is more important. Specifically, is marketing an art or a science?[1] In the main, as discussed in previous chapters, and in the absence of market distortions, consumers ultimately choose what products to consume. Thus, for the most part, consumers drive film content. To assume otherwise is to assume (1) that filmmakers have some hidden agenda that they will pursue at the expense of their profits and in disregard of the bottom line of their now publicly held companies or (2) that there is some kind of outside, third influence, such as the government, that is an active player in the regulation of film content.

As discussed in previous chapters, the first assumption is difficult to support. It is remarkable that the critics of the film industry's moral and political character are erstwhile capitalists (Marxist critics excluded) who forget all that they know about economics when it comes to analyzing the film industry. Granted that Hollywood filmmakers tend to be liberals, there still doesn't seem to be much evidence to suggest that any kind of conspiracy centered in Southern California is intent on corrupting the morals of our youth. This is especially true in the current competitive market for films. A movie executive with an agenda beyond making money is cruising for a financial loss.

There are, of course, subtle exceptions to this rule. Don't cross Hollywood and expect to get away with it! In the 1990s, when the Chinese government looked the other way while Hollywood films, CDs, and other entertainment products were being pirated for a billion Chinese consumers, the result was a literal anti-Chinese film festival that included *Seven Years in Tibet* (1997), *Kundun* (1997), and *Red Corner* (1997). And, yes, it is probably the case that the religious Right takes it on the chin as well when people like Jerry Falwell are depicted in an uncomplimentary manner in films such as *The People vs. Larry Flynt* (1996), a film that celebrates, of all things, *Penthouse* publisher Larry Flynt's role as a defender of civil liberties. But Falwell and his crowd don't go to the movies (to paraphrase a famous line from the film *Apocalypse Now*). Why should Hollywood care what he thinks?

But this brings to mind a more subtle form of censorship produced by the market. If certain groups don't have economic clout or visibility or if they are not an audience for film, their depictions in film can be uncomplimentary or nonexistent. The role of religion in film is an instructive example. Critics of the depiction of religion from the Left argue that the communitarian, cooperative, pacifist tendencies in religion are given short shrift in Hollywood films. For example, in the otherwise excellent film *Witness* (1985), the protagonist police detective John Book, played by Harrison Ford, is forced to hide from some bad guys by living among the Amish. But when the time comes to confront the bad guys, Book and apparently the screenwriters have learned nothing from the Amish. What we get in the end is the traditional gunfight and a terrific kill scene in which one of the villains is literally drowned in amber waves of grain. While that outcome is cathartic, it is not very thoughtful and is in fact a perversion of the story heretofore seen. But when morals are treated in American film, they tend to emphasize the paternalistic, hierarchical values of religion.[2] For example, in *Three Men and a Baby* (1987) and *Look Who's Talking* (1989) the stories conclude that men are happier at work and women are happier at home caring for children within the context of a traditional nuclear family.[3]

By the same token, conservative critics often argue that organized religion is treated with contempt by Hollywood, with its priests depicted as charlatans (or worse) and its adherents as morons. For example, in his book *Hollywood Worldviews: Watching Films with Wisdom and Discernment*, author Brian Godawa analyzes films from a conservative Christian perspective.[4] It is his contention that the existential, postmodern worldview of Hollywood filmmaking depicts a meaningless life in which the characters in film do not act; they simply are.[5] For example, according to Godawa, in the film *Forrest Gump* (1994), the protagonist lives a life that has little or no significance or meaning because he is not motivated by any sort of higher calling. In that sense, the story of *Forrest Gump* is a metaphor for life without God: things happen; wealth is obtained—but for what purpose?

In response to this sometimes shoddy treatment, religious groups have threatened economic retaliation against the entertainment production industry. In the 1920s, groups associated with the Catholic church helped found the production code and the Hays Committee. They backed their calls for censorship with a threatened boycott, a threat made effective by the fact that the market for films at the time, in large part, consisted of lower-class and immigrant groups who belonged to the Catholic church. More recently, groups from the evangelical religious Right, who don't tend to go to the movies, have organized stock ownership programs and economic boycotts in order to pressure entertainment companies into altering the content of their product.

For example, in January 1985, Republican senator Jesse Helms (North Carolina), through an organization called Fairness in Media, promoted a stock purchase program of CBS by religious conservatives. The purpose of this move was to pressure the management of CBS into correcting what Fairness in Media took to be CBS's liberal bias. Fairness in Media sent out a million letters under Senator Helm's signature urging each recipient to purchase twenty shares of CBS stock at a cost of about $1,500 (CBS was trading at about $75 a share at the time). Considering that there were about thirty million shares of CBS stock outstanding, Helms would have had to realize about a 75 percent response rate to gain control of the company. The attempt failed. CBS had a market capitalization of $2.4 billion, too much for an ideologically driven crusade.[6]

Boycotts have been no more successful. In 1996, the 15.6 million members of the Southern Baptist Convention voted to boycott the Disney Corporation. They and other conservatives, including a group called the American Family Foundation, objected to the content of some of the films produced and distributed by Miramax Films (a subsidiary of Disney) and to the fact that Disney accommodated gays who sponsored events at Disney-operated amusement parks. Furthermore, in 1998 the American Family Foundation of Texas managed to pressure the Texas State Board of Education to sell its 1.2 million shares of Disney stock. Disney resisted the boycott, perhaps recognizing that the boycott made by religious conservatives of Miramax's *Pulp Fiction* was a nonstarter (the film grossed over $200 million on an $8 million budget) and that most Americans would ignore a boycott against the nation's top tourist destination anyway. The reward for Disney was one of the great successes of the stock market and of corporate performance in the 1990s: Disney stock grew about 500 percent (split adjusted from 1990 to 2000).

There is absolutely nothing wrong with economic boycotts or stock-purchase programs. However, against the entertainment media, the religious Right is probably barking up the wrong tree. Because religious conservatives are not, by and large, customers for these products, they have little in the way of market leverage against the entertainment industry—that is, unless they enlist the government as an ally. In that regard, the religious Right is much more effective. Not only have religious conservatives been able to use the tax-exempt status of their churches as a subsidy for financing their own television networks, but they have also influenced Congress and the Federal Communications Commission (FCC) to more stringently censor television programming. Perhaps in the future, the religious Right will push for government intervention to control Internet content and, ultimately, the movies.[7]

Economic boycotts are a demonstration of how sensitive the entertainment industry is to the market. If there is money in making films that appeal to religious conservatives, Hollywood won't hesitate for a moment to fill that niche. And perhaps the industry already is, at least to the extent that inexpensively produced niche films and television shows can be produced for, and be profitable in, a limited market. But don't expect Hollywood to bow to the pressure of the religious Right soon, unless the government intervenes or religious conservatives become large consumers of Hollywood's films.

The financial performance of *The Passion of the Christ* has been a momentous event for the entertainment industry, which is why its success was greeted with such glee in conservative circles. In part, the ability of corporations such as Disney to resist the economic pressures of religious conservatives has been based on the assumption supported by surveys such as the one presented in this book that churchgoing people generally don't go to the movies. Whether *The Passion* represents an anomaly or not, the film's box office performance will change the perception of, and thus the clout of, religious conservatives. Media executives can no longer ignore the market potential of churchgoers. The result should be a subtle shift in the content of programming.

The market determines the content of films in two other ways. First, films will be only as good as the skills of the people who make them. On the demand side, there is such a large market for entertainment that even substantially flawed products can enjoy financial success. As such, a couple of recent blockbuster and financially successful disaster films, besides being technical marvels, haven't been half bad in the plot department. *Titanic* (1997) and *Deep Impact* (1998) both had stories to go along with their special effects. Nevertheless, the brain-dead *Twister* (1996) also did well, becoming, as of this writing, the fifty-sixth top-grossing film of all time. That being the case, we probably haven't seen the last *Twister*-type movie.

Another way in which the market censors films is by excluding or ignoring unpopular ideas. Many filmmakers may be liberals, but they sure aren't socialists. As long as corporations are backing and distributing films that are produced about our society, it is doubtful that films critical of the corporate culture will often get made, much less exhibited. But, then again, would there be a market for those films anyway? As noted in the survey in chapter 3, frequent filmgoers tend to be apolitical, especially on issues not related to social interaction. This is a chicken-and-egg problem. Are film corporations suppressing subversive messages that they oppose, or are they responding to the lack of demand? And if there were a demand for anticapitalist messages, would corporations engage in the ultimate irony of sponsoring films critical of themselves?

These problems aside, on balance the range and quality of American motion pictures are the envy of the world. There is still very limited foreign competition for this particular American product (Bollywood, the Indian film industry, produces more films and sells more tickets than Hollywood but garners only about 2 percent of the revenues).[8] This is particularly true in the modern era, well after the demise of the Hollywood studio trust, the advent of television, and the corporatization of the American film industry, which is why it is possible to say that the real golden era of the American film industry is now. The range and quality of Hollywood's best films are unsurpassed and getting better, and the caliber of that product is attributable to the general marketization of the industry. Those who wish to return to the film industry's past, even if those days could be reproduced, are really arguing for a form of censorship different from the one imposed by the market—that is, for one imposed by the industry or through the government. Those forms of censorship, however, would likely produce an inferior product with biases every bit as bad and worse than the occasional brain-dead, corporate-centered, bottom-line filmmaking that is all too common today. At least in the current environment, creative, thoughtful, and even subversive films can get made. Could the same be said for certain periods in the past?

INDUSTRY SELF-CENSORSHIP

When the film industry is under pressure, it often attempts some form of self-censorship. This is something more than a publicity ploy. Throughout most of the 1930s Hollywood operated under a strict production code that imposed severe limitations on film depictions and content. The code was imposed by the movie studios on themselves and was made enforceable by the vertical integration of the industry. Since the studios controlled the distribution and exhibition of films, it was virtually impossible for a film to be exhibited that had not been cleared by the production code censors.

In a sense, the production code came about as a by-product of governmental pressure. From the beginning of the film industry, when nickelodeons were midway attractions at carnivals, the government has attempted to censor film content. One of the first film censorship ordinances in the United States was adopted in 1907 in Chicago, resulting in the establishment of a local film censorship board. A number of other communities and states followed suit.

For film distributors, this patchwork of censorship made distribution difficult not only because it limited the product but also because local censorship made the task of film distribution all the more expensive. Each film print had to be tailored to demands of a different community. In the process, prints were recut so often that they were destroyed, and given the expense and shortage of film stock in the early days of the industry, local film censorship became such a burden that distributors were willing to fight. In 1914 a Detroit film distributor, the Mutual Film Corporation, challenged in federal court an Ohio law that established a state film censorship board. The board was charged with the responsibility of clearing for exhibition "only such films as are . . . of a moral, educational, or amusing and harmless character." The plaintiff, Mutual Film, argued that in addition to violating constitutional protections of freedom of speech and the press, the Ohio law, as a restraint of trade, was in violation of the interstate commerce clause of the U.S. Constitution.[9]

The case was appealed all the way to the Supreme Court, where justice Joseph McKenna, in writing for the majority, dismissed the plaintiff's argument that the

Ohio Censorship Board was a violation of the interstate commerce clause. After all, the censorship board's decisions applied only to films screened in Ohio. Furthermore, as to the matter of freedom of speech, McKenna wrote,

> It cannot be put out of view that the exhibition of moving pictures is a business, pure and simple, originated and conducted for profit, like other spectacles, not to be regarded, nor intended to be regarded by the Ohio Constitution we think, as part of the press of the country, or as organs of public opinion. They are mere representations of events, of ideas and sentiments published and known; vivid, useful, and entertaining, no doubt, but, as we have said, capable of evil, having power for it, the greater because of their attractiveness and manner of exhibition.[10]

In other words, in this decision, the Court ruled that motion pictures were product, not art nor a form of journalism. Therefore, the State of Ohio could treat commercial motion pictures as it did any other product and impose requirements on its marketing and use.

This decision has to be viewed in context. In 1914, prior to the Great Depression, the Court (and federal government) was reluctant to interfere with what was then known as states' rights. Within reasonable limits, states had the authority to regulate their own internal commerce. Thus, at the time, the Court was in no mood to intervene in the sort of action brought by Mutual Film. However, pursuant to the logic of states' rights, states often violated what we now understand to be basic constitutional rights in much more extreme and serious ways than simply censoring movies. For example, Jim Crow laws, which mandated racial discrimination in the South, were justified in part by their supporters as exercises in states' rights.

The result of the Mutual Film decision was to open the floodgates for censorship of American film. Numerous localities in the United States created their own censorship boards. Throughout the 1920s Hollywood fought to comply with the various sensibilities of different state (and sometimes foreign) governments. Censorship, however, was a manageable problem for Hollywood in the 1920s because of the era's general permissiveness and also because of the relative simplicity of editing silent film. Silent films were relatively easy to cut and tailor for local audiences. With the advent of sound, however, it became increasingly difficult to meet the demands of censorship boards in different states and localities. Sound films are technically, and from the perspective of plot development, more difficult to edit. Besides, editing a talking picture was more likely to ruin the print.

With the collapse of the stock market in 1929, the film industry began fearing for its business (money spent on movie admission is, in theory, the ultimate discretionary expenditure). In the late 1920s and early 1930s, the industry began to push against the limits of censorship in order to lure patrons to the theater through the production of more daring and violent films. For example, in concert with the publicity in the press received by real-life mobsters such as Al Capone, Hollywood spawned an entire genre of gangster films. For their time, these films were daring not only in their depiction of violence but also in their treatment of gangsters as glamorous antiheroes.

The film industry, in its quest for increased attendance in the late 1920s, ran headlong into an energized religious movement. In particular, the Catholic church, through the auspices of its organization the Legion of Decency, began to pressure the film industry to adopt a well-defined production code. The Catholic church was particularly effective in this role because of its centralized organization and because it "represented" such a large percentage of the movie-viewing audience. The general backlash against the permissiveness of the Roaring Twenties, especially as depicted in the movies, emerged from several underlying causes.

First, as an entertainment medium, film became increasingly pervasive throughout the 1920s. According to some estimates, by 1930 some forty million people were regular moviegoers in the United States, of a total population of 130 million.[11] In that sense, films were really the world's first mass medium. Much of the audience for these films included recent arrivals who lived in large cities and were disproportionately Jewish or Catholic. What had been a sideshow became a Main Street treat and, to some, a threat. Second, to the extent that the film industry was dominated by first-generation immigrants, often of Jewish descent, Christian Main Street felt a general uneasiness about the potential influence that a bunch of non-Christian "foreigners" had who were perceived to be vaguely in league with international communism and the general conspiracy that got the United States involved in the First World War.[12] In previous chapters, I suggest that vestigial anti-Semitism toward Hollywood still exists today even though most film production and distribution are conducted by publicly held corporations (owned by almost anyone who owns a mutual fund). Finally, with the crash of the stock market and the settling in of hard times, people often turned to religion (and xenophobia) for succor from and an explanation for hard times. In Europe, these economic hard times spawned the politics of fascism. In the United States, the Great Depression spawned the politics of populists such as Huey Long and Father Coughlin.[13]

In reaction to the overt and subtle anti-Semitism that came at the end of World War I, Hollywood acted to preempt the criticism that it was a subversive force representing international interests by forming a trade association, the Motion Picture Producers and Distributors of America (MPPDA), eventually to become in the modern era the Motion Picture Association of America (MPAA). The MPPDA was commonly known as the Hays Office, named after William H. Hays. In 1922 Hays, a former chair of the Republican National Committee from Indiana, resigned as postmaster general in the Harding administration to front for Hollywood as head of the MPPDA. While the MPPDA is more generally known for its activities in the censorship of film through the production code, it was more importantly the agency that made it possible for Hollywood to set up its second monopoly. Everything from labor agreements within the industry to distribution agreements among the studios was coordinated through the MPPDA.[14] That monopoly made it possible for the industry to not only write a production code but to actually enforce it.[15]

Finally, the institution of the production code was probably not completely unwelcome in Hollywood. With the multitude of local codes, compliance for distributors was difficult and expensive. An industry-wide set of standards would save money and provide cover for plotlines and themes that stretched the limit for what was acceptable on Main Street. Indeed, and somewhat ironically, in the earliest years of the production code, Hollywood produced some of its most daring films ever. For example, in the film *Red-Headed Woman* (1932) a secretary played by Jean Harlow basically sleeps her way to the top and gets away with it. In another film from the same year, *Red Dust*, the lead played by Clark Gable has an enthusiastic and thoroughly requited love affair with the wife of one of his employees, but when he changes his mind and sends her back to her husband, he ends up with a prostitute who is hiding from the police, again lustily played by Harlow.

In 1927 the Hays Office published its first production code, to be administered by its own Studio Relations Committee. The code went largely unenforced until after the stock market crash of 1929. A combination of new, more titillating film content, the market crash, and the concomitant reinvigoration of religious movements in the United States forced the MPPDA to become more active in the advance clearance and censorship of film content. In 1930, the MPPDA published a set of general principles to be followed in development of movie scripts:

1. No picture shall be produced which will lower the moral standards of those who see it. Hence the sympathy of the audience shall never be thrown to the side of crime, wrong-doing, evil or sin.
2. Correct standards of life, subject only to the requirements of drama and entertainment, shall be presented.
3. Law, natural or human, shall not be ridiculed, nor shall sympathy be created for its violation.

In one form or another, the production code governed the production and content of movies for the next thirty-five years, after which, in 1966, it was replaced by a rating system.

At first, the enforcement of the code was spotty at best. As noted, some of the raciest commercial films in American film history were made between 1930 and 1933. As in the case of the modern Disney boycott, filmmakers were willing to risk the ire of groups that they believed were not an audience for their films. But when it appeared that the government would get involved and force Hollywood to comply with the production code as a matter of law, the studio heads thought it would be the better part of valor to comply with the code.

In 1933, at the height of the depression, Congress passed the National Industrial Recovery Act (NIRA) that authorized heretofore unprecedented circumventions of a market economy, including a suspension of government antitrust efforts. In exchange for a formal recognition of the legality of certain industrial monopolies, the act required that industries adopt "voluntary" codes of conduct. NIRA was both good news and bad for the movie industry. On the one hand, NIRA would now grant formal recognition to and acceptance of Hollywood's second monopoly. On the other hand, the industry would now have to adopt a voluntary code of behavior that, if ignored, might threaten the monopoly.

Seizing the opportunity to influence the film industry, a combination of religious groups (who objected to the content of Hollywood entertainment) and small-theater owners (who objected to the power that Hollywood had over distribution) lobbied in Washington to use the NIRA as a way to enforce the production code and to give theater owners more power in the film-distribution process, thus setting the foundation for the second Hollywood monopoly. Religious organizations went so far as to call for the inclusion in NIRA guidelines (administered by the National Recovery Administration), mainly encompassing the production code as a matter of law. Hollywood attempted to head off this governmental intrusion by acting to more strictly enforce the production code. In 1934, Joe Breen, a strict Catholic moralist from Philadelphia, was appointed to head the Production Code Administration. The PCA was given the authority to fine any theater owner $25,000 who displayed an unapproved picture. Note that this arrangement helped preserve the vertical monopoly by basically making it illegal for theater owners to screen independently produced films. As it turned out, the code was a small price to pay to preserve Hollywood's second monopoly.[16]

The threat of governmental regulation, periodic boycotts, and the Second World War compelled the PCA to be strict in its enforcement of the production code until well after the end of the war. In addition, to the extent that foreign sales became an important source of revenue for Hollywood in the 1930s, the MPPDA was in constant contact and consultation with foreign governments about the content of its films that were being screened abroad. In particular, the British government, which actively enforced its own production code, demanded that Hollywood export films that not only conformed to British code but also, in its depiction of British colonialism, respected the authority of the Colonial Office in the British government. The Mexican, Chinese, and French governments were also regularly consulted about the content of exported films. But the end of the war brought pressure to bear on the enforcement of the code.

The first signs of the code's erosion came with the breakup of the vertical monopoly. In 1948, in a sweeping decision, the Supreme Court ordered in *United States v. Paramount Pictures, Inc.* the breakup of the vertical monopoly of production and distribution controlled by the large studios (by forcing the studios to divest themselves of the theater chains they owned).[17] The fact that independent theater owners could shop around for pictures to be screened would eventually create a competitive environment in the film industry that would forever change the nature of Hollywood films. Even so, as a practical matter, in the late 1940s and early 1950s, the absence of independent and foreign productions and the de facto collusion of distributors didn't give the *Paramount* decision much force. Nevertheless, after the war, many Hollywood films became darker, more issue oriented, and critical of the veneer of proper society. But even those films were not free from the censor.

Sunset Boulevard, produced in 1950, is representative of the era's films. Not only does the film deal (albeit elliptically) with such subversive themes as the relationship between a gigolo and a faded movie star, but it also attacks Hollywood itself. One feature of the film was particularly disturbing to the censors of its day. The story of *Sunset Boulevard* is told from the perspective of a murder victim who begins and ends the film floating facedown in a swimming pool. So shocking was this artifice for its time that the film was often censored to exclude its eerie opening sequence. Even today, some prints of the film bear the censor's mark.

Also developing as a threat to the second monopoly was television. To compete with television, Hollywood began to probe the boundaries of the code in order to provide the moviegoer with a unique experience that could not be re-created on a black-and-white television set in the living room. In addition, and safe from the censors, were expanded technological innovations, such as wide-screen Cinemascope, experiments with 3-D movies, enhanced color, and improved sound technology, all of which were intended to counter the competition of television.

Ultimately, however, filmmakers began to press against the limits of censorship to provide moviegoers with an experience they could not get on their televisions or radio at home. In part, these explorations in the limits of film were motivated by an influx of films from a reinvigorated postwar European film industry. With the notable exception of those in Britain, European filmmakers were generally under no such code restrictions in their own countries. In the early 1960s, there developed a lucrative niche audience for foreign film as screened in independent theaters in large cities and close to college campuses. In part, this freeing up of American film in the late 1950s and early 1960s was made possible by a series of court decisions that essentially reversed the 1915 *Mutual Films* decision. As we will see, the courts in the United States began to see the film industry as less of a business than a form of artistic expression to be protected under the First Amendment.

Despite the industry's efforts to maintain its audience, film attendance plummeted throughout the 1950s and into the 1960s. Desperate to find a solution to a declining box office, in 1968 Jack Valenti (a former official in the Lyndon Johnson administration), who had come to head MPPDA, scrapped the production code and replaced it with a rating system. The adoption of a rating system represented a significant change in the censorship of American film. No longer would films be filtered for content. Instead, under the new rating system, audiences were filtered for films. The rating system has gone through several iterations. The now familiar G, PG, PG-13, R, and NC-17 (formerly G, M, R, X) rating system was instituted with great success, at least from the perspective of the film producers. The current MPAA movie ratings consist of

G—General audiences: All ages admitted.

PG—Parental guidance suggested: Some material may not be suitable for children (originally, "some material may not be suitable for pre-teenagers"; wording was changed when the PG-13 rating was introduced in 1984).

PG-13—Parents strongly cautioned: Some material may be inappropriate for children under 13.

R—Restricted: Under 17 requires accompanying parent or adult guardian.

NC-17: No one 17 and under admitted.

If a film was never submitted for a rating, the NR (not rated) label would often appear in newspapers and so forth; however, NR is not an official MPAA classification.[18]

The onus is now on film producers to come up with a product that can get a rating that appeals to the largest target audience. Gone, too, are the days when the message of a film was subject to censorship. The Hays Office was notoriously capricious in its judgment of what themes were judged as in violation of the production code. By contrast, the rating system is based on the number of and graphic nature of acts of violence and explicit sex as depicted in a film. The MPAA rating system has administered its own Classification and Ratings Administration, which replaced the old Production Code Administration.

Because there were some fairly well-established guidelines to the assignment of ratings, filmmakers can now predict with a fair amount of certainty what their films' ratings will be. In addition, it is a fairly simple matter to edit a film to conform to a particular rating's requirements. For example, in the film *Eyes Wide Shut* (1999) some scenes of a sexual orgy were obscured (shot out of focus) in order for the film to receive an R rating instead of an NC-17. By the same token, the producers of the film *Sneakers* (1992) actually *added* obscenities to the dialogue in order to move the film from a G to a PG rating. For some audiences a G rating suggests a children's film.

To the extent that the film rating system connotes the character of a film, it also performs the function of an informal system of censorship. It is certainly true that many theaters will simply refuse to screen a movie with the rating NC-17. As a consequence, mainstream Hollywood releases are rarely rated as such. Other consequences for movie content may result from the rating system as well. As we have seen, G-rated films are often perceived as children's films and thus likely to be unpopular with the core movie audience of teenagers. But as conservatives often point out, G films, as rare as they are, tend to do well at the box office. Whether this fact is ignored by Hollywood because of its miscalculation of audience, because of its ideological predilections, or because G films are attended so well precisely because they are so rare is a matter of conjecture. But as long as the rating system is thought to influence the market for a film, it will act as an informal censor and an indicator of the principles that society holds.

The rating system is not beyond criticism. For example, films that depict graphic violence rarely receive more than an R rating, while films that depict graphic sexual activities often receive the dreaded NC-17. That order of priorities may tell us something about a society that would rather have its children see a screen depiction of a man killing his lover than having sex with her (or him). Furthermore, it also says that we trust adults to make the decision whether children should see graphic violence, but we don't trust their judgment when it comes to allowing children to view sex. Nevertheless, disputed priorities aside, the rating system has the virtue of conforming to Supreme Court decisions, allowing filmmakers an opportunity to explore heretofore forbidden topics, while providing a modicum of protection for the young and an advanced warning for parents.

The rating system has undergone minor revisions (with more attention paid to film violence) but has remained essentially unchanged since 1968. As long as theaters are willing to enforce the system, ratings represent a grand compromise that is sensitive to the legitimate demands of a society concerned about its children and its First Amendment rights. However, there is still the problem of enforcement. In a report to Congress in December 2001, the Federal Trade Commission studied the film industry's compliance to trade practices mandated by the commission and to its voluntary restrictions, such as the rating system. While the commission found that the industry had done a commendable job in limiting the advertising of NC-17– and R-rated films to non-target audiences, undercover investigators still revealed a high level of noncompliance in the areas of video rentals of R- and NC-17–rated films to minors and admissions of unaccompanied minors to R- and NC-17–rated films.[19] Should such lax practices continue, it is certain that the film industry will attract more calls for censorship.

The verities of the film business ensure that the censorship of film will always be a bone of contention because it is difficult for the industry to control itself. The irony of the forced dissolution of the vertical monopoly is that theater owners are independent. The studios can no longer force compliance to the code and now the rating system. The collapse of the second monopoly and the rulings by the Supreme Court made production code enforcement impossible. In addition, it became clear that in the last twenty years of its existence the production code did not protect the industry from, and clearly may have been a cause for, falling movie attendance. This conclusion did not escape the film industry's notice. It is unlikely, then, that the industry would or even could return to the era of the production code. Furthermore, as long as social conservatives are not perceived as an important audience for film, their boycotts will not be a credible threat; however, the success of *The Passion of the Christ* may change all that. Consequently, the last resort for those who would censor movie content would be to appeal to the government. But government censorship of the movies in the United States seems unlikely as long as the American majority is aware of and protective of its constitutional rights and the courts are diligent in the same manner as well.

CENSORSHIP BY GOVERNMENT

On December 1, 1997, Michael Carneal walked into the lobby of Heath High School in Paducah, Kentucky, and shot several of his fellow students, killing three and wounding many others. The parents and estate administrators of Carneal's victims sued several video game, movie production, and Internet content–provider firms. According to their complaint, Carneal regularly played video games, watched movies, and viewed Internet sites produced by the defendant firms. These activities, plaintiffs Joe James et al. argue, "desensitized" Carneal to violence and "caused" him to kill the students of Heath High School.[20] Consequently, the distribution of this material to impressionable youth like Carneal constituted a tort in the meaning of Kentucky law, entitling the plaintiffs to recover wrongful death damages from the distributing firms.[21] Moreover, the plaintiffs argued that the defendant firms purveyed defective "products"—namely the content of video games, movies, and Internet sites, triggering strict product liability under Kentucky law.[22] A federal district court dismissed the plaintiffs' claim, and a federal appeals court upheld the dismissal. The court made a similar ruling in regard to the school shootings at Columbine High School in Littleton, Colorado.

Had the court found in favor of the plaintiffs, there could have been a massive chilling effect on the production of games, Internet content, and the movies. This attempt to censor films through civil action based on product liability laws is but one of many attempts since the beginning of film to censor the industry. At one time or another various communities across the country have attempted to impose community standards on the movies through a variety of direct and indirect means. In this last section I examine the continuing evolution of case and civil law in regard to government control over film content. This issue is particularly important (and evolving) now that pay-per-view and cable television have brought first-run unedited feature films to America's living room. Television and films were always treated to a certain extent differently, as the federal government had a "hook" into radio and television content through the broadcast station licensing process. The airwaves are publicly owned and thus allocated and regulated by the federal government. Books and movies, however, are treated differently. Up until recently, it could be fairly argued that if you didn't want to read an objectionable book or see an objectionable movie, you simply didn't have to buy the product. Nowadays, however, to buy cable television is also to buy a lot of programming that would to some audiences be considered obscene and to other audiences, particularly children, even harmful.

The congressionally mandated V-Chip (for parents to censor what their children watch on television) and the new, voluntary rating system adopted by the television networks are just the latest reactions to the perception that viewers need some kind of control over television content. But are these measures enough? Or are they too much? As we shall see, there has been a dramatic evolution in case law in regard to the censorship of film. In fact, the courts have reversed themselves almost completely. From a position of tolerance for local film censorship, the courts are now fairly reluctant to give ground in censoring films regardless of their content. The same, however, cannot be said for television.

In theory the courts should not make, but rather interpret, law. However, when the states or the Congress adopts laws that are unconstitutional or when an issue is so sensitive that politicians avoid it, the courts are often forced to intervene. As we have seen in the era prior to the Great Depression, the federal courts were loathe to get involved in affairs at the state level or in private business. However, because states' rights (and, on occasion, claims to property rights) can sometimes conflict with the Bill of Rights, the federal courts have become substantially more active in overruling the actions of states since the Great Depression and with the advent of the civil rights movement, in the last half century.

As we have seen, the *Mutual Films* decision of 1914 let stand, as an exercise of states' rights, the actions of a film censorship board in Ohio. That ruling legitimized the establishment of film censorship boards in states and localities across the country— that is, until 1952. In 1950 a theater in New York City screened a film made in Italy titled *The Miracle* (which was part of a trilogy called *The Ways of Love*). A New York State film-licensing board had issued a license for the film's exhibition. Pursuant to the 1914 *Mutual Film* decision, states still were allowed to grant licenses to exhibit films. Subsequently, in response to public outrage about the content of the film, the board notified the theater owner that it planned to rescind the film's license on the basis of the film's sacrilegious content. Eventually, the license was suspended, and the film's distributor was sued in state court. The state court upheld the board's decision to rescind the license, and the case was appealed to the federal courts.

Normally, as was the case in 1914, the federal courts at this time would be reluctant to intervene in state matters such as these. However, by 1952 things had begun to change. Beginning in the late 1920s, pursuant to the Fourteenth Amendment (the post–Civil War amendment that nationalized the Bill of Rights), the federal courts had begun to regularly hear cases involving the actions of states. So it was not entirely out of character for the Supreme Court to grant a hearing in the New York film-licensing case (*Burstyn v. Wilson*, 1952). What makes this case so extraordinary is that the Court (as it rarely does) completely and explicitly reversed its earlier rulings when it took the critical step of ruling that commercial films were protected speech in the meaning of the First Amendment. In the *Mutual Film* case, the Court had ruled that films were merely product; in the *Burstyn* case, the Court unambiguously reversed the earlier *Mutual* decision when Justice Tom Clark wrote,

> It is urged [by the defendant New York State Licensing Board] that motion pictures do not fall within the First Amendment's aegis because their production, distribution, and exhibition is a large-scale business conducted for private profit. We cannot agree. That books, newspapers, and magazines are published and sold for profit does not prevent them from being a form of expression whose liberty is safeguarded by the First Amendment. We fail to see why operation for profit should have any different effect in the case of motion pictures.
>
> It is further urged that motion pictures possess a greater capacity for evil, particularly among the youth of a community, than other modes of expression. Even if one were to accept this hypothesis, it does not follow that motion pictures should be disqualified from First Amendment protection. If there be capacity for evil it may be relevant in determining the permissible scope of *community control*, but it does not authorize substantially unbridled censorship such as we have here.
>
> For the foregoing reasons, we conclude that expression by means of motion pictures is included within the free speech and free press guaranty of the First and Fourteenth Amendments. To the extent that language in the opinion in Mutual Film Corp v. Industrial Commission is out of harmony with the views here set forth, we no longer adhere to it.[23] (italics added)

The Court made it clear that films are protected under the First Amendment. But the Court did leave the door open for some kind of "community control" that was something less than a total prohibition on film censorship. There are other exceptions to the First Amendment freedom of speech in regard to films. It was in defining what these exceptions are, those where the First Amendment does not apply, that the Court has expended the greatest amount of energy in delimiting film censorship in the last sixty years. On the one hand, the Court recognizes that there are certain types of speech that can be limited because they are a nuisance or are dangerous. For example, in *Chaplinsky v. State of New Hampshire* (1942) the Court ruled,

> There are certain well-defined and narrowly limited classes of speech, the prevention and punishment of which has never been thought to raise any Constitutional problem. These include the lewd and obscene, the profane and libelous, and the insulting or "fighting" words—those which by their utterance inflict injury or tend to incite an immediate breach of the peace.[24]

This left open the door for the censorship of films that are lewd and obscene. But by what standard were those characteristics to be measured? Only in determining that is *Chaplinsky* on point.

Sometimes the nuisance character of speech is obvious. For example, in *Kovacs v. Cooper* (1949) the court ruled that "when ordinances undertake censorship of speech or religious practices before permitting their exercise, the Constitution forbids their enforcement."[25] However, in this case the Court upheld the constitutionality of an ordinance that forbid the use of sound trucks and other devices that made a lot of noise (even if they were broadcasting protected speech).

In addition, besides the potential for the public nuisance of sound, certain types of speech can be punished for being libelous. But libel laws in the United States are some of the most limited and narrowly defined in the world. According to what is known as the Sullivan test, a publication or statement can only be considered libelous if it can be proved that the statement was false and that it was published with "actual malice," which includes a reckless disregard for its truth.[26] These are exceedingly hard standards to meet in a court of law, and, as a result, very few people who are targets of smears even try.

But what more specifically has a potential for censoring film are obscenity laws, which for years local communities have tried to adopt and enforce. In general in dealing with challenges to these laws, the courts seem to make a distinction between the merely insulting and the obscene. As long as a work of art—a book, a film, or a play—can be arguably said to have some kind of message, to make a point no matter how unpopular, it is to be considered a form of protected speech.

Probably the most important case in regard to obscenity is *Roth v. the United States*, decided in 1957. That case still stands today as the foundation of constitutional law in regard to obscenity. The issue in the case was whether the constitutional rights of the defendant were violated when he was arrested for sending certain types of lewd, indecent, or obscene materials through the mails. In writing for the majority, justice William Brennan argued,

> All ideas having even the slightest redeeming social importance—unorthodox ideas, controversial ideas, even ideas hateful to the prevailing climate of opinion—have the full

protection [of the First Amendment]. . . . But explicit in the history of the First Amendment is the rejection of obscenity as utterly without redeeming social importance.

Brennan defined obscenity as

material which deals with sex in a manner appealing to prurient interest . . . [defined as] to the average person, applying contemporary community standards, the dominant theme of the material taken as a whole appeals to prurient interest.

Finally, Brennan made it clear that the state was under no obligation to prove that a particular piece of obscene material had a direct, demonstrably negative effect on society. It was the lack of any socially redeeming character that defined obscenity for the purposes of censorship.[27]

However, with every solution comes a new set of problems. For one thing, it was not clear that an entire work could be judged obscene merely because a particular passage or scene proved to be objectionable. Furthermore, to the extent that community standards seemed to determine what was obscene, the definition of obscenity was variable. That variability forced any number of obscenity cases into the courts to determine whether the work in question violated community standards. More to the point, judges found themselves having to watch a lot of dirty movies. If for no other reason, that fact forced the courts to come up with a more generic and enforceable standard of obscenity.

Finally, in 1973 the U.S. Supreme Court further refined the standard established in the *Roth* case. In *Miller v. California*, the Court laid out a three-part test for obscenity:

(a) whether the average person, applying contemporary community standards would find that the work, taken as a whole, appeals to the prurient interest, . . . (b) whether the work depicts or describes, in a patently offensive way, sexual conduct specifically defined by the applicable state law, and (c) whether the work, taken as a whole, lacks serious literary, artistic, political, or scientific value. If a state obscenity law is thus limited, First Amendment values are adequately protected by ultimate independent appellate review of constitutional claims when necessary.[28]

Thus, the standard for delineating obscenity became generalized and nationalized. Second, the Court ruled that only the sale of "hard-core" sexual materials (as defined by the Court) could be subject to prosecution. Finally, the Court emphasized the importance of the jury system in finding the fact of obscenity.

Since the *Miller* decision, the courts have upheld a number of state and local ordinances that impose zoning and other restrictions on the licensing and sale of obscene materials. However, because major Hollywood distributors are rarely involved with the production and sale of obscene materials (hard-core pornography in the meaning of the Court's definition), these decisions have largely excluded government censorship of Hollywood film. Thus, we are left with a largely unregulated marketplace in theatrical exhibition of major film productions.

But not many films are released exclusively for theatrical exhibition. Besides being released on VHS and DVD, films are also shown on premium cable channels and broadcast television. It has generally been the case that broadcast television has censored films according to the licensing demands of the Federal Communications Commission. As discussed, because the FCC issues broadcast licenses to radio and television stations, it can rescind those licenses or punish the recipients thereof in many ways. In regard to obscenity, the FCC has been guided by the "compelling interest" standard in broadcast regulation, meaning that the FCC will intervene in a programming matter only if the state has some kind of compelling interest in doing so (the *Sable* decision).[29] As a practical matter, this means that programming content is rarely regulated except when it comes to the protection of children (the protection of whom the state has a compelling interest). This means that the FCC requires that broadcast stations restrict the airing of indecent materials to the hours of 10 P.M. to 6 A.M., when children are less likely to be in the audience.[30] Stations that defy the FCC can either be fined or have their broadcast licenses revoked.

There is now a relatively recent, new element added to the mix. Subscriber-based cable television can air unedited films or shows with pornographic content to home audiences. In 1996 Congress passed the Telecommunications Act, which, among other things, extended the child restrictive (so-called safe harbor) broadcasting hours of 10 P.M. to 6 A.M. to cable television programming. The Supreme Court, however, found this section of the law to be unconstitutional, as it went beyond the absolute minimum intrusion necessary to exercise the state's compelling interest as defined in the *Sable* decision.[31] In English that means that there were other, less restrictive ways to protect children against indecent programming on cable television. Specifically, in the same law, Congress required cable suppliers to provide subscribers with the option of purchasing a lockbox that could be used to block programming that might be objectionable to children. The Court interpreted that provision of the law as being adequate. After all, unlike broadcast television, which may require blanket restrictions, cable television, which is provided by subscription, can be controlled by the subscribers. Thus, the courts have continued the legal tradition of allowing only the bare minimum of censorship of media content.

The reason why FCC regulation of cable television is so important to the film industry is that there exists the potential for its exerting influence on film content. While not as profitable as first-run screenings, the sale of film exhibition rights to cable channels is a lucrative business for the film industry. If the FCC makes it possible to regulate the screening of Hollywood films regarded by some as indecent, a dampening effect may hamper the production of original films. For those low-budget films in particular, which are sometimes the most creative and which are produced with the intent to recoup some of their costs on cable, the FCC regulation of cable television could prove to be a powerful influence on film content.

Finally, one other potential legal threat to the film industry comes from the area of product liability. I have argued here that commercial film is largely product, not art. Although the courts have ruled that it is irrelevant to First Amendment protections whether a film (or newspaper, for that matter) is produced for profit or not, it is possible that with the expansion of product liability case law, filmmakers could be held liable for the content of their films. For example, it seems just a matter of time before a jury awards damages to a smoker at the expense of a cigarette manufacturer.[32] Even though any reasonable adult capable of reading a warning label knows the danger of smoking cigarettes, the fact that there is evidence that tobacco companies knew about the dangers of smoking well before the public did and actually may have tried to enhance the addictive properties of their product may point to some kind of legal culpability on their part.

The same might be said for Hollywood. Because the idea that film violence is associated with actual violence seems to be consensually held by most people, it might be possible to argue that a particular film is directly responsible for a particular act of violence. For example, as discussed in a previous chapter, John Hinckley viewed *Taxi Driver* as many as fifteen times before deciding to attempt to assassinate President Reagan in order to impress Jody Foster. Would President Reagan have had a cause of action against the producer of the film?

So far, the answer is probably not. Even though there is a fairly convincing (albeit flawed) case to be made by behavioral scientists that film violence begets actual violence, the question of product liability has to meet a higher standard. First there is the legal standard of what constitutes a "good" and a "bad" product. There can be such a thing as a good cigarette, at least in the legal sense. A good cigarette or gun or movie in the legal sense is one without manufacturing defects. Thus, if cigarette manufacturers purposely add something to their tobacco that makes their product more dangerous, they may be held liable. However, if they conform in the production of their legal product to a level of reasonable care, they can't be held liable for the consequences of what happens when someone smokes a cigarette. The same general principle holds true for gun manufacturers and, certainly, film producers. It is difficult to conceive of a bad movie in the legal sense—that is, a film with a manufacturing defect that causes harm.

Films are also protected speech in the meaning of the First Amendment. There have been attempts, for example, to hold gun manufacturers responsible for acts of violence committed by handguns. So far the courts have ruled in general that the presumed Second Amendment protection of the right to bear arms trumps any claim to damage caused by firearms. Presumably, the same could be true in the case of films, except as protected by the First Amendment. In the case of motion pictures or guns, we have to make a choice: do we want to restrict the constitutional protections provided to all or act to prevent the actions of deranged individuals, such as John Hinckley, in isolated cases?

So far the answer is no. Probably the best recent test case in this regard is the Kentucky school-shooting case discussed briefly at the beginning of this section. In dismissing the liability lawsuit against the producers of video games and the film *The Basketball Diaries*, the court ruled that the producers of media could not be held liable for criminal acts, for three reasons. First of all, it was not foreseeable that someone would watch *The Basketball Diaries* or play a video game and walk into a school and start shooting; this is based on the principle of "duty care," or the obligation of manufacturers to take reasonable care that a product is not harmful. Second, manufacturers can reasonably assume with a few exceptions that people will not put their products to criminal use. Third, tort liability cannot be applied to speech protected under the First Amendment, which clearly includes the movie but, interestingly, perhaps not the video games. Finally, the defendants did not intend to create harm, nor were they negligent in the marketing of their products.[33] This ruling was so unequivocal that it seems unlikely that the tort law will be used successfully to sue filmmakers in the foreseeable future. But as we have seen, times do change.

In one area, government censorship of film will remain a possibility. Because children are impressionable and are limited in their activities (such as not having the right to vote until age eighteen), it is neither improper nor, according to the courts, unconstitutional to restrict the films they see. Therefore, volunteer but strictly enforced rating systems and the legislatively mandated V-Chip seem completely appropriate.

Another issue to consider is that of local standards. This issue is thorny because the courts still do not provide a completely clear guide in this regard. On the one hand, there is in the federalist system a general guarantee of local autonomy. On the other hand, the protections provided by the Bill of Rights are supposed to be accorded to all Americans, regardless of where they live. Consequently, there are at least two constitutional principles in conflict here. While states' rights are protected under the U.S. Constitution and there seems to be at least some leeway in the law for the judgments of local voters and juries, as long as films are protected expression under the First Amendment, communities that want to restrict the screening of some films seem to have no legal recourse.

But that is not the end of the issue. Market incentives can still be brought to bear, and they are. As a practical matter, film distributors censure what films communities are likely to see. Certain theaters are designated "art houses" and are assigned a special category of film—foreign films, small independent films, and the like. Most other theaters are slated for more mainstream fare. It is no accident that both small theaters all over rural American and suburban cineplexes all show the same films at the same time while more controversial films are slated for limited release (in large cities and on college campuses). The market incentive is at work. The film industry is already sensitive to the needs and demands of local communities without much government intervention.

Feature Films: Five Mystery Films

The Motion Picture Association of America urges exhibitors to abide by a voluntary rating system. Since the MPAA represents an industry that is dependent on good public relations, the rating system is sensitive to market in no other comparable way. Legal standards are a function of the legislative and judicial process. But the rating system is reflective of the market, at least as the raters at the MPAA see it. How films are rated, then, tells us much about the tolerances, demands, and quirks of the viewing public.

In the following exercise, read the description of each film and guess its rating. To test yourself further, see if you can name each movie.

Mystery Film 1

In the performance of his duties as a police officer, a patrolman is shot in the head and left for dead. We witness the shooting from the victim's perspective. The downed and clinically dead officer is then surgically transformed into a cyborg who, as he gains the memory of his former self, seeks revenge against those who "killed" him. Along the way he burns, shoots, and tortures his nemeses. In one scene a man is doused with toxic waste, and as he begins to melt, he is hit by a car. He explodes like a bowl of Jell-O. From inside the car we see the windshield wipers rub off the rest of his remains.

Mystery Film 2

A dancer goes to Las Vegas with the intent of becoming a showgirl. Through grit and determination and her willingness to take her clothes off a lot, she reaches the top of her profession. She also has sexual intercourse with several men, including her boss. In the end, she decides that fame and fortune are not all that they are cracked up to be, so she leaves town to resume a normal life. There is lots of nudity in this film, mainly from the waist up, and simulated intercourse in a number of positions and locales, including a swimming pool.

Mystery Film 3

A religious dissident is convicted of sedition by the colonial power that is occupying his country. He is sentenced to death. He is then tortured and maimed in excruciating detail before he is graphically nailed to a cross, where he is left to bleed to death. The lion's share of this film depicts the graphic torture and execution of this man.

Mystery Film 4

Boy meets girl in Paris. Boy likes girl; girl likes boy. Boy and girl have lots of kinky sex in this film, which includes several scenes of simulated intercourse. There is lots of nudity, including one brief scene of full frontal nudity. In one instance, the couple have a verbal exchange about engaging in anal intercourse using butter as a lubricant.

Mystery Film 5

In this film we follow a day in the life of a pair of hit men for a drug dealer. Among the things we get to see are the execution-style murders of a rival gang, the rape of one man by another (fairly graphically displayed), one man killing another with a samurai sword, and one man shooting another in the testicles with a shotgun. In one vignette, treated as high comedy, one of the hit men accidentally shoots a prisoner in the backseat of their car, blowing the victim's brains all over the upholstery. The hit men are then forced to clean up their mess and pay for their crime with their clothes.

The answers to this test are located at the end of this chapter.

EXERCISE

The MPAA posts its ratings and the reasons for its ratings of most films made after 1968 (www.filmratings.com). Review the film ratings, especially those at the risqué (NC-17) end of spectrum. Do you agree with the MPAA's rating standards, and what do those standards say about us as a society?

Answers to quiz:
Mystery film 1—*Robocop* (1987): R
Mystery film 2—*Showgirls* (1995): NC-17
Mystery film 3—*The Passion of the Christ* (2004): R
Mystery film 4—*Last Tango in Paris* (1972): X (equivalent of the modern NC-17)
Mystery film 5—*Pulp Fiction* (1994): R

NOTES

1. Theodore N. Beckman and William R. Davidson, *Marketing* (New York: Ronald Press, 1967) 21.

2. See Joel W. Martin and Conrad E. Ostwalt Jr., eds., *Screening the Sacred: Religion, Myth, and Ideology in Popular American Film* (Boulder, Colo.: Westview, 1995), especially sec. 3, "Ideological Criticism."

3. These are a couple of examples cited by Margaret Miles in her book *Seeing and Believing: Religion and Values in the Movies* (Boston: Beacon, 1996).

4. Brian Godawa, *Hollywood Worldviews: Watching Films with Wisdom and Discernment* (Downers Grove, Ill.: InterVarsity Press, 2002).

5. Existentialism is the belief that there is no God and thus no preordained characteristics of man, commonly called human nature. Accordingly, "Man simply is. Not that he is simply what he conceives himself to be, but he is what he wills, and as he conceives himself after already existing—as he wills to be after that leap towards existence. Man is nothing else but that which he makes of himself." That realization precipitates what is known as the *existential crisis.* Jean-Paul Sartre, "Existentialism," in *Existentialism from Dostoevsky to Sartre,* ed. Walter Kaufmann (New York: Meridian, 1969), 291.

6. Throughout the 1980s CBS suffered a severe decline in ratings and revenues (a decline of about 25 percent). During that period, CBS went from being the most avant-garde to the

least (and least profitable) of the major television networks, with the oldest viewing audience. Eventually, in 1995, the company disappeared as an independent entity when it was sold to Westinghouse. James Roman, ed., *Love, Light, and a Dream: Television's Past, Present, and Future* (Westport, Conn.: Praeger, 1998) 5.

7. See Clyde Wilcox, *Onward Christian Soldiers? The Religious Right in American Politics* (Boulder, Colo.: Westview, 1996); or Kathryn C. Montgomery, *Target, Prime Time: Advocacy Groups and the Struggle over Entertainment Television* (New York: Oxford University Press, 1990), 8.

8. *Business Week Online*, "Bollywood vs. Hollywood," December 2, 2002, www.businessweek.com/magazine/content/02_48/b3810019.htm (accessed August 23, 2005). What constitutes an American film is a matter of some contemplation, since much of the production of American films is now outsourced or done overseas.

9. Article 1, section 8, clause 3, of the U.S. Constitution empowers Congress "to regulate Commerce with foreign Nations, and among the several States, and with the Indian Tribes." Since the Great Depression, the federal courts have often used the commerce clause as a justification for ruling as unconstitutional a variety of actions taken by the states.

10. *Mutual Film Co. v. Industrial Commission of Ohio*, 236 U.S. 230 (1915), http://caselaw.lp.findlaw.com/scripts/getcase.pl?court=US&vol=236&invol=230 (accessed August 5, 2005).

11. Margaret Thorpe, *America at the Movies* (New Haven, Conn.: Yale University Press, 1939).

12. Because there were several Jews prominent in the Bolshevik Revolution, Jews have often been painted as agents of international communism.

13. Populism is the political doctrine that supports the rights and powers of the common people in their struggle with the privileged elite.

14. Even today booking agents collude to ensure that competing theaters do not show the same films. The fact that this seems to be a clear antitrust violation provides one explanation for why Hollywood is such an active player in national electoral politics.

15. For an excellent history of the founding and enforcement of the Hollywood production code, see Steven Vaughn, "Morality and Entertainment: The Origins of the Motion Picture Production Code," *Journal of American History* 77, no. 1 (June 1990): 39–65.

16. This explains why Hollywood so enthusiastically embraced the code even after the U.S. Supreme Court declared the NIRA unconstitutional in 1935.

17. *United States v. Paramount Pictures, Inc.* 334 U.S. 131 (1948).

18. For a good short discussion of the development of the rating system, see "MPAA Film Rating System," *Wikipedia: The Free Encyclopedia*, http://en.wikipedia.org/wiki/Movie_ratings#History (accessed August 5, 2005). In addition, the MPAA has its own movie ratings site at www.mpaa.org/movieratings.

19. Federal Trade Commission, "Marketing Violent Entertainment to Children: A One-Year Follow-Up Review of Industry Practices in the Motion Picture, Music Recording, and Electronic Game Industries," December 2001, http://news.findlaw.com/hdocs/ftc/ftcviolentcertpt/20501.pdf (accessed February 21, 2005).

20. Excerpted from the appeal from *Joe James v. Meow Media, Inc.*, 2002 Fed App. 0270P (6th Cir.), http://pacer.ca6.uscourts.gov/cgi-bin/getopn.pl?OPINION=02a0270p.06 (accessed August 5, 2005).

21. "A tort is an act that injures someone in some way, and for which the injured person may sue the wrongdoer for damages. Legally, torts are called civil wrongs, as opposed to criminal

ones." 'Lectric Law Library, "Legal Definition of *Tort*," www.lectlaw.com/def2/t032.htm (accessed December 31, 2004).

22. *Joe James v. Meow Media, Inc.*

23. *Burstyn v. Wilson*, 343 U.S. 495 (1952) http://caselaw.lp.findlaw.com/scripts/getcase.pl? navby=case&court=US&vol=343&invol=495 (accessed August 5, 2005).

24. *Chaplinsky v. State of New Hampshire*, 315 U.S. 568 (1942) http://caselaw.lp .findlaw.com/cgi-bin/getcase.pl?navby=case&court=us&vol=315&invol=568 (accessed August 5, 2005).

25. *Kovacs v. Cooper*, 336 U.S. 77 (1949) http://caselaw.lp.findlaw.com/scripts/getcase.pl? court=US&vol=336&invol=77 (accessed August 5, 2005).

26. *New York Times Co. v. Sullivan*, 376 U.S. 254 (1964), http://caselaw.lp.findlaw.com/ scripts/getcase.pl?court=us&vol=376&invol=254 (accessed August 5, 2005).

27. *Roth v. United States*, 354 U.S. 476 (1957), http://caselaw.lp.findlaw.com/scripts/ getcase.pl?court=US&vol=354&invol=476 (accessed August 5, 2005).

28. *Miller v. California*, 413 U.S. 15 (1973), http://caselaw.lp.findlaw.com/scripts/getcase .pl?court=us&vol=413&invol=15 (accessed August 5, 2005).

29. *Sable Communications of Cal., Inc. v. FCC*, 492 U.S. 115 (1989) http://caselaw.lp. findlaw.com/cgi-bin/getcase.pl?navby=case&court=US&vol=492&invol=115&pageno= 126 (accessed August 5, 2005).

30. The FCC defines indecent speech as "language or material that, in context, depicts or describes in terms patently offensive in terms of community standards for the broadcast medium, sexual or excretory activities or organs." U.S. Federal Communications Commission, "Indecent Broadcasts Restricted to 10 P.M.–6 A.M.," www.fcc.gov/eb/broadcast/opi.html (accessed August 23, 2005).

31. *United States v. Playboy Entertainment Group, Inc.* (98-1682) 529 U.S. 803 (2000), http://supct.law.cornell.edu/supct/html/98-1682.ZS.html (accessed August 5, 2005).

32. A Florida jury did just that (award damages to a smoker), only to be reversed in a higher court on what was basically a technicality.

33. *Joe James v. Meow Media, Inc.*

SUGGESTED READING

Black, Gregory. *Hollywood Censored: Morality Codes, Catholics, and the Movies*. New York: Cambridge University Press, 1996.

Koppes, Clayton, and Gregory Black. *Hollywood Goes to War: How Politics, Profits, and Propaganda Shaped World War II Movies*. Berkeley: University of California Press, 1990.

Lasalle, Mick. *Complicated Women: Sex and Power in Pre-Code Hollywood*. New York: St. Martin's Press, 2001.

Leff, Leonard, and Jerold Simmons. *Dame in the Kimono: Hollywood, Censorship, and the Production Code*. Lexington: University of Kentucky Press, 2001.

Oshima, Nagisa. *Cinema, Censorship, and the State*. Boston: MIT Press, 1992.

Ryan, Michael, and Douglas Kellner. *Camera Politica: The Politics and Ideology of Contemporary Hollywood Film*. Bloomington: Indiana University Press, 1988.

Wilcox, Clyde. *Onward Christian Soldiers? The Religious Right in American Politics*. Boulder, Colo.: Westview, 1996).

Conclusion

The central question in this book is, what do commercial films have to do with politics? The answer as it has been laid out in the preceding chapters is multifaceted and complex and can really be summed up in two parts. First, we must consider the degree of the film industry's influence on American politics. At various times, the industry's influence has more or less depended on the market for films, the technology of the time, and the political economy of the film industry itself. But the main question here is one of cause and effect. Do films promote certain types of behaviors and spread certain beliefs that are outside the mainstream of society? Or are they in the main a reflection of prevailing attitudes in society? The answer is, probably a little of both but more one than the other.

Second, the film industry is an instructive lesson in the politics of government–industry relations in the United States. But beyond that, how we have regulated how we regard the film industry tells us much about American political culture. The fact that the film industry has such a high profile and that it was in large part founded by an immigrant group outside the mainstream of American cultural life is an instructive example of how we regard and treat the "outsider." Thus, in the main, this study of film politics is the study of American political culture. Furthermore, tangentially, the study of politics and film tells us something about presidential, congressional, and regulatory process. In general, however, the story of politics and film is the story, through metaphor, of American political development in the twentieth century.

THE FILM INDUSTRY IN AMERICAN HISTORY

The role of commercial film in American history is a relatively recent one, really only since the turn of the twentieth century. But quickly after its introduction, the film medium became the first medium entertainment for the masses. Up until then, theater, music, and the arts had been the relative province of the elite. But by the early 1920s, movies were regularly viewed by a large and growing segment of the American public. The problem for the elite then was how to react to this entirely new phenomenon. The answer, it seems, was to censor the content of films by establishing, with the blessing of the courts, film censorship boards at the local community level. Ultimately, the Hays Office and the production code were established as a form of censorship at the source. By gently intimidating studio owners, most of whom were first-generation immigrant Jews, and by intimating that their position in society was tenuous at best and subject to revocation, Main Street America was able to manipulate the content of film. The moguls, having experienced religious persecution firsthand in Europe, and for reasons related to their business, were more than willing to go along.[1]

This regime of elite control, better known as the golden era of Hollywood cinema, was reinforced by the vertical integration of the movie industry. Theater owners could show their product only with the permission of the studios because Hollywood had an effective monopoly over the production and distribution of films. Thus, the content of commercial films for the period from 1933 to just after the end of World War II was relatively homogeneous and, while often brilliant in execution, bland in character.

But as economists tell us, monopolies are bound to erode. The recovery of the European film industry, the advent of television, and the hunger among audiences for something new began to chip away at the edifice of the golden era. The movie genre of film noir ushered in a new and more daring style of Hollywood cinema. While the Hays Office still exerted substantial control over film content, censorship at the local level was limited by the antitrust breakup of the vertical monopoly (in the *Paramount* decision of 1948) and the Court's reversal of its view that commerical films were not constitutionally protected speech (in the *Burstyn* decision of 1952). In some sense, the last gasp of the golden era was the imposition of the Hollywood blacklist when a number of filmmakers, writers, and actors (many of whom happened to be Jewish) were accused of being communists and were forbidden from working in the industry. The result was to intimidate the rest of the industry, including the moguls, who were beginning to pass the torch to a new generation.

Subject to the limitations of the blacklist code, uninspired filmmaking in the 1950s could not prevent film attendance from continuing to plummet. By the early 1960s the film industry collapsed and was largely bought out by large industrial conglomerates. Eventually the parts of the movie industry were reconfigured, and the industry became what it is today, a modern commercial enterprise. The studios are a shadow of what they once were. They are subsidiaries of larger corporations that outsource the production of films. The result is a more commercial film, one that is more sensitive to the audience it hopes to attract. Critics and moralists from both the Right and Left can object to this arrangement. After all, strictly speaking, business is not moral; it is not immoral; it is amoral. Conservatives argue that the appeal of commercial films to the lowest common denominator degrades the morals of our society. Leftists argue that the corporate monopoly in American film reinforces the corporate control of our economy and of our politics by reinforcing the belief in the status quo and excluding from the screen certain messages considered subversive by the industrialists who now produce films.

But both these critiques seem just a bit disingenuous. If industrial filmmaking is simply the act of satisfying a demand, then the fact that films may seem immoral says more about our society and the audience for film than it does about the businesses that produce them. Furthermore, if there is a market for biblical epics, the film industry has every incentive to tap that market. *The Passion of the Christ* may or may not be a milestone in that regard. The same kind of argument can be made to counter the criticisms of the Left. If there were a market for movies extolling workers' rights, the film industry has an incentive to produce those films. Furthermore, the vibrant market for so-called independent films (even though most indies are ultimately distributed by member companies—the major studios—of the MPAA) demonstrates that films with alternate messages can get screened. Could it be that progressive films don't get screened because there really isn't a market for them?

If the content of film is more a reflection than a driver of the public mood, the movie industry tells us more about who we are than who we will be, which brings to mind the next major question addressed in this book: What behaviors would the screening of biblical epics or calls to a workers' revolution be likely to produce anyhow? What are the causes and effects of commercial film?

CAUSE AND EFFECT

While there is certainly evidence to suggest that film is both a cause and an effect, the direction of causality is more one way than the other. Because the film industry is a business and, particularly in the modern era, produces films to meet a market demand, it seems fairly clear that the demand is driving the supply. There is a market for certain types of films, and the selection of those films tells us something about the audience that consumes those products. But the relationship is not as simple as that. Research indicates that the messages in media "activate" and then reinforce certain biases, preferences, and behaviors. So, in that sense, films could drive behavior.[2] But there are a couple of caveats that should be added to this conclusion. First of all, movies are one of the least obtrusive and affecting of the media. While watching the same film over and over may result in a cumulative effect on behavior (as doing so did to John Hinckley in watching *Taxi Driver*), most moviegoers will see a film once or twice. And even if viewers are avid moviegoers and even if different films reinforce similar messages, there is an absolute limit on how often one can go to the movie theater. Consequently, it is more likely that television, video games, and even recorded music will play a more prominent role in reinforcing the existing beliefs of those who watch, play, and listen to them. Furthermore, it's not just negative or objectionable messages that are reinforced in the media. Little has been done to measure the countervailing influence of positive messages in the media and whether, on balance, the positive outweighs the negative. Finally, the commercial film attracts a surprisingly narrow audience.

In the days before the advent of television, film entertainment was practically the only game in town, with the exception of radio. As suggested, the movies may have been the first truly mass entertainment. A phenomenally large percentage of the American public went to the movies regularly in the 1920s, 1930s, and 1940s. But with the advent of television and other media outlets competing for the public's free time, moviegoing populations became more narrow and more distinct. Besides the fact that television, video games, and radio compete for the attention of the film audience, viewers have other ways of screening a movie than by doing so in a theater. Broadcast television, DVDs, videotapes, paid movie channels, and television channels that air commercially uninterrupted films all compete for the public's entertainment dollars. The consequence is that the most lucrative moviegoing public can be fairly described as being relatively young and affluent and without children and religious or civic obligations to occupy their time. It is for this target audience that most Hollywood films are made, and because of that, the content of film, while reflecting American society to be sure, reflects a relatively narrow segment of that society.

Now it may be the case that rather than try to attract an audience they already have, Hollywood filmmakers can go out and seek audiences that don't go to the movies. But that is really not how marketing generally works in a capitalist system. It is not an accident that the audience for films exhibits the kind of profile they do. Nothing that Hollywood can do will make it easier for the parents with children to get out for an evening's entertainment or for churchgoers to subsume their religious obligations or for the poor to pay to see a film in a first-run theater. These are the realities of the market that drive not only the audience for movies but the content of films as well. The drives for film censorship therefore represent not just, as the proponents of censorship suggest, a desire to protect the community but an attempt by one part of the community, those who don't go to the movies, to impose its control over those who do go to the movies.

SUBJECTIVE EVALUATIONS

The American Film Institute just released its list of the top American comedy films. By and large the list makes lots of sense (see www.afionline.org). With interest, I did notice that the film *Shampoo* made the list. *Shampoo* (starring Warren Beatty, Julie Christie, and Goldie Hawn) is a morality tale about the loneliness of a serial womanizer. In the end, the main character, played by Beatty, is left standing alone on a hill pondering his fate. He has just lost the only woman he ever really loved; in fact, we get a sense that she may be the only woman he ever will love. To me, this movie is hardly a comedy. In fact, calling *Shampoo* a comedy is like calling Mozart's opera *Don Giovanni* a comedy. To go one step further, *Shampoo* is *Don Giovanni*. Now, *The Producers* (1968), with Zero Mostel and Gene Wilder, that's a comedy.

I bring this up to illustrate a central point to this book. Our evaluation of films, the parts that are really important to most of us, is highly personal; it doesn't include the technical quality of the film or the obscure references to film history that are the historical nods to the inside Hollywood crowd. In that sense, my reaction to *Shampoo* is hardly to think of it as a comedy. (A kind of subplot in the film concerns the election of 1972, but that part made no impression on me at the time, and I may have to look at the film again from a different, older perspective.)

By the same token, one of the funniest films ever made in my opinion is *Showgirls* (1995; starring all of Elizabeth Berkeley and Gina Gershon). I don't know whether the producers of the film meant this to be a comedy. But when I saw this film a couple of years ago with a good friend of mine, we couldn't stop laughing. Some of the funniest scenes in film history are in this film. But let me issue a warning. If you don't tolerate nudity, foul language, and simulated sex, don't rent this film. This film is not about any of those elements, but there is plenty of each. And maybe, too, you won't get the joke. That's okay. That doesn't mean you don't have a sense of humor. It just means that you don't have my sense of humor. And thank goodness, too. What a boring world that would be if everyone thought like me.

All of this discussion of "different strokes for different folks" is pretty harmless until we get to the politics of film. The ideas that I consider harmless or even right on the mark, other people consider objectionable. There is certainly some consensus as to what constitutes harmful films, particularly as they affect children. Thus, the film-rating system is heavily weighted toward parental involvement. There is also a certain amount of consensus concerning the harm of screening hard-core pornography. So, as the rating system is enforced, it tends to be much more stringently imposed on films that are sexually explicit than on films that are violent or have some other kind of social or political message.

Right now, as of the writing of this book (2005), there is quite a controversy concerning news coverage of the war in Iraq. The heart of this controversy goes to the subjective evaluations of what people will see when they view the images of dead Americans or dead Iraqis or of American soldiers torturing Iraqi prisoners of war.[3] The conservative presumption is that opponents of the war want the public to see all the gruesome images and thus turn against the policies of George W. Bush. Despite the well-meaning objections to showing American war casualties, in respect to the families of the dead, the flip side of the argument is that supporters of the war want to insulate the public against the inevitably troubling images in order to maintain public support to "stay the course." This is not a new controversy.

As far back as World War II, there was quite of a bit of disagreement concerning the depiction of American dead and wounded in the documentary film *The Battle for San Pietro* (1945). Ultimately, because of its record of American dead, the film was heavily censored by the War Department. Even today it is difficult to find a version of the film that is not heavily edited. During the Korean and Vietnam wars, the same controversy flared up on occasion, to the point at which contemporary films often speak of current wars in metaphor. It is hard not to associate the fictional re-creation of the Korean War in *MASH* (1970) or the slaughter of the American Indian in *Little Big Man* (1970) or the senseless World War II bombing of an Italian village in *Catch-22* (1970) with the Vietnam War that was actually going on at the time. Even in times of peace, war films can attract quite a bit of controversy. Steven Spielberg's *Saving Private Ryan* (1998) was attacked from the political Right, ostensibly for its depiction of cowardice among American troops during World War II. I say "ostensibly" because one gets the sense that there is also a political agenda behind the attacks that reflect more the Left-Right debate in the United States than the actual content of the film.[4]

What this suggests is that the reaction to film at the societal and even at the individual level tells us as much about the audience as it does about the film itself. The reaction to *The Passion of the Christ* is instructive in this regard. Beyond evaluations of the technical merits of the film, the range of reactions to the film is a veritable metaphor for the spectrum of American political debate. While the *Passion* is just one of the most obvious examples in this regard, film criticism in general can be regarded as metaphor even when the connection between the film being evaluated and public life is much more subtle.

But besides being an instructive indicator of where the film audience stands, subjective evaluations are not really that important until they are translated into action. That being the case, much of the politics of films involves the attempt of one group or another to censor the content of films.

CENSORSHIP AND CONTROL

Beyond the crocodile tears shed for the morality of our youth, much of what passes for concern for morality is really an attempt at another purpose. What I am suggesting is that the politics of censorship are not as much about morality as they are about control. As discussed, many of the early attempts to censor films were engaged as a kind of class warfare. The nickelodeon version of film was considered too crass and vulgar for the common man or woman, filled with too much sex and violence. From the elite perspective, film was a danger to the masses. The films of the carney sideshow had none of the refinement of, say, the bloodbath at the end of a typical Shakespearean tragedy.

Furthermore, when the movie industry fell into the hands of people with funny accents and apostolic religious beliefs, the problem was no longer the corruption of the masses by the medium but the corruption of the medium by the masses. The next phase of movie censorship came as an attempt to weed out "foreign influences" that had pervaded American films. The only thing that was particularly remarkable about this second era of censorship was that it was orchestrated by the Catholic church in what is basically a Protestant country.

Maybe in the case of adults controlling what children see there is a justification for this kind of control. Children are assumed to be in their minority and thus unable to make responsible decisions for themselves. But adults are assumed to be able to make their own decisions. That is the definition of an adult. Thus, censorship of what adults see is nothing more than control. Viewed from that perspective, the golden era of Hollywood film was not so golden after all. Yes, some great films were made during that era, as they are today. But what viewers were allowed to see was controlled. So, before we start waxing poetic about that great era of Hollywood cinema, let us consider the implications of what was going on at the time. Who was being un-American and who wasn't: the censors or those who wanted to defy them?

The golden era of censorship ended when the government intervened, as it should when there is gross distortion of the free market, and broke up the Hollywood monopoly. Nevertheless, one gets the sense that the days of vertical-integration monopoly were numbered in any event with the advent of television and the recovery of the postwar European film industry. Nonetheless, without the intervention of the government the breakup would have taken many years, and that fact alone makes the government's actions in this case commendable.

So without the tool of monopoly to control the content of film, those who wished to control had to resort to other measures to assert their authority. In American politics, one of the primary tactics of achieving policy goals is through personal attacks. If one could demonstrate that filmmakers or newscasters were sick or crazy or disloyal, then one could intimidate them and thus discredit their wrongheaded politics. Taking advantage of the Red Scare at the end of World War II, Senator Joseph McCarthy and his minions sought to discredit their political rivals by labeling them *communist*. It is no accident that the two main targets of the McCarthy era were opposition politicians and entertainers. The attack on the first group is completely understandable, and the second diabolically brilliant. It is not just enough to defeat your opponents in politics—that is only temporary—but if you can control the interpretation of that defeat and reinforce the message that emerges, that is real victory.[5]

But eventually McCarthy fell victim to his own devices, and no one was more deserving. So discredited was McCarthy that the term *McCarthyism* has been coined in the English language as a pejorative word. After McCarthy, the question for politicians became how to discredit political opponents without looking like McCarthy. The answer was science. After all, if scientific evidence could be brought to bear to prove that their opponents were sick or crazy, then their opponents would be discredited or intimidated. Thus, the junk science of media psychology was born. Literally hundreds of studies were conducted looking for a connection between media depictions of violence and actual behavior, with the same (surprise!) results. The weight of the evidence suggested that the media cause violence, with the inescapable conclusion that those who produce the entertainment media are either sick or crazy or undeniably evil.

I argue in chapter 4 that much of what passes for evidence that the media cause violence is simply wrong or can be completely misinterpreted. (To be fair to the researchers, their results are often misinterpreted or exaggerated by people with a political agenda.) But let's just assume, for the sake of argument, that research is right—that media depictions of violence cause violence. Okay—now what?

I suppose we could return to the good old days of the production code and the Hays Commission. But, no, that wouldn't work. What made the production code work was the fact that the censorship board's decisions could be enforced. Films that did not meet code standards were simply not screened in the theaters that the studios owned or controlled. Nowadays films would be screened whether they were approved or not, as the vertical integration of the film industry no long exists (to the same extent).

Who would form a film censorship board? Our society, in the political sense, is now as diverse as it ever has been. With the advent of the Voting Rights Act and other legislation that eased restraints not only on black participation but on the participation of other voters, it is highly unlikely that any consensus would form about the composition of the board or its message. Certainly, it would no longer be the case that the Catholic church would be ceded the right to speak for moviegoers or the elite.

Additionally, what kind of censorship should be permitted and, more important, how much? This is a slippery-slope argument. Once we begin to censor film for content, there is no telling what direction that will go. Presumably, if violent films make people more violent, or sexy films make people more prone to having sex, then liberal films will make people more liberal and conservative films will make people more conservative. The battle over film content will ultimately become a battle for our hearts and minds, and the outcome will in no way reflect the market demand for entertainment: it will simply be the outcome of a battle for control. Fortunately, up to now, the courts do not allow it. However, times do change. The Supreme Court has taken a 180-degree turn from the original notion that film is product, not art. One gets the sense that the Court could at some point turn away from *Miller* (regarding the three-point obscenity test) and lift the First Amendment protections currently enjoyed by commercial films. One landmark lawsuit could allow the censorship of film, either directly or indirectly, through the artifice of liability law or some other legal principle that we haven't even thought of yet.

We have to consider what we will have lost if we subvert the First Amendment to censor movies. On balance, would it be worth it to keep *Taxi Driver* off the market if it meant that President Reagan wouldn't have been shot by John Hinckley? This is a classic security versus freedom argument. Reagan also might not have been shot had the private ownership of handguns been forbidden. But I can already hear the objections of the gun-ownership crowd. The right to bear arms is protected by the U.S. Constitution. The same could be said for the untrammeled right to screen *Taxi Driver* in the theater. Hinckley would have done something anyhow (but probably not shoot Reagan to impress Jodie Foster). Freedom of expression is the cornerstone of a free society. Movies don't kill people; people kill people and so on. I can't accidentally kill my next-door neighbor with a videotape.

Of course, it is true that film censorship was never mandatory, mainly because studio owners of the golden era were intimidated by their own immigrant ancestry, by the context of world fascism, and by unclear court decisions on the status of film. Nowadays, owners of the studios *are* the elite. The religious Right cannot intimidate them. In fact, they are probably more frightened of their shareholders. Furthermore, it is not clear that the religious Right goes to the movies. Therefore, from the market perspective, the religious Right has little or no leverage (although the success of *The Passion* could change all that). Thus, the likelihood of voluntary compliance with something like the code in the modern era is quite unlikely.

Now, it is possible that if it were patently clear that movie violence caused actual violence, appeals could be made to the collective conscience of studio executives. And, indeed, theater owners have made a half-hearted attempt to enforce the ratings system (more actively after the Columbine incident). But more than that is unlikely. This,

I have argued, is a function of the fact that the film industry is increasingly being publicly held and the distribution end of the business is more often than not part of a large conglomerate. Studio executives couldn't restrain themselves if they wanted to. Corporate headquarters wouldn't allow it. If it is clear to the studios that films with a certain type of content are more salable, then market forces will prevail.

The reason that I focus on feature films in saying this—that voluntary compliance with some kind of code is unlikely—is that the market for films is about the least encumbered of any in the entertainment media. Political activists have some leverage in the market for television because the FCC issues broadcasting licenses. Through the licensing procedure, political pressure can be brought to bear to influence television programming content. The same can be said for radio. But in the market for movies, there is no FCC (except when movies are aired on cable or broadcast television). Short of an unexpected court ruling that attaches to film some sort of product liability or dictates that film exists as product and not expression, there exists for film a market that is about as free as one can be.

Even so, marketization has its own bias, which is mainly associated with the availability of money to finance production. Money for production and distribution is readily available for *Rocky VI* or *Star Wars II: The Next to the Last Episode* and other such tedious nonsense. And I suppose corporate America will be reluctant to finance and screen films that are critical of corporate America or are controversial in general. In a recent case, Miramax Films (owned by Disney) refused to distribute *Fahrenheit 911*, a film directed by Michael Moore critical of President George W. Bush. Studio heads probably regret that decision, as the film was eventually distributed and screened and was an enormous financial success. Given the variety of outlets for films these days, it seems certain that most films of a certain quality that are produced and directed by established filmmakers will be distributed and screened in some medium.

But that is a bias in content that is present in all American media. This would alarm a Marxist to be sure—the capitalist conspiracy to control the thoughts and minds of the proletariat and all that—but it is more likely that because of our preference for free market liberalism, Americans get the films that they want to watch. We are limited in what we see not because of some kind of plot orchestrated by the ruling class.

Nevertheless, because *The Blair Witch Project* (1999; one step above a bunch of kids in their backyard with a video camera) can get made and screened, one gets the sense that anything can get made and screened. And, with the fragmentation of the market that allows for an economic return on films made for almost the smallest niche, I would have to say that now is the golden age of American cinema. There is more product now of a wider variety and better quality than ever before. American movies are so popular in France that the French government has been "forced" to set quotas on the number of American films that can be screened in French cinemas—hence, the present golden age of American cinema.

In terms of content, what exists now is a pretty benign environment. I have pointed out that we should mostly ignore the junk science that supports the politics of control. Most of us who go to the movies see what we want to see and aren't much the worse for wear. People who don't go to the movies, cultural conservatives, are horrified by what we watch in the movies and on television. Let us not forget for a minute that the culture wars are not about culture—they are about control—and that attacks on our persons are really attacks on our politics.

That last point is why I think it is so important to discuss film and politics in the same context. Films are meant to be entertainment, but they also tell us something about who we are as a people. The debate over film content as part of the culture wars tells us something about the politics of our society. We are engaged in a constant struggle over the untrammeled rights of expression guaranteed to us under the U.S. Constitution. There will always be those in society who are not satisfied with their own status unless they can control others as well.

The intersection of film and politics is just a piece in the complex mosaic of American politics. While at a superficial level, many people would not see a connection between politics and film, in this book I have outlined some of the ways that the film industry both reflects and even in some cases drives the politics of the country. Ideally, in reading this book, students of politics will begin to consider how this and other seemingly innocuous aspects of our national life affect our larger society. By the same token, I hope that students of film, in reading this book, will be more reflective about the importance of the work that they do. Ultimately, if all I have done in this book is to introduce readers to a slightly different perspective on politics through the study of film, then I have more than succeeded at my task.

Feature Film: *Kill Bill: Vol. 2* (2004)

Whenever a film is roundly applauded, I want to make the effort to go out and see it just to get a sense what the gold standard is. The fact is that I saw *Kill Bill: Vol. 1* and didn't really care for it. Violence, even cartoon violence, is really not my cup of tea these days; it is hard to enjoy happy killing on-screen, especially when there is real violence taking place in the Middle East. So when I walked out at the end of *Kill Bill: Vol. 1*, I had pretty much decided to take a pass on *Kill Bill: Vol. 2*. But when practically every film reviewer in America praised the film, I dragged myself down to the theater, and, in some sense, I wasn't disappointed: *Kill Bill: Vol. 2* was as disheartening an experience as I had expected it to be.

I keep looking for signs of sentient life on planet Earth, but when films like *Kill Bill: Vol. 2* and *The Passion of the Christ* lead in the box office, I despair for the future of humankind. What does the success of this film and that of *The Passion* have in common? They are both essentially snuff films that appeal to widely disparate audiences. And while I would kind of expect *Kill Bill* to do well, given the target audience for most American films, I am

Kill Bill: Vol. 1. *Courtesy of M.P. & T.V. Photo Archive.*

still a little perplexed about the popularity of *The Passion*. After all, there is a great tradition of pacificism that comes out of the Christian religion, and it is my understanding that the outstanding feature of the modern faith is the de-emphasis on the crucifixion and the focus on the substantive doctrines of the religion.

However, I am beginning to think that the tolerance for violence in our society is endemic, and it is not the movies that have caused us to be this way. In a society where a man's making love to a woman is considered obscene but a man's killing a woman is not, there are some seriously misplaced priorities. A society that discourages the news reporting of the real violence of war but winks at the simulated violence of movies is a society that is in trouble. In *Kill Bill: Vol. 2* a woman's eye is plucked out and then graphically squished between the toes of our "hero." In the theater I was in, laughter rippled through the audience. I know it's a movie; I know it's not real, but am I crazy when I think that's not funny?

Quentin Tarantino had essentially one original idea. In *Pulp Fiction* he explored an unusual narrative form. Even then the idea was not that original. Film plots have been relying on the device of flashbacks since the beginning. However, in the past, directors used some kind of indicator to warn the audience that what we were seeing was a flashback. Tarantino leaves it to us to guess. Eventually, we catch on and find that the old narrative devices were not really that necessary. That is something of a creation I suppose, but it is hardly *Citizen Kane* (come to think of it, that movie used the same device). Other than that, *Pulp Fiction* and *Kill Bill* are just atmospheric cut-and-paste. In academics we call that plagiarism; in Hollywood it is called homage. I am aware that *Kill*

Bill: Vol. 2 contains numerous historical references to films, television shows, and comic strips of the past and that these references are really winks to the filmetic cognoscenti. I suppose in some sense it makes the film a bit more interesting.

But while Tarantino tries to remake the kung fu action film, I get the sense that he doesn't understand or, more likely, doesn't want to understand what made those films unique. What made *Enter the Dragon* (1973) a great film despite the relatively primitive production values or the acting, which was a little less than wooden, was the magnetism of a star, kung fu master Bruce Lee. Some films can be built around a star. The James Bond films with Sean Connery come to mind. But Uma Thurman can't carry this film. Tarantino is clearly smitten with her, and she is a lovely actress; she just can't carry this film. And without much of a plot and without much dialogue, this film without a star is less homage to *Enter the Dragon* than it is to *Saturday Night Live.*

Don't agree? What do you think?

EXERCISE

Review a current popular film and write an essay on how that film will be viewed in fifty years. What will that film say about the values of our culture, and what ideas in those films will be current and enduring as opposed to fleeting and obsolete?

NOTES

1. In general, American Jews responded to the anti-Semitism sparked by the Great Depression "by increasing their efforts to assimilate or by keeping a low profile. This attitude is reflected in the screen portrayal of the Jew during the 1930s and 1940s." Patricia Erens, *The Jew in American Cinema* (Bloomington: Indiana University Press, 1984), 4. For a more positive take on this, see Ted Baehr, "How Church Advocacy Groups Fostered the Golden Age of Hollywood," in *Advocacy Groups and the Entertainment Industry,* ed. Michael Suman and Gabriel Rossman (Westport, Conn.: Praeger, 2000), chap. 7.

2. For a recent example of this kind of finding, see Nicholas A. Valentino, "Crime News and the Priming of Racial Attitudes during Evaluations of the President," *Public Opinion Quarterly* 63, no. 3 (Autumn 1999): 293–320. In the summary of his findings, the author states, "These results suggest that implicitly racial issues are connected in memory and can be simultaneously activated by common news coverage." See also, Roberto Franzosi, "Narrative Analysis—or Why (and How) Sociologists Should Be Interested in Narrative," *Annual Review of Sociology* 24 (1998): 517–54.

3. Pictures showing the torture of Iraqi prisoners by American troops were initially suppressed by most major news organizations in the United States (with the exception of CBS, which

originally aired the pictures) but were widely displayed in news outlets in Europe and the Middle East. Because the pictures were widely available on the Internet, the pictures were eventually (after about twenty-four hours) on all mainstream American news outlets. Such is the power of the Internet to make news (and a lot of faux news) available to anyone with a computer and a telephone line.

4. For example, see the column written by Ken Masugi, senior fellow at the conservative Claremont Institute, titled "Saving 'Private Ryan' from the Conservatives," www.leaderu.com/humanities/masugi.html (accessed August 5, 2005). At the end of the column, he writes, "How can a conventional liberal such as Spielberg make such an impressive movie? One might recall that the morally obtuse Woody Allen has made deeply spiritual films about morality and the family such as *Bullets Over Broadway* and *Mighty Aphrodite*. It is good that bad men are hypocrites. That is the only way they can be tolerated. The answer to this paradox may lie in a fact this low: Spielberg is simply a whore of the marketplace, and what sells is patriotism. What does not sell are political depictions of America such as the Clinton clone movie *Primary Colors* or the even more repulsive *Bulworth*. In at least that regard, we Americans are good, or at least better than our filmmakers and a lot of our critics."

5. See Larry Ceplair and Stephen Englund, *The Inquisition in Hollywood: Politics in the Film Community, 1930–1960* (Garden City, N.Y.: Doubleday, 1980); or Robert Griffith, *The Politics of Fear: Joseph R. McCarthy and the Senate*, 2nd ed. (Amherst: University of Massachusetts Press, 1987).

Filmography with Commentary by the Author

Note: **Boldface** denotes a feature film.

2001: A Space Odyssey (1968). Directed by Stanley Kubrick. Starring Keir Dullea and Gary Lockwood. This movie caused a sensation when it was released. Based on a novel of the same name by Arthur C. Clarke, this film may seem quaint by today's standards, at least in terms of its special effects, but the story is still fresh, suggesting that the human race got its start as the result of a nudge by some higher form of being, perhaps even God.

The African Queen (1951). Directed by John Huston. Starring Humphrey Bogart and Katherine Hepburn—a terrific adventure film made in the 1950s that nevertheless did little to forestall the studio's collapse.

All Quiet on the Western Front (1930). Directed by Lewis Milestone. Starring Lew Ayers. Based on a novel of the same name, this antiwar film is probably one of the greatest of all time. The film, which won the Academy Award for Best Picture, fed into the disillusionment that America felt in the aftermath of its participation in World War I.

Amadeus (1984). Directed by Milos Forman. Starring Tom Hulce and F. Murray Abraham. *Amadeus* won the Academy Award for Best Picture of 1984, when *Beverly Hills Cop* made the most money.

America, America (1963). Directed by Elia Kazan. Starring Stathis Giallelis. This film is simply amazing. A long, slow, and detailed account of the immigrant experience as seen from the perspective of Kazan's uncle. Change the faces and the locations, and this film could be the family history of 80 percent of those who now live in the United States. *America, America* deserves more attention, but Kazan has been on the outs in Hollywood ever since he decided to name names during the McCarthy era.

Animal House (1978). Directed by John Landis. Starring John Belushi, Tim Matheson, Karen Allen, John Vernon, Verna Bloom, Tom Hulce, Peter Riegert, and Donald Sutherland. Believe it or not, *Animal House* is one of the most influential films of the last thirty years. I don't say that with a total sense of sadness. A lot of what is skewered in this movie needs to be skewered. But anything can be taken to an extreme. *Animal House* promotes a style of nihilism that has come to define a generation.

Apocalypse Now (1979). Directed by Francis Ford Coppola. Starring Marlon Brando and Martin Sheen. *Apocalypse Now* is Coppola's somewhat muddled attempt to examine the meaning and the causes of the Vietnam War. *Apocalypse Now* is at the same time brilliant and flawed but is well worth a look. I recently viewed the rereleased director's cut, and I'm still confused.

Around the World in Eighty Days (1956). Directed by Michael Anderson. Starring David Niven, Cantinflas, and Robert Morley. This is another in a series of larger-than-life (some would say bloated) 1950s-era epics. *Around the World* is colorful and a lot of fun but should almost certainly be viewed on the big screen.

Back to the Future (1985). Directed by Robert Zemeckis. Starring Michael J. Fox, Christopher Lloyd, and Lea Thompson. Top-grossing film of 1985, *Back to the Future* spawned two sequels, each sillier than the previous.

The Basketball Diaries (1995). Directed by Scott Kalvert. Staring Leonardo DiCaprio. I haven't seen this film, but it is noteworthy in that it is reputed to be the "inspiration" for the school shootings at Columbine High School in Colorado.

Batman (1989). Directed by Tim Burton. Starring Jack Nicholson, Michael Keaton, and Kim Basinger. This is an entertaining, stylish comic. Burton creates a re-markable world in Gotham City. *Batman* is interesting in its depiction of a 1930s character that, if you really think about it, was a model of fascism, right down to the black Nazi-like uniform with the bat symbol that recalls a swastika. That may sound outlandish, but that's how far removed we are from the world in which Batman was introduced.

The Battle for San Pietro (1945). Directed by John Huston. This film is an excellent documentary that generated quite a bit of controversy because it showed actual American dead and wounded. The government generally sought to censor scenes of American casualties during the Second World War.

The Battleship Potemkin (1925). Directed by Sergei Eisenstein. *Potemkin* is a drama-tized account of a mutiny in the Russian navy in 1905. The Soviet government ordered that this film be made on the twentieth anniversary of the revolt. The film is an iconic example of film technique and propaganda.

Ben Hur (1959). Directed by William Wyler. Starring Charlton Heston, Jack Hawkins, and Stephen Boyd. When the film industry came under economic pressure in the 1950s, Hollywood produced a series of biblical epics that conformed to the production code and at the same time attempted to counter the perceived corrosive market influence of the introduction of television. This movie is a monumental film based on a New Testament story and is well worth seeing.

Beverly Hills Cop (1984). Directed by Martin Brest. Starring Eddie Murphy and Judge Reinhold. *Beverly Hills Cop* was the top-grossing film of 1984. In terms of car chases, this film stresses quantity over quality.

The Big Sleep (1946). Directed by Howard Hawks. Starring Humphrey Bogart and Lauren Bacall. This film is one of the earliest examples of the film noir genre. Film noir brought to the screen the darker side of American life and thus reflected a subtle change in the control and motivation of the film industry. Sometimes convoluted and difficult to follow, *The Big Sleep* is nevertheless one of the most finely crafted detective films of its time.

The Birth of a Nation (1915). Directed by D. W. Griffith. Starring Lillian Gish, Mae Marsh, Henry Walthall, Miriam Cooper, Mary Alden, and Ralph Lewis. Obviously, any film made in praise of the Ku Klux Klan is likely to be controversial in the modern era. As a historical piece, this film tells us a lot about the political sensibilities of the early twentieth century, like it or not. But it is as a film event that *Birth of a Nation* is most important. One of the first feature-length films released in the United States, this movie was wildly successful at the box office and inspired a film industry aimed at a respectable mainstream audience.

Blade Runner (1982). Directed by Ridley Scott. Starring Harrison Ford, Rutger Hauer, and Sean Young. A visually stunning and suspenseful story of the future when the environment is darkly fouled and technology has advanced to the point that it can produce "replicants" or imitation human beings fashioned to perform difficult or unpleasant tasks. The future may be now. This is a thoughtful film that muses on the ethics of cloning and what it means to be human.

The Blair Witch Project (1999). Directed by Daniel Myrick and Eduardo Sánchez. Starring Heather Donahue, Joshua Leonard, and Michael C. Williams—a fascinating film where less is more. The film grossed $140 million on a budget of $35,000 (three zeros, not six). Small, independent, and creative films can get made and distributed in the modern business environment. It just doesn't happen that often.

Boogie Nights (1997). Directed by Paul Thomas Anderson. Starring Burt Reynolds, Luis Guzman, Julianne Moore, Rico Bueno, John C. Reilly, Nicole Ari Parker, Don Cheadle, Heather Graham, William H. Macy, and Mark Wahlberg. This film is about the porn industry in the 1970s and 1980s. I shouldn't really like this film, but it is one those guilty pleasures. Seriously, it is an interesting look at one of the seamier sides of life. Really, I swear.

Braveheart (1995). Directed by Mel Gibson. Starring Mel Gibson. This is the story of the thirteenth-century Scots' rebellion against the English. Lots of swordplay and brutality are depicted in this film. What is particularly interesting about *Braveheart* is that many in the Republican Party saw this film as a metaphor for their takeover of Congress in 1994, except for the disembowelment of the hero at the end of the film and the complete failure of his revolution.

Brave New World (1998). Directed by Leslie Libman and Larry Williams. Starring Peter Gallagher and Leonard Nimoy—a made-for-television adaptation of the Aldous Huxley novel. This film is an interesting example of how cable television networks can produce films that are reasonably well made and adaptable to a multiseries presentation that is beyond the capacity of most films in theatrical release.

The Bridge on the River Kwai (1957). Directed by David Lean. Starring Alec Guinness, William Holden, Sessue Hayakawa, and Jack Hawkins. This is a grand, superb meditation on the meaning of duty. It is thought provoking and for its time surprisingly antiwar.

Bullitt (1968). Directed by Peter Yates. Starring Steve McQueen, Jacqueline Bisset, and Robert Vaughn. This film is a stylish crime drama that features the best car chase in film history. An interesting subtext in the story explores intergovernmental rivalry. McQueen portrays a cop who plays by his own rules.

Bulworth (1998). Directed by Warren Beatty. Starring Warren Beatty. *Bulworth* is a cynical, dispiriting look at American politics. If our system is this badly off, it's going to take more than an election to solve the problem. Fortunately, the film didn't make money; filmgoing audiences are just not that political.

The Caine Mutiny (1954). Directed by Edward Dmytryk. Starring Humphrey Bogart, Jose Ferrer, Van Johnson, and Fred MacMurray. Based on a novel and play of the same name by Herman Wouk, this film is a wonderful examination of military competence, duty, courage, and social class.

Casablanca (1942). Directed by Michael Curtiz. Starring Humphrey Bogart, Claude Rains, Ingrid Bergman, and Paul Heinreid. In this, one of the greatest dramas ever made, everything works. *Casablanca* also happens to include some wonderful musings on heroism and loyalty to one's country, one's ideals, and one's spouse.

Casino (1995). Directed by Martin Scorsese. Starring Robert De Niro, Sharon Stone, and Joe Pesci. A tale well told of mobster control of precorporate Las Vegas. *Casino* has a high body count and is often cited as an example of the growing violence of mainstream Hollywood cinema.

Celsius 41.11: The Temperature at Which the Brain . . . Begins to Die (2004). Directed by Kevin Knoblock. This documentary attempts to counter charges made against President Bush by the 2004 Democratic presidential candidate, Senator John Kerry, and filmmaker Michael Moore. The film did not do well at the box office, suggesting that filmgoers are generally not Republicans and that the film media will probably not become the medium of Republican attack ads.

Chariots of Fire (1981). Directed by Hugh Hudson. Starring Ian Holm, Ben Cross, and Ian Charleson. One of the sedate films that dominated the box office in the 1980s, when it was "morning in America."

The China Syndrome (1979). Directed by James Bridges. Starring Jane Fonda, Jack Lemmon. This unfortunately titled film refers to the apocryphal scenario in which the melting core of a nuclear reactor burns its way all the way through the earth and comes out the other side. This somewhat shrill film reflects concerns about the safety of nuclear power plants at the time of the Three Mile Island nuclear power plant accident. Interestingly, *The China Syndrome* opened twelve days before the accident and thus benefited by the film's prescience.

Citizen Kane (1941). Directed by Orson Welles. Starring Orson Welles and Joseph Cotton. This film is a metaphorical study of the life of newspaper magnate William Randolph Hearst. This film is considered by many to be one of the most finely crafted American films. Besides the brilliance of its art, *Citizen Kane* is an astute examination of the intersection of wealth, journalism, and politics.

The Client (1994). Directed by Joel Schumacher. Starring Susan Sarandon and Tommy Lee Jones. Titled after a John Grisham novel of the same name, *The Client* tells the tale of a young boy who is a witness against the mob. The boy finds a lawyer who inexplicably obstructs attempts by the district attorney to use the boy in his investigation. There is a lot of weird reasoning in this movie, the upshot of which is that we live in a community but owe nothing to it.

Cold Mountain (2003). Directed by Anthony Minghella. Starring Jude Law and Nicole Kidman. Titled after a popular novel of the same name, *Cold Mountain* is a love story set in the North Carolina mountains during the Civil War. The film is interesting in its treatment of the Civil War from the perspective of Southern mountain folk.

Coming to America (1988). Directed by John Landis. Starring Eddie Murphy. *Coming to America* is a twist on the typical immigrant-experience movie. Although Murphy does not come to the United States from poverty (he is an African prince), he has a more or less typical immigrant experience even though he is black. Many blacks in the United States are the descendants of slaves, but many are not. We tend to forget that the black community in the United States is not a monolith. This film reminds us that blacks in the United States, just like everybody else, come from a variety of backgrounds. The film is also kind of funny but clearly not Murphy's best role, which was in *Bowfinger*, a comedy must-see.

Conan the Barbarian (1982). Directed by John Milius. Starring Arnold Schwarzenegger. In this film, the future governor of California takes on various monsters and beds good-looking women on his way to the throne. Who says life doesn't follow art?

Coneheads (1993). Directed by Steve Barron. Starring Dan Aykroyd and Jane Curtin. Who would have thought that one of the best movies depicting the immigrant experience would be a comedy about pointy-headed aliens on Earth? This film could substitute Vietnamese, Mexicans, the Irish, or the Italians for the Coneheads, but it wouldn't be half as funny.

Contact (1997). Directed by Robert Zemeckis. Starring Jodie Foster, Matthew McConaughey, and Tom Skerritt. This film is an earnest, bordering on preachy, look at the search for life on other planets. In particular, *Contact* is thought provoking because it explores in an intelligent way the intersection of science and religion.

The Contender (2000). Directed by Rod Lurie. Starring Joan Allen, Jeff Bridges, and Gary Oldman. Watching this film makes me think that maybe there really is a liberal conspiracy running Hollywood. Allen plays a transparently liberal atheist vice presidential nominee who is beset by Monica Lewinsky–like charges of sexual misconduct (or should I say *Bill Clinton–like*?). Eventually, her opponents are vanquished and she is triumphantly cleared of all charges. Give me a break.

The Cook, the Thief, His Wife, and Her Lover (1989). Directed by Peter Greenaway. Starring Richard Bohringer, Helen Mirren, and Michael Gambon. This film tests the limits of, shall we say, good taste. For right-wing film critic Michael Medved, *The Cook* became the stalking horse of an attempt by Hollywood to undermine the morals of our youth. The fact that the film opened in nineteen theaters, was rated NC-17, and was seen by almost no one didn't seem to make a difference to Medved.

Dances with Wolves (1990). Directed by Kevin Costner. Starring Kevin Costner. With an earlier run of successful films—*Bull Durham, The Untouchables, Field of Dreams*—there was a time when Kevin Costner was on top (before *Waterworld* and *The Postman*). *Dances* recalls what for Costner must have been happier days. This film represents the latest installment in the evolution of Hollywood's interpretation of the Indian Wars. Far from the typical heroic Indian fighter as depicted in film, Costner goes native and actually ends up battling the American army.

Dave (1993). Directed by Ivan Reitman. Starring Kevin Kline, Sigourney Weaver, Frank Langella. This is a cross between *Mr. Smith Goes to Washington* and *Gabriel over the White House*. Through a series of improbable events, an average guy gets to be president. He fixes the country's problems and beds the real president's wife. Yeah...right. This film plays to the feeling that if we could just get rid of the "politicians" in Washington, we could find effortless solutions to our problems. If only it were so easy. Having said all that, this film is enjoyable to watch when not taken too seriously.

The Day of the Jackal (1973). Directed by Fred Zinnemann. Starring Edward Fox. This film is a taut political thriller about an attempted assassination of French President Charles De Gaulle. *The Day of the Jackal* is based on actual events, as a group of disgruntled French military officers did attempt to assassinate President De Gaulle in retaliation for his decision to support Algerian independence.

Deep Impact (1998). Directed by Mimi Leder. Starring Robert Duvall, Téa Leoni, Elijah Wood, Vanessa Redgrave, Morgan Freeman, and Maximilian Schell. This is a really good character-driven disaster film. Along with *Armageddon* and the insufferably politically correct *Independence Day*, there seemed to be at the time a concern in Hollywood and apparently among the viewing public that the world was coming to an end.

The Defiant Ones (1958). Directed by Stanley Kramer. Starring Tony Curtis and Sidney Poitier. In this film Hollywood tackles race relations through the plot gimmick of chaining together a black man and a white racist. If you think about it, there is a definite allegory here to forced busing.

Dirty Harry (1971). Directed by Don Siegel. Starring Clint Eastwood. Inspector Harry Callahan is a rogue cop who chafes against the restraints of the bureaucracy and the court system. We are tempted to approve of the shooting and torturing of suspects in his custody until we consider the consequences of such behavior for our legal system. Who made Callahan judge, jury, and executioner? This film appeals to some of our baser instincts.

Doctor Zhivago (1965). Directed by David Lean. Starring Omar Sharif, Julie Christie, Geraldine Chaplin, Rod Steiger, Alec Guinness, and Tom Courtenay. Adapted from a Boris Pasternak novel of the same name, this film is both giant and modest. At its grandest, the film tells the story of the Russian Revolution as a backdrop to a modest love triangle. Recounting the grand sweep of history from the perspective of an individual is a device that has to be handled carefully. It can shortchange or render insignificant a major world event. Lean creates a fine balance that captures both the grand sweep of the Russian Revolution and the power of romance. The film is one of the most visually stunning movies ever made.

Double Indemnity (1944). Directed by Billy Wilder. Starring Fred MacMurray, Barbara Stanwyck, and Edward G. Robinson. *Double Indemnity* is a classic crime drama and morality tale. The film anticipates the film noire genre.

Driving Miss Daisy (1989). Directed by Bruce Beresford. Starring Jessica Tandy, Morgan Freeman, and Dan Aykroyd. Based on a play by the same name, this film treats a delicate topic, racism in the South, awkwardly. Freeman's performance was nominated for an Academy Award. His performance as the servant is so good that it makes us wince.

The Elizabeth Smart Story (2003). Directed by Bobby Roth. Starring Dylan Baker, Lindsay Frost, and Amber Marshall. This made-for-television movie was released within a year of the event. While based on a true story, the account is at least partially fictionalized. *The Elizabeth Smart Story* is an example of the best and the worst of the television medium: On the one hand, television can respond quickly to this sort of news; on the other, the movie is probably inaccurate and the primary source of information for most of those who watch it.

Enemy at the Gates (2001). Directed by Jean-Jacques Annaud. Starring Jude Law, Ed Harris, and Rachel Weisz. *Enemy at the Gates* is a film about the battle for Stalingrad during World War II from the Russian/Western perspective. Only in the aftermath of the Cold War could such a sympathetic film be made about the Red Army. Nevertheless, Nikita Khrushchev makes an appearance in this film and is treated roughly, probably as a stand-in for Stalin. This is a strange film, as it recounts an event that was probably a creation of communist propaganda.

E. T. (1982). Directed by Steven Spielberg. Starring Drew Barrymore and Peter Coyote. The top-grossing film of the year, *E. T.* is a well-made sweet.

Exodus (1960). Directed by Otto Preminger. Starring Paul Newman, Eva Marie Saint, Ralph Richardson, Peter Lawford, Lee J. Cobb, and Sal Mineo. This is a gassy epic about the founding of the state of Israel. Read the book.

Eyes Wide Shut (1999). Directed by Stanley Kubrick. Starring Tom Cruise and Nicole Kidman. Any film directed by Stanley Kubrick is worth seeing. *Eyes Wide Shut* is a meditation on the dehumanization of the modern world, in this case focusing on the act of sexual intercourse. The producers were forced to obscure certain images in the film in order to obtain an R rating.

Fahrenheit 9/11 (2004). Directed by Michael Moore. Featuring George W. Bush and starring Michael Moore. Moore directed this highly controversial documentary that claims that the Bush administration was negligent, if not indirectly complicit, in the terrorist attack on the World Trade Center on September 11, 2001. This inflammatory film enjoyed unexpected success at the box office and was quite predictably attacked as blood libel by supporters of the president.

The FBI Story (1959). Directed by Mervyn LeRoy. Starring Jimmy Stewart and Vera Miles. As the name implies, this story is about some of the most notorious cases assigned to an FBI agent. The movie reminds us that at one time the government was viewed with favor.

The Fifth Element (1997). Directed by Luc Besson. Starring Bruce Willis, Ian Holm, Gary Oldman, Milla Jovovich, and Chris Tucker. *The Fifth Element* is like my old Renault: it looked great but didn't work very well. This film is worth watching just for the visual artistry. The story, on the other hand, is hard to figure. It has something to do with good versus evil—I think.

The Firm (1993). Directed by Sidney Pollack. Starring Tom Cruise, Jeanne Tripplehorn, Gene Hackman, and Hal Holbrook. Inspired by a John Grisham novel of the same name, *The Firm* puts on display some perverse values. A supposedly brilliant young attorney goes to work for a law firm whose primary purpose, unbeknownst to him, is to shield the Mafia's proceeds from taxes. He is surprised to find that the firm is engaged in all sorts of illegal activities, including murder. He then refuses to help the FBI investigate the firm because he is afraid of being disbarred. And he is supposed to be a hero?

Forrest Gump (1994). Directed by Robert Zemeckis. Starring Tom Hanks, Robin Wright, Gary Sinise, and Sally Field. This was a wildly successful and popular movie. The message of it is hard to decipher. In a weird twist on the "anyone can make it in America" story, are the filmmakers saying that a total idiot can be wildly successful in America by sheer happenstance? Doesn't that sort of devalue the accomplishments of the rest of us?

The Fountainhead (1949). Directed by King Vidor. Starring Gary Cooper and Patricia Neal. Every pimply-faced teenager flirts with libertarianism after reading Ayn Rand's book of the same name. This film is a passable reflection of the Rand novel. However, *Lonely Are the Brave* is a more thoughtful, nuanced musing on the subject.

The French Connection (1971). Directed by William Friedkin. Starring Gene Hackman, Fernando Rey, and Roy Scheider. *The French Connection* is a fascinating and thrilling crime drama starring one of the best actors in the business, Gene Hackman. As they say, this movie is based on a true story. It depicts an investigation by the New York City Police Department into an international drug-trafficking scheme. The film is an absorbing look at crime, police investigation, and bureaucratic politics.

Gabriel over the White House (1933). Directed by Gregory La Cava. Starring Walter Huston. In its day, this film was quite successful. It depicts divine intervention in the White House. We tend to forget that in the 1930s totalitarianism in the world was ascendant and the efficacy of democracy was in question. It is rumored that newspaper publisher William Randolph Hearst, who was flirting with fascism at the time, wrote some of the dialogue for this film. The film seems preposterous now, but it was taken seriously at the time and that makes *Gabriel* an important historical artifact.

Gangs of New York (2002). Directed by Martin Scorsese. Starring Leonardo DiCaprio, Daniel Day-Lewis, and Cameron Diaz. This is an example of a type of film that is technically exquisite, visually stunning, and plotwise incomprehensible—the victory of form over substance.

Gentlemen's Agreement (1947). Directed by Elia Kazan. Starring Gregory Peck and Dorothy McGuire. *Gentlemen's Agreement* is Hollywood's take on anti-Semitism.

Peck plays a gentile newspaper reporter who pretends to be Jewish in order to experience unfair discrimination. An interesting film but kind of strange in the sense that anti-Semitism becomes somehow more distasteful when viewed through the eyes of someone who is not Jewish.

The Getaway (1972). Directed by Sam Peckinpah. Starring Steve McQueen, Ben Johnson, and Ali McGraw. No morality tale this. In a kind of weird twist on the rags-to-riches story, the film says that if you are a tough, smart, principled, and determined bank robber, you can get a piece of the American pie. I don't think the censors of the production code era would have passed on this.

Ghandi (1982). Directed by Richard Attenborough. Starring Ben Kingsley, Candice Bergen, Edward Fox, John Gielgud, Trevor Howard, John Mills, and Martin Sheen. This film depicts the life of one of the great men of our time. This is a fine movie that handles complex ideas with ease—won more awards than money.

Ghostbusters (1984). Directed by Ivan Reitman. Starring Dan Aykroyd, Bill Murray, Sigourney Weaver, Rick Moranis, and Harold Ramis. This was the top-grossing film of 1984 and a marketing sensation.

The Godfather (1972). Directed by Francis Ford Coppola. Starring Marlon Brando, Al Pacino, and James Caan. *The Godfather* is an operatic study of the life of a Mafia kingpin, a cinematic masterpiece that is both finely crafted and fabulously entertaining. This film is the apotheosis of the classic American immigrant story and is also, interestingly enough, a musing on the dynamics of a free, unfettered market.

The Godfather: Part II (1974). Directed by Francis Ford Coppola. Starring Al Pacino, Robert Duvall, Diane Keaton, Robert De Niro, John Cazale, Talia Shire, and Lee Strasberg—perhaps the best sequel ever made. Flashbacks to the old country and the growth of the family olive oil business in New York and, finally, Vito Corleone's passage into a life of crime are so truthful they are almost newsreels but better. *The Godfather: Part II* captures the flavor of the immigrant experience and at the same time is a wonderful character study of a man's descent into depravity.

The Gold Rush (1925). Directed by Charlie Chaplin. Starring Charlie Chaplin. This is Chaplin's comedic take on the conquest of the West—prospectors eating their boots.

The Grapes of Wrath (1940). Directed by John Ford. Starring Henry Fonda and Jane Darwell. *The Grapes of Wrath* is based on the John Steinbeck novel of the same name. The central character of this film, Tom Joad, is an "Okie" who during the Great Depression sets out on the road with his family to look for work. So realistic, it often looks like a documentary. So heart wrenching, it could only be true to life. If there were one overarching question posed by this film, it would be, why are the Joads in the fix they are in and what should be done about it?

The Greatest Show on Earth (1952). Directed by Cecil B. DeMille. Starring Betty Hutton, Cornel Wilde, Charlton Heston, and Dorothy Lamour. This is a colorful, chaotic, and predictable film—more 1950s escapism.

The Greatest Story Ever Told (1965). Directed by George Stevens. Starring Max Von Sydow. This is one of the many movie versions depicting the life of Jesus. In the commercial sense, this probably *is* the greatest story ever told in that it keeps on being successfully remade time after time. *The Greatest Story Ever Told* is the gospel according to George Stevens. While I can't judge it on its ecclesiastical merits, it is a well-made film. It is certainly less inflammatory than Mel Gibson's *Passion*. Look for a cameo by John Wayne.

Guess Who's Coming to Dinner (1967). Directed by Stanley Kramer. Starring Spencer Tracy, Katherine Hepburn, Sidney Poitier, and Katherine Houghton. This museum piece is from a time when mixed-race marriages were really quite remarkable. It is worth watching if only to see how far we have come in the last forty years.

Hamlet (1990). Directed by Franco Zeffirelli. Starring Mel Gibson, Glenn Close, Alan Bates, Paul Scofield, Ian Holm, and Helen Bonham Carter. This film is actually a well-made rendition of the classic Shakespeare play with the exception of a weird allusion to incest between Hamlet and his mother. Also, the casting of Gibson as Hamlet seems a little strange. Such a choice wouldn't be made under the old studio star system. Nevertheless, he does fine, showing the kind of frenetic energy that carried him through the *Lethal Weapon* series.

Hester Street (1975). Directed by Joan Micklin Silver. Starring Carol Kane, Steven Keats, and Mel Howard. *Hester Street* is another film about the immigrant experience except from the Jewish perspective. Nevertheless, change the faces, accents, and locales, and this could be about the families of most Americans. The film is a pleasure to watch, understated and beautifully filmed.

High Noon (1952). Directed by Fred Zinnemann. Starring Gary Cooper and Grace Kelly. *High Noon* is the prototype Western; everything after this is derivative. But beyond the Western setting, this film is really a story about an individual, his courage, his love, and how alone one person can be even within a community. Cooper does a truly wonderful job of acting in this film. His face creases with disappointment and disillusionment with each rejected plea for help. Everything comes out okay in the end, but one wonders if the resolution isn't a little contrived. Can a man really make it completely on his own without the help of his neighbors? Grace Kelly is completely miscast—what is she doing in this film?

Homicide (1991). Directed by David Mamet. Starring Joe Mantegna and William H. Macy. I will say flat out that any film produced by Mamet is worth seeing. *Homicide* is one of his less well-known films, and there is no reason to expect it wouldn't be. This is his rumination on what is to be Jewish in America—a secular Jew, that is, who is just trying to fit in. Because of the limited audience for this topic, it never gets much play. But it is a must-see for anyone interested in fine filmmaking.

House of Wax (1953). Directed by Andre de Toth. Starring Vincent Price. *House of Wax* is a gimmicky horror film that was the first studio release in 3-D. Under pressure of foreign competition, the break-up of the second (golden era) monopoly, and the emergence of television, Hollywood introduced a number of technical gimmicks, including 3-D, to keep patrons in the theater. This film is an example of this sort of industry trend.

The House of Yes (1997). Directed by Mark Waters. Starring Parker Posey, Josh Hamilton, Tori Spelling, Freddie Prinze Jr., and Genevieve Bujold. A brother and sister dress up like John and Jackie Kennedy, reenact the Kennedy assassination, and have sex—with one another. I'm dead serious. Who says Hollywood can't explore new horizons?

I Am a Fugitive from a Chain Gang (1932). Directed by Mervyn LeRoy. Starring Paul Muni. Depicts the real nature of Southern prison camps in the 1930s. So impressed was the audience by this film, *Fugitive* sparked a national prison reform movement. This film is often cited as an example of the power of film to provoke progressive reform.

Invaders from Mars (1953). Directed by William Cameron Menzies. Starring Helena Carter, Arthur Franz, Jimmy Hunt, and Leif Erickson. In this film Martians come from the Red Planet (get it?) to take over our minds. This film scared the heck out of me when I was a kid and is still a lot of fun to watch.

The Invasion of the Body Snatchers (1956). Directed by Don Siegel. Starring Dana Wynter and Kevin McCarthy. The allusion to the Cold War in this film is unavoidable (although Siegel maintains that he intended nothing of the kind). Beyond that, this film is well made and darn scary. The film was such a downer that it was released with a happier ending. Fortunately, in most modern prints the original ending has been restored.

It's a Wonderful Life (1946). Directed by Frank Capra. Starring James Stewart and Donna Reed. This film is a perennial Christmas favorite. An example of the type of filmmaking that cultural conservatives would like to see more of.

The Jackal (1997). Directed by Michael Caton-Jones. Starring Bruce Willis, Sidney Poitier, Richard Gere, and Diane Venora. *The Jackal* is a gimmicky remake of the excellent thriller *The Day of the Jackal* (1973). The plot of this film is incomprehensible and contains at least one truly insulting homoerotic stunt pulled for no other reason than to shock the audience.

Jason and the Argonauts (1963). Directed by Don Chaffey. Starring Todd Armstrong. This film is primarily interesting for its special effects that were (and still are) spectacular in their day.

Judas (2004). Directed by Charles Robert Carner. Starring Johnathon Schaech, Jonathan Scarfe, and Tim Matheson. The ABC television network tried to cash in on the craze for *The Passion of the Christ*, as one of Jesus's disciples goes to the dark side.

Jurassic Park (1993). Directed by Steven Spielberg. Starring Sam Neill, Laura Dern, Jeff Goldblum, and Richard Attenborough. This is an ambitious film that has a lot of ground to cover in terms of plot, special effects, and Spielberg's special brand of homespun kitsch. The pace in this film is so frenetic that it's almost too fast to follow. The best parts of the film are, in order, the special effects; the lawyer getting eaten by the dinosaur (the audience cheered in the theater where I watched the film); and last, and certainly least, the wheezy subplot involving Neill's uneasiness with children. Meditations on the science of cloning are sort of interesting, too.

Kill Bill: Vol. 1 and **Kill Bill: Vol. 2** (2003, 2004). Directed by Quentin Tarantino. Starring Uma Thurman, Lucy Liu, Vivica Fox, Daryl Hannah, David Carradine, and Michael Madsen. *Kill Bill* is a stylish and bloody homage to kung fu movies and comic strips. The film would have worked better as one film, not two, but the lure of the extra buck was too strong. I think Tarantino is stuck on Thurman.

Kundun (1997). Directed by Martin Scorsese. Starring Tenzin Thuthob Tsarong. This film is part of the 1997 anti-Chinese trilogy, which includes *Red Corner* and *Seven Years in Tibet*. At the time, China was accused of failing to enforce copyright laws, which allowed the widespread pirating of Hollywood films and popular music. There may be a debate about the politics of Hollywood, but one thing can unite the industry: a threat to their bottom line. About this time, Hollywood began to display a remarkable concern for the people of Tibet.

Lady and the Tramp (1955). Directed by Clyde Geronimi and Wilfred Jackson. This movie is one of the best feature-length Disney animation films. This sort of clean escapism was especially prevalent in the 1950s, even as the film industry began to encounter economic hard times.

La Femme Nikita (1991). Directed by Luc Besson. Starring Anne Parillaud. *La Femme Nikita* is a French action film that, if it were made in English, could pass for an American action film. In fact, it was remade as an almost exact copy, but in English, titled *Point of No Return* (1993). The French government views with growing alarm the infiltration of American culture into France. This film should stoke those concerns.

The Last Emperor (1988). Directed by Bernardo Bertolucci. Starring John Lone. *The Last Emperor* is a grand, sweeping film that recounts the life of the last emperor of China. *The Last Emperor* treats the communist revolution in China with remarkable balance, although it is not strictly an American film.

Last Tango in Paris (1972). Directed by Bernardo Bertolucci. Starring Marlon Brando and Maria Schneider. *Last Tango in Paris* is considered by many film insiders to be a masterpiece of form and expression. It is remarkable how dated this film feels, not because of its antiquity, but because of its daring.

Life of Brian (1979). Directed by Terry Jones. Starring Graham Chapman, John Cleese, Terry Gilliam, Terry Jones, Eric Idle, and Michael Palin. This is Monty Python's hysterical send-up of the New Testament. Given the current political climate, one wonders how this project would be greeted were such a script proposed today.

Little Big Man (1970). Directed by Arthur Penn. Starring Dustin Hoffman, Faye Dunaway, and Chief Dan George. *Little Big Man* is the first modern, and some would say the first politically correct, Western. The film looks at the Indian Wars from the Native American perspective. The Indian side is treated as something other than a caricature; in fact, whites are more likely to be caricatured. The film's treatment of General George Armstrong Custer couldn't be more different than an earlier portrayal in *They Died with Their Boots On* (1941). The contrast between the two Custers is a study in the evolution of American thought in regard to the conquest of the West.

The Littlest Rebel (1935). Directed by David Butler. Starring Shirley Temple and Bill "Bojangles" Robinson. *The Littlest Rebel* is a marker along the path of the depiction of race relations in American film. In this film Temple negotiates an end to the Civil War through dance.

Lonely Are the Brave (1962). Directed by George Miller. Starring Kirk Douglas, Gina Rowlands, and Walter Matthau. This was Kirk Douglas's favorite film. *Lonely Are the Brave* is ostensibly another modern Western, but it is really so much more. The story is about the conflict that exists between freedom defined as "absence of constraint" and the demands of conformity imposed by living in modern civilization. No other film is quite as good at capturing in its complexities and pathos the death of the old West.

Look Who's Talking (1989). Directed by Amy Heckerling. Starring Kirstie Alley and John Travolta. *Look Who's Talking* is a feel-good movie that reinforces traditional (some would say paternalistic) values. The film grossed $300 million on a $12 million budget and spawned a franchise.

Lost in Space (1998). Directed by Stephen Hopkins. Starring William Hurt, Mimi Rogers, Lacey Chabert, Heather Graham, Jack Johnson, Gary Oldman, and Matt LeBlanc. Loud, annoying remake of a modestly successful television series—a typical example of film as product.

Lost in Translation (2003). Directed and written by Sophia Coppola. Starring Bill Murray and Scarlett Johansson. Directed by Sophia Coppola, Francis Ford

Coppola's daughter, *Lost in Translation* is the well-anticipated follow-up to her promising feature-length directorial debut, *The Virgin Suicides*. Every industry has its nepotism, and Hollywood is no exception. But this film is so much more. *Lost in Translation* is an interesting exploration of culture clashes and, from the American perspective, getting along in a foreign environment.

Malcolm X (1992). Directed by Spike Lee. Starring Denzel Washington. The fact is that for many moviegoers this sort of film is the only information they will ever get about the civil rights movement—and this would not be an entirely bad source. While Lee does take some liberty with the facts and bends on occasion to his stylish side, this film captures well a portion of the black power movement that often goes unexplained to white audiences. Washington's performance is terrific.

The Man in the Iron Mask (1998). Directed by Randall Wallace. Starring Leonardo DiCaprio, Jeremy Irons, Gerard Depardieu, Gabriel Byrne, and Anne Parillaud. One of the many remakes of an Alexandre Dumas novel, this film is remarkable only to the extent that its story line is a complete sop to the ethics of popular culture.

MASH (1970). Directed by Robert Altman. Starring Elliott Gould, Donald Sutherland, Tom Skerritt, Sally Kellerman, and Robert Duvall. This film is a commentary on the Vietnam War, in metaphor. A lot more than war is skewered in this film. The army and bureaucracy in general also take a hit.

Master and Commander: On the Far Side of the World (2003). Directed by Peter Weir. Starring Russell Crowe and Paul Bettany. This film is a ripping yarn that is also an impressive technical achievement. It is an example of the best of commercial Hollywood filmmaking, with some interesting accommodations made to anti-French and pro-British sentiments that existed in the United States in the lead-up to the Iraq War.

The Matrix Reloaded (2003). Directed by Andy Wachowski. Starring Keanu Reeves and Laurence Fishburne. This film is an incomprehensible sequel to the equally confusing *Matrix* (1999). Here is a plot description, as posted on the Internet Movie Data Base: "Neo and the rebel leaders estimate that they have 72 hours until 250,000 probes discover Zion and destroy it and its inhabitants." This film is too loud for a good snooze—but somebody gets it; it did almost $300 million at the box office.

McCabe and Mrs. Miller (1971). Directed by Robert Altman. Starring Warren Beatty and Julie Christie. In this film *MASH* goes to the old West. Altman's films have a wonderful free-form approach, like an abstract painting. I suspect that this film is a pretty accurate depiction of life on the frontier. In that sense, when the 1960s meet the old West, there seems to be a remarkable resemblance. The film also has a great soundtrack by Leonard Cohen.

Meet John Doe (1941).   Directed by Frank Capra. Starring Gary Cooper and Barbara Stanwyck. This film is about the triumph of the common man. It is a paean to the populist politics of its day. Of course, as it turned out, the populism of the common man was not always so benign as it is portrayed in this film. In the 1930s Senator Huey Long exploited populism of the Left in his "share the wealth" movement, and Father Charles E. Coughlin exploited the populism of the Right in his protofascist proposal to establish a regime of "social justice" that would resist, among other things, the influence of an international conspiracy of Jewish bankers.

Mildred Pierce (1945).   Directed by Michael Curtiz. Starring Joan Crawford. This is a "women's film" before there was such a thing. Joan Crawford won an Oscar for her lead role in this rags-to-riches-to-rags story.

Mississippi Burning (1988).   Directed by Alan Parker. Starring Gene Hackman and Willem Dafoe. This is a strange movie that depicts the battle over civil rights in the South. This film has generated a lot of controversy, as it depicts the FBI in a favorable light during a time when the FBI was actually using its resources to discredit the Reverend Martin Luther King.

Moscow on the Hudson (1984).   Directed by Paul Mazursky. Starring Robin Williams. *Moscow on the Hudson* is a modern immigrant story that self-consciously tells the immigrant tale. It is not a particularly remarkable or original film. The combination of *America, America; Hester Street;* and *The Godfather* and *The Godfather: Part II* do a better job. As they say in Hollywood when they reject a script, "I think we've been there before."

Mr. Deeds Goes to Town (1936).   Directed by Frank Capra. Starring Gary Cooper and Jean Arthur. *Deeds* is another of Capra's common-man pictures. I feel guilty saying anything cynical about this film, so I'll just say nothing.

Mr. Smith Goes to Washington (1939).   Directed by Frank Capra. Starring James Stewart, Claude Rains, and Jean Arthur. This is a classic political film. Stewart plays Jefferson Smith, who is literally a Boy Scout sent to the U.S. Senate. In the end, good triumphs, but I find the film's plot solutions troubling. If you think about it, democracy does not prevail in *Mr. Smith*. Smith, the good guy, isn't even elected, and his opponent has the upper hand until, in an unlikely fit of conscience, he decides to recant and confess his sins. In reality, I hope, the checks-and-balances system works better than this.

Mulholland Drive (2001).   Directed by David Lynch. Starring Naomi Watts and Laura Harring. This film is a lot of fun but completely impossible to describe. Oddball films such as this can get made, but it is unlikely that they will turn up in your neighborhood cineplex.

My Darling Clementine (1946).   Directed by John Ford. Starring Henry Fonda, Ward Bond, Walter Brennan, Linda Darnell, and Victor Mature. This film is my favorite

Western—a semifictionalized account of the gunfight at the OK Corral. While much of this film is standard Western fare, it contains a lot of intelligent musings about the struggle to establish order in a state of nature. More so than most, this film captures that moment of transformation that is important to the beginning of any civilization.

My Dinner with Andre (1981). Directed by Louis Malle. Starring Wallace Shawn and Andre Gregory. This is an unusual film, a little picture on the big screen that happens to work.

Mystic River (2003). Directed by Clint Eastwood. Starring Sean Penn, Tim Robbins, Kevin Bacon, Laurence Fishburne, Marcia Gay Harden, and Laura Linney. This film is more form than substance, featuring lots of fine acting and film technique but a disjointed plotline. This film is an example of poor plot continuity.

Natural Born Killers (1994). Directed by Oliver Stone. Starring Woody Harrelson and Juliette Lewis. This is a frenetic killing spree on film. I suppose *Natural Born Killers* could be seen as a study in the genesis of a couple of serial killers, but it also can be seen as a study in the lengths to which people will go to become famous. This film wasn't really all that successful at the box office, which means that this sort of thing isn't going to get made often, at least on a high budget.

Nicholas and Alexandra (1971). Directed by Franklin J. Schaffner. Starring Michael Jayston and Janet Suzman. This film is a rather sympathetic view of the last days of Tsar Nicholas II. Only the Cold War could have stimulated nostalgia for the good old days of the Russian tsar. Nicholas II wasn't the worst tsar, but he wasn't better than nothing. Nevertheless, the film is wonderfully made, and Janet Suzman is worth watching in any role.

North by Northwest (1959). Directed by Alfred Hitchcock. Starring Cary Grant, Eva Marie Saint, James Mason, and Martin Landau. A hazy plot doesn't get in the way of Grant and Hitchcock doing their thing in top form. One of the era's better films but not better earners.

One from the Heart (1982). Directed by Francis Ford Coppola. Starring Frederick Forrest and Terri Garr. This film is a visually stunning but largely plotless love story. Coppola practically went bankrupt to produce this film, and yet it really works as a piece of art. Unfortunately, art doesn't sell, and neither did this film. Nevertheless, I believe it is a hidden gem and is well worth seeing, especially on the big screen.

On the Waterfront (1954). Directed by Elia Kazan. Starring Marlon Brando, Eva Marie Saint, Lee J. Cobb, Rod Steiger, and Karl Malden. In this film the heroic protagonist fights against corrupt union bosses by ratting them out. Kazan admitted that this film was something of a personal statement after he was ostracized by Hollywood for naming names in front of the House Un-American Activities Committee.

Ordinary People (1981). Directed by Robert Redford. Starring Donald Sutherland, Mary Tyler Moore, Timothy Hutton, and Elizabeth McGovern. In this enormously well-made drama, talk therapy works. This is an example of a film that is more a critical than a box office success.

Out of Africa (1985). Directed by Sidney Pollack. Starring Robert Redford, Klaus Maria Brandauer, and Meryl Streep. *Out of Africa* is a big picture for the big screen, an example of why the market for films shown in the theater still exists.

Paint Your Wagon (1969). Directed by Joshua Logan. Starring Lee Marvin, Clint Eastwood, and Jean Seberg. This film could be described as "American West, the musical." Where else can you watch perennial tough guys Marvin and Eastwood sing? The film is a lot of fun and puts the myths of the West to song.

The Passion of the Christ (2004). Directed by Mel Gibson. Starring James Caviezel. No one can say that Gibson doesn't put his money where his mouth is. This tremendously controversial film raises more questions than it answers. Is this an accurate interpretation of the New Testament? Is the film anti-Semitic? How much money will this film make in the end? Will this be the model for more specialty, message-centered, self-financed films to come?

The People vs. Larry Flynt (1996). Directed by Milos Forman. Starring Courtney Love, Woody Harrelson, and Edward Norton. This film is a well-made biopic about one of the most prolific pornographers in America, Larry Flynt. It is also a good lesson on the meaning of the First Amendment.

Peter Pan (1953). Directed by Clyde Geronimi and Wilfred Jackson. This animated Disney film was one of the top-grossing films of the 1950s. Films of this type did well in the 1950s even as the film industry staggered.

Planet of the Apes (1968). Directed by Franklin J. Schaffner. Starring Charlton Heston, Roddy McDowall, Kim Hunter, James Whitmore, and Maurice Evans. In this film are intelligent musings on everything from time travel to the meaning of human intelligence to the wages of the nuclear arms race.

Platoon (1986). Directed by Oliver Stone. Starring Charlie Sheen, Tom Berenger, and Willem Dafoe. The interpretations of what happened in Vietnam evolve with time. Before the world was completely explored, territories that were blank on the map were labeled "here there be tigers." In this movie, Vietnam is uncharted territory.

Point of No Return (1993). Directed by John Badham. Starring Bridget Fonda and Gabriel Byrne. Dorothy Parker once said, "The only ism Hollywood believes in is plagiarism." This film is an almost exact remake in English of a movie made in France two years earlier—a classic example of film as product.

The Postman (1997). Directed by Kevin Costner. Starring Kevin Costner. Why do some films succeed while others fail? This film was a monumental failure. It is worth a watch, if you can find it, just to get an idea of what not to do when making a film.

The Producers (1968). Directed by Mel Brooks. Starring Zero Mostel and Gene Wilder. This film is far and away one of the funniest ever made. It anticipates modern forms of tax shelters.

Pretty Woman (1990). Directed by Garry Marshall. Starring Richard Gere and Julia Roberts. In this movie, the best-looking, healthiest, most intelligent, nonaddicted streetwalker on the planet beds and weds a billionaire client. If this is a "women's film," then I would like to see what a male-chauvinist film looks like.

Primary Colors (1998). Directed by Mike Nichols. Starring John Travolta and Emma Thompson. Based on an insider account of Bill Clinton's run for the Democratic presidential nomination in 1992. John Travolta plays a fictional Southern governor who emerges as his party nominee for president. This film is a realistic depiction of the campaign process and the pressures that are imposed on the candidate, his family, and supporters. Further, Travolta's performance captures well the infuriating duality and complexity of Clinton's—excuse me, Governor Jack Stanton's—personality.

Raiders of the Lost Ark (1981). Directed by Steven Spielberg. Starring Harrison Ford, Karen Allen, and Denholm Elliot. In this film, Indiana Jones, a mild-mannered archaeology professor, fights the Nazis. The plot is kind of loony but sort of antic-ipates the wildly successful *Left Behind* series of novels, which is taken more than seriously by a lot of supporters of the current administration (George W. Bush).

The Rainmaker (1997). Directed by Francis Ford Coppola. Starring Matt Damon, Danny DeVito, Claire Danes, and Jon Voight. This film is based on the John Grisham novel. It is in my opinion the best of the courtroom dramas based on Grisham novels, which include *The Firm, The Client*, and *Runaway Jury*. What makes this film reassuring is that the system actually works. Apparently, however, that message doesn't resonate. *The Rainmaker* was only modestly successful at the box office, whereas *The Firm* and *The Client* were box office hits. I suspect that tells us more about ourselves than it does about the films.

Rambo: First Blood (1982). Directed by Ted Kotcheff. Starring Sylvester Stallone and Richard Crenna. This enormously popular film, which spawned two sequels, com-bines two strains of American anomie: anger at the loss of Vietnam and rebellion against abusive authority. Put them together and add the skills of an elite mem-ber of the Special Forces, and you get a pretty high body count, not to mention some pretty spectacular kill scenes. What else could a sixteen-year-old boy or his equivalent ask for?

The Reagans (2003). Directed by Robert Allan Ackerman. Starring James Brolin and Judy Davis. This made-for-television movie generated so much contro-versy that CBS decided not to air it. Instead the movie was shown on the

Showtime cable network. The Reagan presidency is still too controversial for prime time.

Red Corner (1997). Directed by Jon Avnet. Starring Richard Gere. Part of the 1997 anti-Chinese trilogy (*Kundun, Red Corner, Seven Years in Tibet*). See *Kundun.*

Red Dust (1932). Directed by Victor Fleming. Starring Clark Gable, Jean Harlow, Gene Raymond, and Mary Astor. This film and *Red-Headed Woman* were made before the enforcement of the Hollywood production code. Modern students are amazed at the liberties taken in both dialogue and plot.

Red-Headed Woman (1932). Directed by Jack Conway. Starring Jean Harlow and Chester Morris. See *Red Dust.*

Reds (1981). Directed by Warren Beatty. Starring Warren Beatty and Diane Keaton. This is one of the few mainstream Hollywood films to treat the Left and associated socialist movements (including the Bolshevik Revolution) as positive and noteworthy endeavors. The film is a biographical study of Jack Reed, a left-wing American journalist who covered the Russian Revolution and is now buried in the Kremlin. The film actually made some money but clearly wouldn't stimulate much interest in similar projects pursued as anything else but labors of love, as was the case with this film.

Road Trip (2000). Directed by Todd Phillips. Starring Breckin Meyer, Seann William Scott, Amy Smart, Paulo Costanzo, D.J. Qualls, and Tom Green. *Road Trip* is the new millennium's answer to *Animal House.* Not as good because it isn't as bad.

The Robe (1953). Directed by Henry Koster. Starring Richard Burton, Jean Simmons, and Victor Mature. This film is yet another 1950s biblical epic. The first film released in CinemaScope.

RoboCop (1987). Directed by Paul Verhoeven. Starring Peter Weller and Nancy Allen. *RoboCop* is a surprisingly complex and fun film. The city of Detroit has descended into chaos. The problem of policing the city is outsourced to a giant corporation that turns out to be in cahoots with the criminals, an important insight into outsourcing. This film is interesting from a number of perspectives; everything from corporate culture to popular culture to bioethics is in play. Verhoeven has a mischievous sense of humor; look closely for multiple subtle digs at modern American society.

Sands of Iwo Jima (1949). Directed by Allan Dwan. Starring John Wayne. This film is the archetypical World War II drama. It's all here. The gruff drill sergeant whips green recruits into a fighting machine. Sergeant Stryker is one of the few American film heroes who is celebrated for doing everything "by the book."

Saving Private Ryan (1998). Directed by Steven Spielberg. Starring Tom Hanks. This film set the technical standard for modern war films. Spielberg's depiction of the landing at Omaha Beach on D-day is one of the most unrelenting, breathtaking, and graphic depictions of the horrors of war ever portrayed in the movies. The plot of the movie is a little strange and almost trite. But that shortcoming is more than compensated for by the technical quality of the film. Parenthetically, Spielberg was attacked by some commentators on the Right for depicting American troops in an unflattering light by including occasional displays of cowardice and cruelty, including the shooting of German prisoners of war.

The Searchers (1956). Directed by John Ford. Starring John Wayne, Vera Miles, Ward Bond, Jeffrey Hunter, and Natalie Wood. *The Searchers* is a deeply thoughtful Western that confronts, among other things, the issue of racism head on—which is unusual for the period in which it was made. This may be Wayne's best role. His subtle performance spans the spectrum of emotions, from rage to forgiveness and tenderness. Wayne was never considered the most accomplished actor, playing more a persona than a character. But in this film, he at least displays range within the limits of his persona.

Sergeant York (1940). Directed by Howard Hawks. Starring Gary Cooper, Walter Brennan, and Joan Leslie. In this film Cooper plays a pacifist who learns the value of killing his fellow man. In the lead-up to World War II, isolationist America had to be convinced of the importance of going to war to defend its freedom.

Seven Years in Tibet (1997). Directed by Jean-Jacques Annaud. Starring Brad Pitt. Part of the 1997 anti-Chinese trilogy (*Kundun, Red Corner, Seven Years in Tibet*). See *Kundun*.

Shaft (1971). Directed by Gordon Parks. Starring Richard Roundtree. This film is a prime example of the *blaxploitation* ("black-exploitation") genre. It is about this time that, in association with the black power movement, it became cool to be black. As a result, this film had a surprisingly large white audience.

Shampoo (1975). Directed by Hal Ashby. Starring Warren Beatty, Julie Christie, Goldie Hawn, Jack Warden, and Lee Grant. This film is a bedroom farce that turns out to be a 1970s version of *Don Giovanni*.

Shane (1953). Directed by George Stevens. Starring Alan Ladd, Jean Arthur, Van Heflin, Brandon De Wilde, and Jack Palance. *Shane* is pretty much standard Western fare. It is exceptionally well made and is interesting in how it depicts the roots of the Western range wars. Otherwise, *High Noon* is a better Western to watch as being representative of the era.

Show Boat (1936). Directed by James Whale. Starring Irene Dunne, Allan Jones, Charles Winninger, and Paul Robeson. One of several remakes of the titular novel by Edna Ferber, in this film Hollywood tentatively begins to examine issues of racism in the old South.

Showgirls (1995). Directed by Paul Verhoeven. Starring Elizabeth Berkeley and Gina Gershon. One of the funniest films ever made, though perhaps unintentionally.

Verhoeven actually showed up to collect his Razzie Awards for Worst Director and Worst Picture of 1995.

The Silence of the Lambs (1991). Directed by Jonathan Demme. Starring Jodie Foster and Anthony Hopkins. The fictional serial killer Hannibal Lecter portrayed in this film has become part of our popular discourse. He represents the extreme of evil and depravity. This film was tremendously successful at the box office and sparked a number of sequels and spin-offs. Some would suggest that this film set a new low for mainstream Hollywood cinema's exploitation of the lurid and depraved to attract audiences to the theater.

Sleeping Beauty (1959). Directed by Clyde Geronimi. This is a prototypical 1950s hit, a children's fairy tale. Nevertheless, as a work of art, it is a superb film.

Sling Blade (1996). Directed by Billy Bob Thornton. Starring Billy Bob Thornton. This film is interesting as an example of an indie film that hit the big time, the suburban multiplex cinema. The corporatization of American cinema doesn't mean that small-budget films can't get made and can't get screened. It isn't easy, but at least it's possible—and *Sling Blade* is proof.

Smokey and the Bandit (1977). Directed by Hal Needham. Starring Burt Reynolds, Jackie Gleason, and Sally Fields. The first installment in what was to become a franchise. At the risk of sounding too academic, this film highlights a quintessential component of American liberalism, the myth of the individual. Reynolds and his trucking buddies take on the bumbling establishment. Certainly, the story resonated with a large segment of the public. The film grossed $363 million (inflation adjusted) and ranks sixtieth in the top-grossing films of all time.

Sneakers (1992). Directed by Phil Alden Robinson. Starring Robert Redford and Sidney Poitier. *Sneakers* is a middling caper film. It is reported that the producers actually added obscenities to the dialogue in order to obtain a PG rating so that it wouldn't appear to be a children's film.

Spartacus (1960). Directed by Stanley Kubrick. Starring Kirk Douglas, Jean Simmons, Laurence Olivier, Charles Laughton, and Tony Curtis. This is a 1950s-style toga epic with superb direction and an achingly poignant story. Blacklisted screenwriter Dalton Trumbo was credited for having written this script after having ghostwritten through much of the 1950s. Look for a scene in the film, unusual for the time and cut from some versions, in which the character played by Olivier makes a pass at Curtis.

Starship Troopers (1997). Directed by Paul Verhoeven. Starring Casper Van Dien, Dina Meyer, Denise Richards, Jake Busey, Neil Patrick Harris, and Clancy Brown. Intelligent insects from outer space have attacked Earth. From there on the movie moves from one frenetic battle to another. It is never clear to me what this film is about. I have a suspicion the plot represents some kind of metaphor for human shortcomings. There is some suggestion here that the war didn't have to happen at all if we humans had been more sensitive to the insects' interests. But apparently because of our speciesism, we can't conceive of an intelligent bug.

Star Wars (1977). Directed by George Lucas. Starring Harrison Ford, Alec Guinness, Mark Hamill, Carrie Fisher, James Earl Jones, and Peter Cushing. *Star Wars* is the first installment of Lucas's life's work. When this film came out, it created a phenomenon. As far as I am concerned, the plot is incomprehensible, but the special effects continue to amaze. Only the future can tell whether the *Star Wars* series will be considered a masterpiece. I suspect it will be if only because it is the most ambitious project ever undertaken in the history of film. The series comprises two trilogies that were produced in somewhat reverse chronological order. The first trilogy, episodes four through six, includes *Star Wars*, *The Empire Strikes Back* (1980), and *Return of the Jedi* (1983); the second trilogy, episodes one through three, includes *The Phantom Menace* (1999), *Attack of the Clones* (2002), and *Revenge of the Sith* (2005).

Stolen Honor: Wounds That Never Heal (2004). Directed by Carlton Sherwood. This documentary attacks the Vietnam War record of the 2004 Democratic presidential nominee, Senator John Kerry. The film did not do well at the box office, indicating that the film medium is not a good place for attack documentaries or that the audience for film is generally not Republican.

Stripes (1981). Directed by Ivan Reitman. Starring Bill Murray, Harold Ramis, Warren Oates, and John Candy. Signals the end of the Vietnam era. Service in the army is again treated as a benign, constructive right of passage.

Striptease (1996). Directed by Andrew Bergman. Starring Demi Moore. This is the worst film ever made. The film pays homage to Moore's surgical breast enhancement.

Sunset Blvd. (1950). Directed by Billy Wilder. Starring William Holden, Gloria Swanson, Erich Von Stroheim, and Nancy Olsen. This film is perhaps one of the best ever made. It is well executed, acted, and written from beginning to end. At the same time, the film paints a generally dark, depressing portrait of growing old and of getting started in industrial America.

Taxi Driver (1976). Directed by Martin Scorsese. Starring Robert De Niro, Jody Foster, Cybill Shepherd, and Harvey Keitel. I don't know of another film that captures an emotion, alienation, as well as *Taxi Driver* does. This film is a textual, thrilling, and bloody masterpiece. *Taxi Driver* is for those of you who want to know where serial killers come from.

The Ten Commandments (1956). Directed by Cecil B. DeMille. Starring Charlton Heston, Yul Brynner, Anne Baxter, and Edward G. Robinson. This film is the granddaddy of all biblical epics. Parenthetically, publicists for the film encouraged the placement of monuments to the Ten Commandments at sites all over the country, including public areas, sparking part of the current controversy over the display of religious symbols in public places.

Terms of Endearment (1983). Directed by James L. Brooks. Starring Shirley MacLaine, Debra Winger, Jeff Daniels, and Jack Nicholson. This is a gloopy drama that uses every trick in the book to pull at our heartstrings. For some reason, this won the Academy Award for Best Picture. *Return of the Jedi* made the most money.

Thelma and Louise (1991). Directed by Ridley Scott. Starring Susan Sarandon, Geena Davis, Brad Pitt, Michael Madsen, and Harvey Keitel. This is a so-called women's film where the protagonists solve their problems by driving off a cliff.

They Died with Their Boots On (1941). Directed by Rauol Walsh. Starring Errol Flynn and Olivia de Havilland. This film is a largely fictional biography, if such a thing is possible, of George Armstrong Custer. Basically untrue from beginning to end, the film is nevertheless tremendously enjoyable with a delightful over-the-top performance by Flynn. In this film, Custer is portrayed as a playful, willful scamp, which couldn't be more different from his portrayal as a murderous megalomaniac in the 1970s film *Little Big Man.*

The Thing (1951). Directed by Christian Nyby. Starring James Arness, Margaret Sheridan, Kenneth Tobey, Douglas Spencer, James R. Young, Dewey Martin, and Eduard Franz. A science fiction standard, this film is seen by many scholars as a metaphor for the infiltration of communism into the United States. Frankly, I don't see the connection, or at least it is better made in *The Invasion of the Body Snatchers* or *Invaders from Mars.*

Three Men and a Baby (1987). Directed by Leonard Nimoy. Starring Ted Danson, Steve Guttenberg, and Tom Selleck. This feel-good movie reinforces traditional, some would say paternalistic, values.

Titanic (1997). Directed by James Cameron. Starring Leonardo DiCaprio and Kate Winslet. This film is titanic in more ways than one. It was made at a titanic cost, produced at titanic risk, and experienced titanic gains at the box office. Besides the money, however, it's a darn good film—an example of the best of American commercial filmmaking. It also has an interesting riff on societal stratification.

Tootsie (1982). Directed by Sidney Pollack. Starring Dustin Hoffman and Jessica Lange. The intersection of quality and quantity, *Tootsie* was the top-grossing film of the year. It is a seriously funny comedy about a serious topic, the discrimination against women on the job.

Training Day (2001). Directed by Antoine Fuqua. Starring Denzel Washington and Ethan Hawke. This film is noteworthy in that the main character, a thoroughly corrupt undercover police officer, is black and that the decision to make him black is unremarkable. That plot device is a positive marker along the path of race relations in the United States. For this film, Washington won the Academy Award for Best Actor, an award that he deserved for his portrayal of Malcolm X.

Triumph of the Will (1935). Directed by Leni Reifenstahl. Featuring Adolf Hitler. This film documents a Nazi rally in Nuremberg in 1934. *Triumph* is the prototype of modern propaganda technique. Watch this film and then compare it to the events staged by modern presidents to gain support for their public policies.

The Truman Show (1998). Directed by Peter Weir. Starring Jim Carrey and Laura Linney. A spooky musing on the probity of reality television, this film was made before the nascent television genre was even in vogue.

Twister (1996). Directed by Jan de Bont. Starring a special effect. During this film, I went out for popcorn and found the longest line. Twister ranks seventy-second of top-grossing films of all time (inflation adjusted) and the beginning of the end of sentient life on Earth.

Unforgiven (1992). Directed by Clint Eastwood. Starring Clint Eastwood, Morgan Freeman, and Gene Hackman. Another in a string of modern Westerns, starting with *Little Big Man* and perhaps *The Searchers*, that takes a more critical view of the myths of the American West. Eastwood's particularly unique take is his depiction of violence and revenge. As if to pay penance for his earlier portrayals as Dirty Harry, Eastwood as filmmaker makes sure that we see the horrors of violence and the futility of revenge.

An Unmarried Woman (1978). Directed by Paul Mazursky. Starring Jill Clayburgh and Alan Bates. This is a "women's film." At the time when it was released, it represented a departure in the depiction of not only women but also men. The character played by Bates is more desirable as a love interest because of his sensitivity and intelligence than because of his body. How this type of women's film morphed into *Pretty Woman* and *Working Girl* is anyone's guess.

The Untouchables (1987). Directed by Brian De Palma. Starring Kevin Costner, Robert De Niro, Andy Garcia, Charles Martin Smith, and Sean Connery. In this film, federal agent Eliot Ness sets out to break the back of the Chicago crime mob led by Al Capone. This film is a ripping yarn, technically superb, well written, and well performed. There is one glaring fault in this film. Eliot Ness, a by-the-book agent, murders a suspect in his custody. This is so out of character and is such a sop to emotions of the viewers that it ruins the film.

Wag the Dog (1997). Directed by Barry Levinson. Starring Dustin Hoffman and Robert De Niro. Along with *Bulworth*, this film is a cynical, dispiriting look at American politics. If politics have sunk this low in the United States, it will take more than elections to turn things around.

Way Down East (1920). Directed by D. W. Griffith. Starring Lillian Gish and Richard Barthelmess. This film is a fascinating period piece that was probably outdated even in its day. Adapted from an enormously popular nineteenth-century melodrama, this story says a lot about the status of women at the turn of the twentieth century. But for what the story lacked in freshness, in the technical sense the film was quite cutting edge.

Ways of Love (1948). Directed by Roberto Rossellini. Starring Anna Magnani. This Italian film became a test of the legal principle that film was product, not art, and therefore not protected under the First Amendment. As a result of a legal challenge to this film, the Supreme Court reversed its previous decision and ruled that film was indeed art.

Witness (1985). Directed by Peter Weir. Starring Harrison Ford and Kelly McGillis. This is an interesting chase movie that takes place largely within a Pennsylvania Amish community. This fish-out-of-water story could have worked had Weir had the courage to devise an ending that wasn't a complete sop to the audience.

The Wizard of Oz (1939). Directed by Victor Fleming. Starring Judy Garland, Frank Morgan, Ray Bolger, Bert Lahr, Jack Haley, Billie Burke, and Margaret Hamilton. This is the ultimate road movie. What is it about this movie that has made it stand the test of time? See Roger Ebert's 1996 discussion of this at http://rogerebert .suntimes.com/apps/pbcs.dll/article?AID=/19961222/REVIEWS08/401010348/ 1023 (accessed June 1, 2005).

Working Girl (1988). Directed by Mike Nichols. Starring Harrison Ford, Melanie Griffith, and Sigourney Weaver. According to my standards, this film is one of the worst ever made. To be sure, the film is more than technically competent, but the problem is that for a self-purported women's film, it is nothing of the kind. In the end, the only way that Tess gets ahead is by sleeping and cheating her way to the top. This film would play better in the former Soviet Union because it puts on display the essential corruption of the capitalist system.

X2 (2003). Directed by Bryan Singer. Starring Patrick Stewart, Hugh Jackman, Ian McKellan, Halle Berry, Famke Janssen, James Marsden, Anna Paquin, Rebecca Romijin-Stamos, Brian Cox, and Alan Cumming. This film is a prime example of Hollywood film as a commodity. A sequel to the enormously successful *X-Men*, *X2* carries on the tradition—it has become the 160th top-grossing film of all time (inflation controlled). Not bad for a lot of banging, crashing special effects. In all fairness, the film does include some interesting musings about racism.

Index

Burton, Tim, 100, 182
Busey, Jake, 202
Bush, George H. W., 31n2
Bush, George W., 1–2, 58, 105, 126, 134, 171, 175, 184, 188
Bush, Jeb, 1
Butler, David, 194
Byrne, Gabriel, 195, 198

Caan, James, 190
cable television, 45, 155, 159
Caine Mutiny, The, 130, 184
Cameron, James, 204
Candy, John, 203
Cannes Film Festival, 2
Cantinflas, 182
capitalism, 102–3, 108, 109
Capra, Frank, 138, 192, 196
Carneal, Michael, 154
Carner, Charles Robert, 193
Carradine, David, 193
Carrey, Jim, 205
Carter, Helena, 192
Carter, Helen Bonham, 191
Casablanca, 184
Casino, 88, 184
Catch-22, 171
Caton-Jones, Michael, 192
causality, 5–7, 63, 75–77, 85
Caviezel, James, 198
Cazale, John, 190
CBS, 121, 145, 163n6
Celsius 41.11, 126, 184–85
censorship, 143–61; establishment of, 168; film as product/art and, 7–8; by government, 154–61; industry self-censorship, 42, 147–54; in market, 143–47; motivations behind, 9, 57, 170, 172, 176; questionable basis for, 83; rating system versus, 152–54; slippery slope of, 174; by states and localities, 147–48, 155–56, 158
Century City, 44
CEO Sumner Redstone, 58
Chabert, Lacey, 194

Chaffey, Don, 192
Chaplin, Charlie, 97, 190
Chaplin, Geraldine, 187
Chaplinsky v. State of New Hampshire, 157
Chapman, Graham, 194
Chariots of Fire, 135, 185
Charleson, Ian, 185
Cheadle, Don, 183
children: effect of violence in media on, 83–84; rating system and, 153–54; television content and, 159, 161
China, 125, 151
China Syndrome, The, 16, 28, 185
Christie, Julie, 170, 187, 195, 201
Cinerama, 124, 141n5
Citizen Kane, 5, 26, 43, 177, 185
Civic Culture, The (Almond and Gabriel), 4
civil rights movement, 135–36
Clark, Tom, 156
Clarke, Arthur C., 181
classical liberalism, 20–22
Classification and Ratings Administration, 153
Clayburgh, Jill, 205
Cleese, John, 194
Client, The, 103–4, 185, 199
Clinton, Bill, 16, 27, 125, 186, 199
Close, Glenn, 191
CNN, 46
Cobb, Lee J., 188, 197
Coca-Cola, 44
Coen brothers (Joel and Ethan), 97
Cohen, Leonard, 195
Cold Mountain, 18, 45, 185
Cold War, 130
Columbia Pictures Sony, 58
Columbine High School, Littleton, Colorado, 77, 155
comedy, 170–71
Coming to America, 22, 185
communism, 173
community, sense of, 18, 24, 25, 136–38
Comstock, George, 82
Conan the Barbarian, 26, 185–86

About the Author

Daniel P. Franklin is associate professor of political science at Georgia State University in Atlanta, Georgia. He is the author of *Making Ends Meet: Congressional Budgeting in the Age of Deficits* and *Extraordinary Measures: The Exercise of Prerogative Powers in the United States* and is coeditor of *Political Culture and Constitutionalism: A Comparative Approach.* He teaches courses on American government, politics of the presidency, and politics and film.